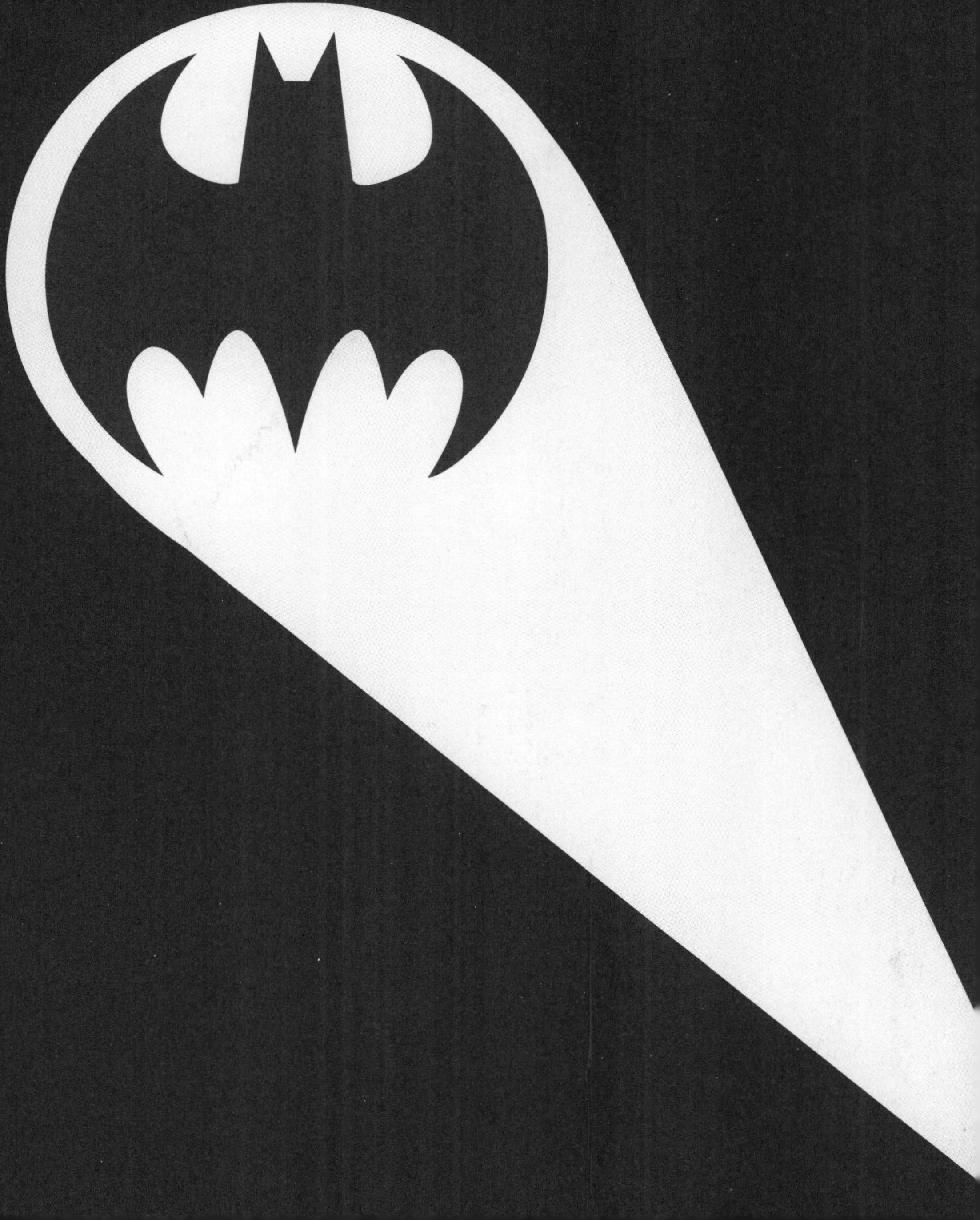

BATMAN™

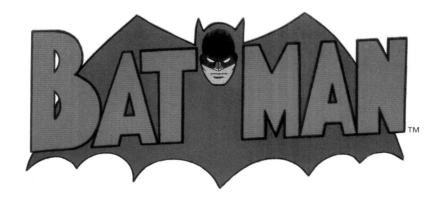

DK | Penguin Random House

LONDON, NEW YORK, MELBOURNE,
MUNICH, AND DELHI

Senior Editor: Alastair Dougall
Senior Designer: Jon Hall
Designer: Ray Bryant
Original Cover Artwork: Jorge Jiménez
Senior Production Controller: Mary Slater
Production Editor: Marc Staples
Managing Editors: Sarah Harland, Emma Grange
Managing Art Editor: Vicky Short
Publishing Director: Mark Searle

Dorling Kindersley would like to thank:
Benjamin Harper and Josh Anderson at Warner Bros. Global Publishing;
Joe Daley, Benjamin Le Clear, Hank Manfra, Mike Pallotta, Leah Tuttle, Erin Vanover, Steve Sonn at DC.

Many thanks to: Alex Allan, Hannah Dolan, Nathan Martin, Simon Beecroft, Lisa Lanzarini, Robert Perry, Ron Stobbart, Catherine Saunders. Editorial assistance: Pamela Afram, Neil Kelly, Julia March, Emma Grange. Design assistance: Clive Savage, Toby Truphet, Satvir Sihota, Rhys Thomas. Index: Helen Peters

First American Edition, 2022
Published in the United States by DK Publishing
1450 Broadway, Suite 801, New York, NY 10018

Page design copyright © 2022 Dorling Kindersley Limited.
DK, a Division of Penguin Random House LLC
22 23 24 25 26 10 9 8 7 6 5 4 3 2 1
001—326311—Feb/2022

A catalog record for this book is available from the Library of Congress.
ISBN 978-0-7440-4821-6

DK books are available at special discounts when purchased in bulk for sales promotions, premiums, fund-raising, or educational use. For details, contact: DK Publishing Special Markets, 1450 Broadway, Suite 801, New York, New York 10018
SpecialSales@dk.com

Printed and bound in China

For the curious

www.dk.com

BATMAN™

THE ULTIMATE GUIDE

WRITTEN BY

MATTHEW K. MANNING
DANIEL WALLACE

FOREWORD BY

TOM KING

CONTENTS

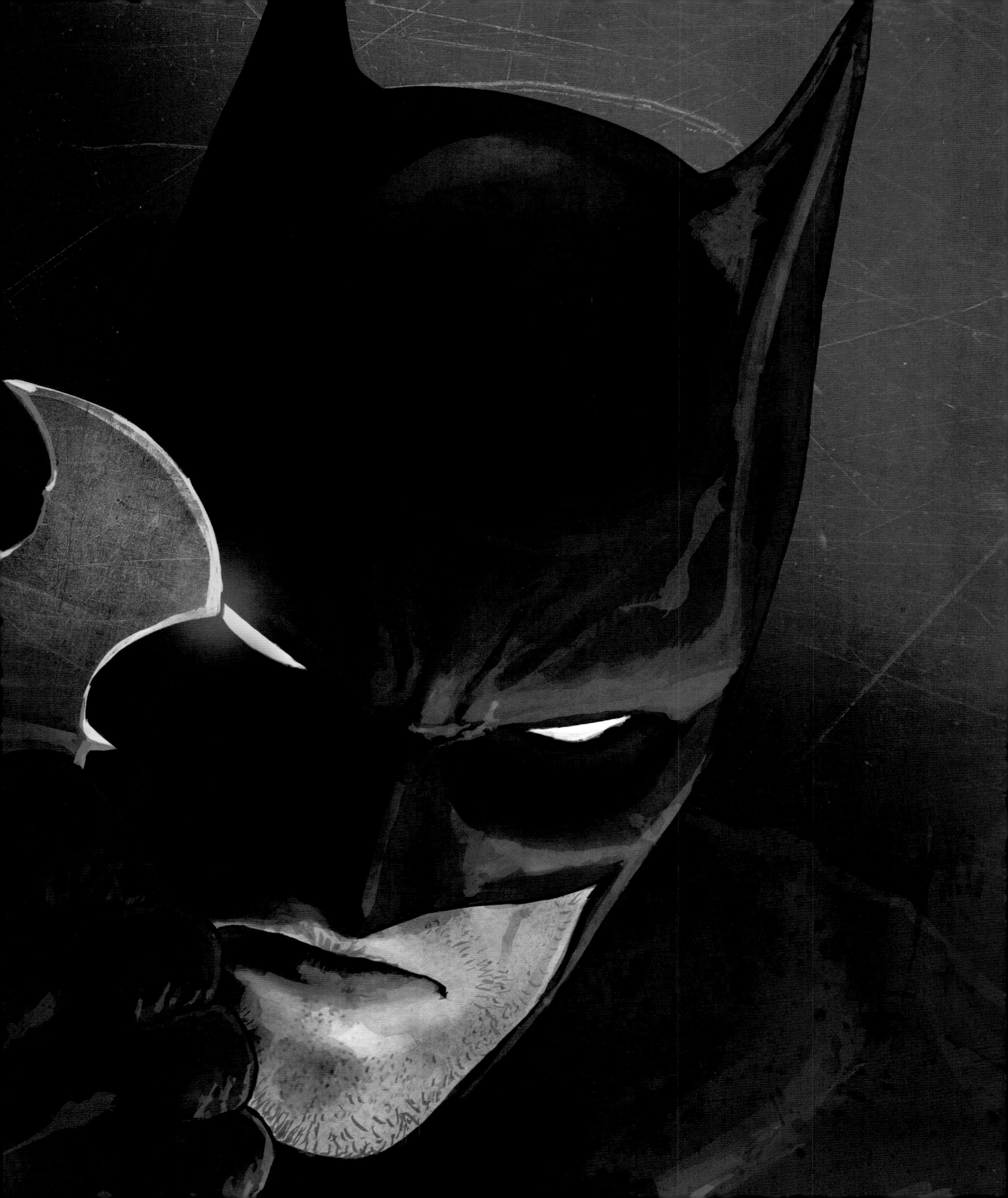

FOREWORD

There are awkward moments at signings. A very kind fan will give you a book and ask for a signature and you say thank you and you sign your name and while you sign, for those very few seconds, a quiet falls between the two of you—two strangers in a very strange interaction unsure who should speak or if anyone should speak both knowing full well that the reason you get and give a signature is to have a small record of this moment, to connect to someone, and so this moment should be a moment and not a silence. To combat this tepid void, I often ask a question:

"Who is your favorite Super Hero?"

Now, there's obviously some bias in my audience as I wrote Batman for many years and many, many issues; but, with that slant acknowledged, I note that about 80 percent of the people say "Batman." The answer is so ubiquitous that it's not a conversation and definitely not a moment, so I inevitably follow up with, "Why Batman?" in hopes of filling up more of this time and finding something over which two people might quickly connect. What follows that simple follow-up often astounds me.

Some people shrug; some say it was watching the animated series when they were a kid; some people just say Batman's cool. But most people say, "Because he doesn't have powers, because he's human, because he's like me." Despite Batman's wealth, his all-powerful gadgets, his ability to jump and swing and fight as no man ever has or will—Batman's audience still sees him as I see him, as just a man in a funny suit walking amongst the gods.

And this—this absurdity—inspires them, inspires me, inspires us.

As I flip through this beautiful book I am reminded of that simple truth. For all the wonderful complications all these wonderful comic creators added over 80 years—in the end Batman is just a man who took the pain of his youth and transformed it into a mission for justice. He is the epiphany each of us hope for: that our greatest tragedy is actually an opportunity to punch harder, to swing higher, to solve all the intricate mysteries that come our way—to walk, as Batman walks, among the gods.

And even in the small awkward moments that make up most of life, that is something to connect us all.

Tom King
Washington, D.C., 2021

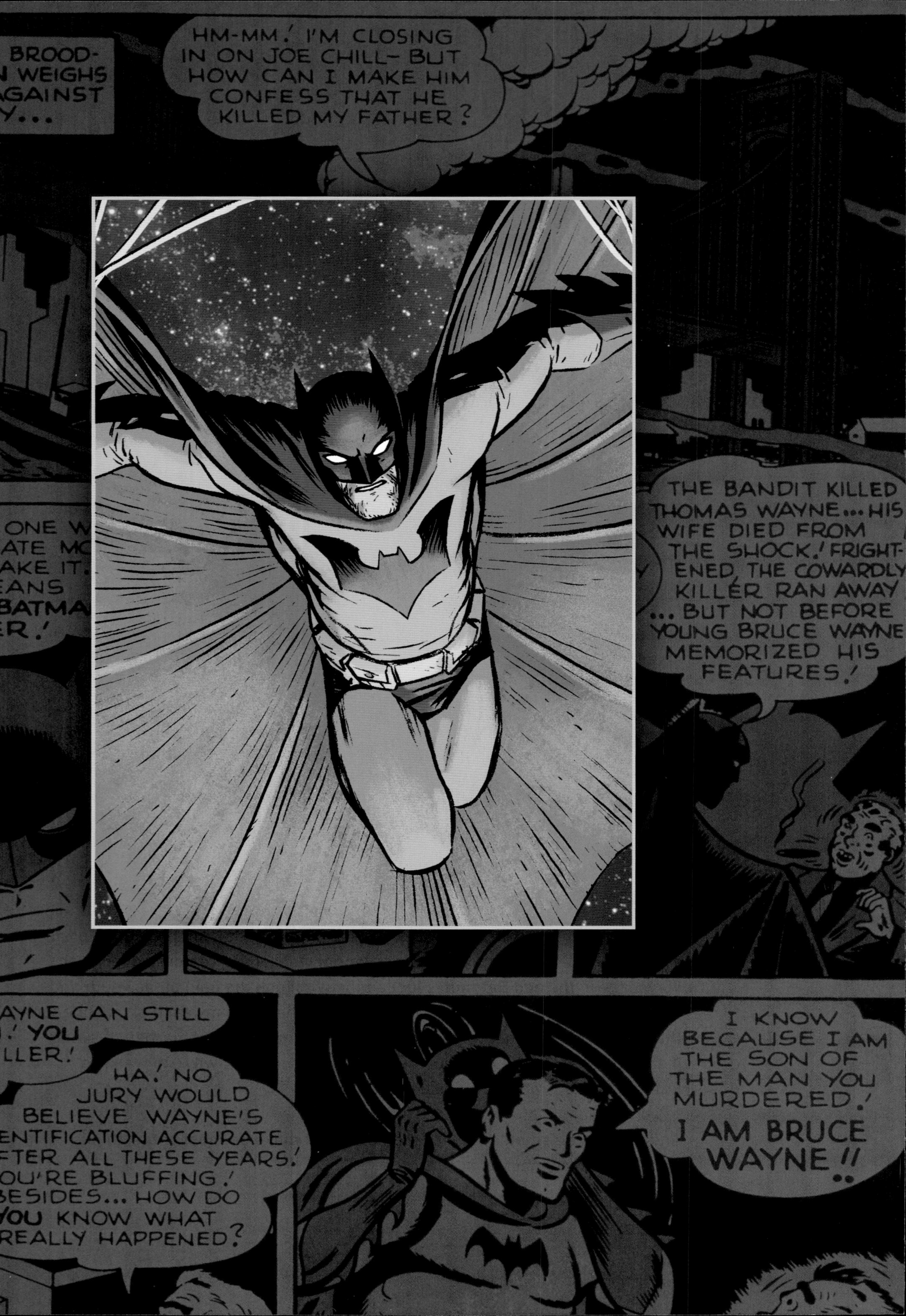

HM-MM! I'M CLOSING IN ON JOE CHILL— BUT HOW CAN I MAKE HIM CONFESS THAT HE KILLED MY FATHER?
THE BANDIT KILLED THOMAS WAYNE... HIS WIFE DIED FROM THE SHOCK! FRIGHTENED, THE COWARDLY KILLER RAN AWAY ... BUT NOT BEFORE YOUNG BRUCE WAYNE MEMORIZED HIS FEATURES!
HA! NO JURY WOULD BELIEVE WAYNE'S
I KNOW BECAUSE I AM THE SON OF THE MAN YOU MURDERED! I AM BRUCE WAYNE!!

INTRODUCING...

BATMAN

Batman adapts. In a fantastic world populated by hyper-focused costumed Super-Villains, deadly secret societies, and other-dimensional doppelgangers, he has no choice. Ever since a young Bruce Wayne swore an oath on the graves of his parents to protect Gotham City, he simply can't bring himself to quit. He has dedicated his life to become the World's Greatest Detective, the crime-fighting hero known as Batman. So he endures and he evolves. Because if he's anything, Batman is forever.

When masked men and noir detectives dominated pulp literature, Batman was born. When bright and positive Super Heroes commanded the newsstands, a smiling Caped Crusader traded punches with colorful clowns. When science fiction gripped the nation, a not-so-Dark Knight battled aliens and went on time-traveling adventures. When readers' tastes grew more sophisticated, Batman embraced his Gothic roots. When graphic novels challenged adults with their storytelling potential, a Dark Knight grew even darker. And when Super Heroes conquered the Hollywood box office, Batman led the way, invented anew for each unique audience.

Batman has spent his life training for every eventuality, to escape every death trap, to defeat every opponent. Likewise, the very concept of Batman changes to blend in seamlessly with each new decade's developments. Today, as real-world billionaires fall under increasing scrutiny, Batman no longer has an unlimited budget for gadgets and vehicles. The Dark Knight is giving a more streamlined approach a try, all the while embracing a brave new era of social consciousness and online innovation. His supporting cast has also become more diverse, and his outlook now favors reformation rather than punishment. Batman is justice personified, but today's Dark Knight is not above questioning how he goes about achieving that justice.

Everyone has a favorite Batman, whether it's the lighthearted hero of the 1960s, the living gargoyle of the 1989 film, or the brooding detective of the 2000s. Yet no one version is the character's absolute true form. Batman is ever-changing; he is as malleable in spirit as his shape-shifting adversary Clayface is in form. There's a reason they say that the Dark Knight can best any foe if given enough time to prepare. Batman is ready for anything that comes his way, perfectly primed for today's infinite frontier. Because now and always, Batman adapts.

Matthew K. Manning

THE BIRTH OF BATMAN

Batman was an instant sensation. His popularity helped to usher in the age of the comic book Super Hero.

Comic books were a new medium in the 1930s. Everyone was looking for ways to turn them into moneymakers. Some publishers simply reprinted comic strips taken from the nation's daily newspapers, but DC decided to make a big play for original content in the genres of humor and adventure. *Detective Comics* launched in 1937 with a focus on tough guys and private eyes, but it was a very different kind of hero who would give them their biggest hit. After issue #27's cover announced the "amazing and unique adventures of the Batman," *Detective Comics*—and DC as a company—would never be the same.

The new hero looked almost vampiric in his dark cloak, and he owed a debt to the grim pulp heroes of the era including the Shadow and the Spider. He became DC's second breakout star following Superman's debut in *Action Comics* the previous year. The non-superpowered, nocturnal Batman and the brightly colored Man of Steel couldn't be more different, but the two characters defined the polar extremes of the vast storytelling landscape offered by the Super Hero genre. DC spent most of the next decade filling in the middle ground with costumed heroes of every conceivable stripe.

Bob Kane and Bill Finger collaborated on Batman's creation. Kane provided most of the art and Finger the scripting. Soon joined by inker Jerry Robinson, the team created nearly all of Batman's core elements—including Robin, the Batmobile, Gotham City, and Batman's bizarre Rogues Gallery— in just a few short years.

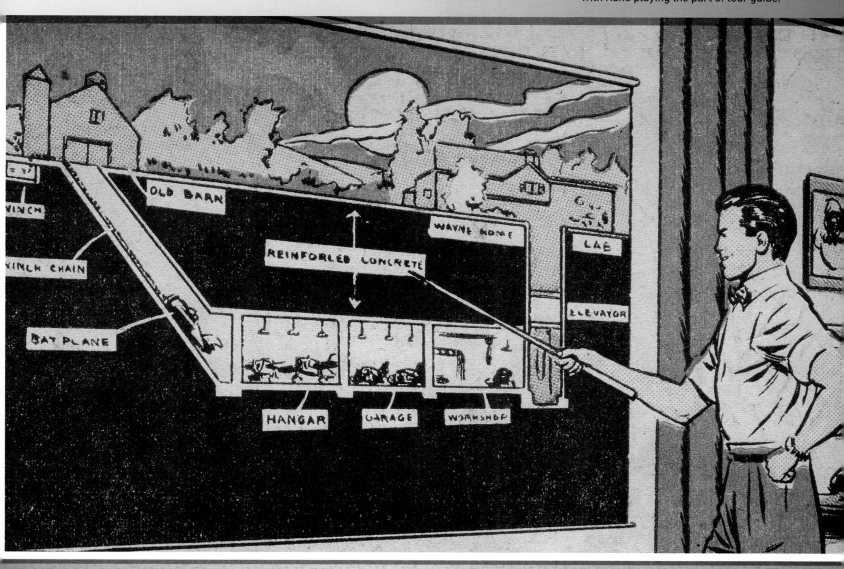

Bob Kane himself became a comic book character when he appeared on the pages of DC's *Real Fact Comics* #5 (1946). Readers were treated to a detailed tour of the Batcave with Kane playing the part of tour guide.

BOB KANE

Artist Bob Kane found work at the Max Fleischer animation studio during the 1930s, but hoped to apply his illustration skills to the new medium of comics. After gaining experience at DC on the *Adventure Comics* feature "Rusty and His Pals," Kane came up with his own idea for a new Super Hero he thought could become as popular as Superman. He enlisted writer Bill Finger as his creative partner, and sold his Batman concept to *Detective Comics* editor Vin Sullivan. Under the terms of his deal, Kane received a byline on all stories. In 1943 Kane left comics to concentrate full-time on the Batman newspaper strip, but returned and remained involved with DC through the 1960s.

BILL FINGER

Writer Bill Finger met Bob Kane at a party and soon the two had struck a deal to collaborate as comics creators. During development of the Batman pitch, Finger refined Kane's concept for the hero. Out went a red costume and domino mask, and in came a cape, a blue-gray color scheme, and Batman's cowl with its trademark white eye-slits. Finger's scripts demonstrated a deep understanding of visual storytelling, and he emphasized Batman's potential as a detective by introducing Sherlock Holmes-style investigation to the stories. Soon made a DC staffer, Finger was instrumental in the development of many of Batman's best-known adversaries. He also helped develop the Golden Age version of the Green Lantern character with artist Martin Nodell.

JERRY ROBINSON

Jerry Robinson was just 17 years old and studying journalism at Columbia University when his artistic skills came to the attention of Bob Kane. Kane immediately signed him on as a comics inker and letterer. He and Bill Finger had just gotten Batman off the ground, and Robinson was able to contribute key concepts to the Dark Knight's legend during its developmental stage. Robinson is credited with illustrating a Joker playing card that led in part to the final design of Batman's archenemy, and also with suggesting the name for Batman's sidekick, Robin. As Batman gained popularity, Robinson began to share inking duties on the comics with George Roussos, and when Bob Kane moved on to the Batman newspaper strip, Robinson took over as penciler.

DETECTIVE COMICS

Issue #27

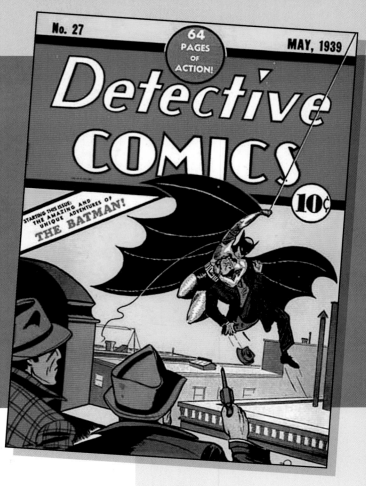

"As the two men leer over their conquest, they do not notice a third, menacing figure standing behind them. It is the Batman!"

MAIN CHARACTERS: Batman; Commissioner Gorden
SUPPORTING CHARACTERS: Lambert; Lambert Jr.; Alfred Stryker; Steven Crane; Paul Rogers; Jennings
LOCATIONS: Commissioner Gordon's home, Lambert Mansion, Stryker laboratories, Wayne Manor

BACKGROUND

Detective Comics launched with the goal of telling stories about sleuths and private eyes—Super Heroes weren't in its mission statement. But after *Action Comics* delivered a breakout star in Superman, editor Vincent Sullivan hoped he could cause lightning to strike twice. *Detective Comics* #27 is where Batman began. Many of the building blocks of the Batman legend—including his double identity as Bruce Wayne, his relationship with Commissioner Gordon, and the white eye-slits of his pointed cowl —made their first appearances in this short, six-page story.

Leading off an issue that contained mostly forgotten figures like Buck Marshall and Cosmo the Phantom of Disguise, the dark-garbed vigilante pursued his own brand of justice and exhibited a cruel edge. Batman was both a Super Hero and a detective, and the newcomer soon pushed the other *Detective Comics* features out of the spotlight.

PUBLICATION DATE
May 1939

EDITOR
Vincent Sullivan

COVER ARTIST
Bob Kane

WRITER
Bill Finger

PENCILER
Bob Kane

INKER
Bob Kane

LETTERER
Bob Kane

The Story...

Danger and death traps abound as Gotham City gets its first taste of Batman, who solves a murder mystery by relying on fisticuffs and smart detective work.

News of a costumed "Batman" has Gotham City buzzing when wealthy man-about-town Bruce Wayne decides to visit his friend, Police Commissioner Gordon **(1)**. Their talk is interrupted by a telephone call: Lambert, an industrialist known as "the Chemical King," has been stabbed to death at his home. Gordon sets off to investigate the crime scene, while a seemingly bored Wayne agrees to accompany him, remarking that the case may prove an amusing diversion.

At the Lambert mansion **(2)**, it turns out that the late tycoon had three business partners—Steven Crane, Paul Rogers, and Alfred Stryker—any of whom may have had a motive to kill him to secure control of the Apex Chemical Corporation. Lambert's son, who found his father's body, reveals that valuable business documents are missing from a safe **(3)**. Lambert's former partner, Steven Crane, then reports a threat on his life and demands police protection.

Batman arrives too late to prevent Crane's murder **(4)**, but confronts the two assassins as they flee **(5)**. After knocking them out, Batman drives off to investigate the two remaining businessmen with connections to Lambert. They are already together: Paul Rogers has paid a visit to Alfred Stryker to warn him of the danger they are in. Stryker then reveals himself to be the true villain behind the murderous scheme.

Stryker's hulking manservant, Jennings, captures Rogers and places him beneath a huge bell jar suspended from the ceiling in Stryker's laboratory **(6)**. As the jar lowers toward the floor, the gloating goon announces that Rogers' will die the moment the jar forms an airtight seal and fills with poison gas **(7)**. Only seconds remain when Batman appears at an open window. He slides beneath the gas chamber, plugging the valve the instant it begins to spray its toxin **(8)**. Using a wrench to smash the glass, Batman frees himself and Rogers.

Stryker pulls a knife and tries to kill Rogers, but Batman disarms him **(9)**, and reveals the evidence he has gathered about Stryker's plot. Stryker pulls a gun. Batman deflects a shot and counters with a punch, sending Stryker tumbling over a railing into a vat of acid **(10)**. Batman delivers a grim eulogy as the villain expires: "A fitting end for his kind."

The next day, Bruce Wayne visits Commissioner Gordon to hear the official version of the case. An unimpressed Wayne calls Gordon's report of the horrific events a "lovely fairy tale" before taking his leave **(11)**. However, Wayne's bored socialite routine soon proves to be merely an act; a final plot twist reveals that Bruce Wayne and Gotham City's strange new Batman are one and the same **(12)**.

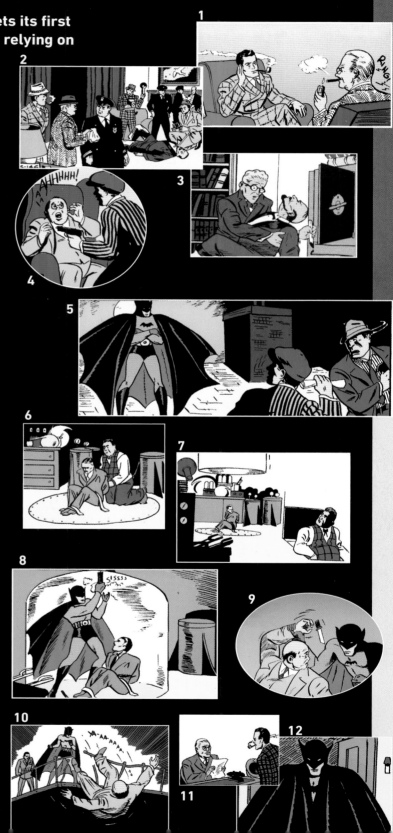

BATSUIT

ARMORED ALL OVER

The Batsuit offers Batman a powerful defense against fists, knives, and bullets—not to mention Mr. Freeze's ice blasts or The Joker's acid-squirting flowers. It is constructed of 15 micro-layers of Nomex-reinforced fabric, the innermost providing insulation against extremes of heat and cold. Covering the whole thing is a shell of triple-weave Kevlar. The Batsuit's silhouette strikes terror into the hearts of criminals everywhere, but the outfit is more than a tool of intimidation. Packed with microelectronics, it is the most advanced combat suit ever built.

The cowl's ears contain an antenna and transmitter, which allow Batman to maintain constant contact with the Batcave's information resources.

Batman's cowl is made of Kevlar around a steel frame. Built-in electronics give Batman night vision, allow him to hear distant whispers or to shut out external sounds, and to transmit voice commands.

The bat-symbol on the suit's chest often serves as a target for enemy gunfire; consequently it carries the thickest layer of armor.

Armored gauntlets protect against knife strikes. The three sharpened prongs can cut ropes—and create an intimidating visage.

Not all heroes have the spatial awareness to use a cape effectively as part of their costume. In the wrong hands, a cape can become unwieldy.

FIREPROOF

Both the suit and cape are constructed from fire-retardant materials that dissipate heat quickly, allowing Batman to continue fighting in conditions that would force many heroes to retreat. Batman has full confidence in the strength of his suit, and will sometimes surprise enemies by charging when they think they have him safely pinned behind a barrier of flame. The Batsuit is also resistant to most acids and corrosives, and has almost no electrical conductivity.

The outer layer of the Batsuit can be electrified with a charge of 200,000 volts to shock enemies who get too close for comfort.

The layers of the Batsuit insulate against cold but also permit excess body heat to escape via microscopic pores.

Smart armor reacts to pressure, remaining flexible while Batman is moving and becoming rigid when stabbed or crushed.

BACK VIEW

The cape billows out behind Batman when he leaps at criminals, creating a false outline that momentarily confuses them and often draws inaccurate gunfire. Its ends are weighted with lead, allowing the cape to be swung as a bludgeoning weapon. If an enemy grabs on to the cape, Batman operates its quick-release clasp and jettisons both cape and enemy!

BECOMING A BAT

The most important layer of protection offered by the Batsuit is the effect that it has on startled victims. Dark colors and the cape's irregular outline provide perfect nighttime camouflage, so Batman can appear and disappear without warning. It's not surprising that some believe him to be a vampire or demon. Batman encourages such rumors, which bolster his fearsome reputation.

Batman is protected from top to toe. Steel-toed boots are thermally insulated and have high-grip rubberized soles.

BATSUIT VARIANTS

While always remaining instantly recognizable, the Batsuit has gone through many changes over the years. Batman constantly updates it to take advantage of advanced materials and technology, or to provide protection from strange new enemies. Once superseded, older variants are rarely abandoned. Most are kept at the ready in the original Batcave, or stored in vacuum-sealed cylinders for display in the trophy room.

ORIGINAL
Batman's first costume was a cloak and a gray bodysuit with an integral bulletproof vest.

EARLY VARIANT
The stiff, winglike internal structure of this cape permitted Batman to glide for short distances.

1940'S
Batman perfected his gadget-packed Utility Belt with this version of the costume.

1950'S
Shorter ear points and a wider mask gave Batman a friendlier appearance.

1960'S
Batman added a yellow oval around the bat-symbol to draw gunfire toward his ballistic chest armor.

1970'S
A long, flowing cape helped Batman to disguise his silhouette when he lurked in the shadows.

POST-KNIGHTFALL
After reclaiming his identity from Azrael, Batman adopted a darker Batsuit to better blend in with the darkness.

NO MAN'S LAND
Batman introduced new armored materials into his suit while defending post-quake Gotham City.

BATMAN INC.
As the Batman brand went global, Batman adopted an amalgam of his most familiar costumes.

THE NEW 52
This segmented Batsuit included stylistic armored touches such as bat-shaped knee guards.

REBIRTH
Batman's *Rebirth* suit featured a purple inner cape lining and a yellow-outlined Bat-Symbol.

MODERN
Similar to the suit Batman employed after *No Man's Land*, the modern suit takes a back-to-basics approach.

ALTERNATIVE REALITIES

In branching timelines and on parallel Earths, Batman and his successors have demonstrated some unique spins on the traditional Batsuit.

DAMIAN WAYNE
In one possible future, Bruce's son Damian gained supernatural abilities, including powers of instant healing.

KINGDOM COME
An aged Batman wore an armored suit to deal with a new age of heroes whose methods he found unethical.

BATMAN BEYOND
Batman passed the torch to Terry McGinnis in the alternate future setting of Neo-Gotham City.

FUTURE STATE
Tim "Jace" Fox took the place of the seemingly absent Bruce Wayne to heroically rebel against the oppressive forces of the Magistrate.

SPECIALIZED DESIGNS

Batman keeps a number of specialty Batsuits ready for use, while others have been worn just once, under unique circumstances.

WHITE LANTERN
The White Lantern Ring of Life replaced Batman's usual costume with an all-white suit of blinding purity.

GREEN LANTERN
Batman has worn a Green Lantern ring and costume on more than one occasion, but only temporarily.

BLACK LANTERN
The Black Lantern Ring of Death transformed a skeleton into a black-clad, undead bat-horror.

SUIT OF SORROWS
Created during the Crusades, the Suit of Sorrows bestows great strength on those with pure hearts, like Batman.

RAINBOW BATSUITS
Batman wore a series of brightly colored costumes to draw attention away from an injured Robin.

ZEBRA BATSUIT
When a villain accidentally imbued him with energy, Batman saw his costume change to this striped variant.

SPECIALTY BATSUITS
Arctic, aquatic, slalom, desert, inferno, and other Batsuits are maintained in perfect condition in the Batcave.

ZUR-EN-ARRH BATSUIT
Left without his memory, Batman fashioned this multi-colored suit out of mismatched scraps.

OTHER BEARERS

Bruce Wayne isn't the only person to have put on the cape and cowl of Gotham City's most famous hero.

DICK GRAYSON
After Bruce Wayne's disappearance in time, the original Robin stepped into his shoes—and Batsuit.

DOCTOR HURT
Claiming to be Thomas Wayne, Doctor Hurt appeared in Thomas's bat-themed masquerade costume.

TIM DRAKE
After meeting a grim future version of himself as Batman, Tim Drake vowed never to follow that dark path.

JASON TODD
The second Robin went rogue and tried to become a new, better Batman employing his own uncompromising methods.

AZRAEL
Jean-Paul Valley became a new, more dangerous Batman when Bruce Wayne suffered a back-breaking injury.

HUGO STRANGE
This obsessive villain knows Batman's secret identity and has impersonated him more than once.

JIM GORDON
Taking a break from his role as Commissioner, Jim Gordon adopted an armored Batsuit after Batman was believed dead.

UTILITY BELT

As much a part of the Dark Knight's identity as his cape and cowl, the Utility Belt is a literal lifesaver, filling an essential, multifunctional role. Over the years, the belt's design has varied from incorporating spring-loaded compartments to utilizing simple workman's tool pouches. To wrong-foot criminals, Batman constantly and secretly upgrades the many gadgets concealed in his Utility Belt. Here are just a few that he has employed at various times...

HIDDEN TREASURES

Batman's Utility Belt is boobytrapped with electrical current, but an enemy or two has still managed to dissect it over the years. The corrupt soldiers of the Colony were able to explore about 30 percent of its content after taking Batman captive. However, the Dark Knight escaped using one last gadget they didn't expect: a smoke bomb stored in a false tooth.

ALWAYS PREPARED

Batman has a specialized tool for any situation, but they would be worthless if he couldn't get his hands on them at just the right moment. The Utility Belt is both a field kit and a mobile weapons locker, packing maximum power into a compact and wearable form.

LIGHTS, CAMERA...

One of the belt's compartments held a miniature camera, which captured high-resolution video and still images in ultraviolet and infrared ranges beyond visual perception. All images were instantly uploaded and archived on the Batcomputer's servers. Batman also used its powerful camera flash to dazzle attackers.

DIGITAL CAMERA

SECURE CONSTRUCTION

Featuring solid components made from titanium, the Utility Belt is a triumph of user design. It balances ease of use with the ability to thwart unauthorized access, while using every centimeter of available space within a slim shape that lies flat against the body. The buckle's complex lock releases only after it registers a pre-programmed finger pattern. It also contains a tracking beacon and an explosive charge that can be triggered remotely should the belt fall into the wrong hands.

REMOVABLE BUCKLE AND LOCKING MECHANISM

COMMUNICATIONS

A removable belt compartment has concealed a computer and digital communicator. This device responded to vocal and gestural commands, and possessed a backup touch screen and button array. Though Batman's cowl contains its own dedicated communication system, this device had the added functionality of holographic recording and three-dimensional playback.

PALM-TOP COMMUNICATOR

FIELD EQUIPMENT

Much of the contents of the Utility Belt comprise general and mission-specific field equipment. Common items have included a first-aid kit containing a wide spectrum of antidotes for various toxins, an oxygen rebreather, lock picks, and an acetylene torch capable of cutting through the hull of a battleship. When facing specialized foes Batman might choose to carry flamethrowers, defoliants, electromagnetic pulse generators, or even rare substances like Kryptonite.

MEDICAL KIT AND FIELD DRESSINGS

GRAPPLING HOOK

Earlier versions of the Utility Belt featured a jumpline reel within the buckle—this could be attached to a weighted hook and then thrown by hand.

WEAPONS COMPARTMENTS

Several sections of the belt contain folding Batarangs or mini Batarangs. At one time these were dispensed via spring-loaded ejectors. Titanium cylinders held stacks of tear gas, smoke, and pellets designed to stun an assailant with a sudden flash-bang. One segment contained a magazine of anesthetic darts and a collapsible dart shooter. All of the Utility Belt's weapons compartments have quick-release covers.

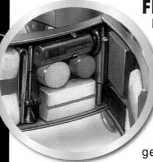

ANYTHING BUT GUNS

The trauma of his parents' murder left Batman with an aversion to firearms. In Batman's view, crooks frequently harm innocents with indiscriminate fire. But even a well-aimed gun will take a life, and a fundamental principle of Batman's crime-fighting credo is his "no killing" rule. His Batarangs and other custom tools require considerable skill to wield, but are designed only to incapacitate their targets. Batman's inner circle have been carefully trained in their use.

BAT-GRENADES

An entire room of enemies can be subdued with a single Bat-grenade. These single-use devices have many tactical applications, including bringing down large structures through controlled explosions and disorienting a crowd of enemies with a concussive blast. Grenades have timers that vary from five seconds to 40 minutes, or they can be activated remotely via radio signal. Large canister grenades can be rolled into rooms or affixed to doorframes where they are triggered by a tightening activation cord. Small pellet grenades can be thrown by the handful or stuck to a wall with a dab of contact cement.

CONCUSSION GRENADE

Firing pin attached to a pull cord

WEAPONS

EXPLOSIVE PELLETS

These hardened gelatin spheres break upon impact, releasing smoke screens or irritants like tear gas. Other pellets are packed with flash-bang charges that temporarily leave foes deaf and blind. The pellets are carried within impact-resistant cylinders on Batman's Utility Belt to prevent accidental detonation.

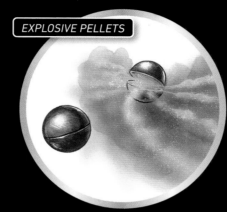
EXPLOSIVE PELLETS

Batman's arsenal of non-lethal weapons isn't for amateurs. Each device requires the strong arm and careful aim of a seasoned expert.

AEROSOL SPRAYS

AEROSOL SPRAY

Depending on the mission, any number of hand-held aerosol canisters may be clipped to Batman's Utility Belt. Knockout sprays also induce temporary amnesia. Supercooled sprays freeze electronics and render adhesives brittle. Tracking sprays tag targets with infrared paint, which Batman can detect through the filtered lenses in his cowl. Any aerosol canister can be placed freestanding in a room and set for timed release.

BAT-CUFFS

BAT-CUFFS

With a stranded-metal cable core surrounded by sapphire-impregnated nylon, these restraints are too strong to be broken by any human being, save those who possess superpowers.

HARD-IMPACT BATARANG

SPINNING BATARANG

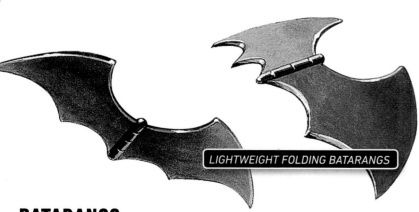
LIGHTWEIGHT FOLDING BATARANGS

CUTTING BATARANG

BATARANGS

Batman's signature weapon is the Batarang, a bat-shaped throwing tool usually cast from a hardened steel alloy. Though the name is derived from the Australian boomerang, not all Batarangs are designed to return to Batman's hand. Some are modeled on throwing knives, darts, and even flying discs. Hard-impact Batarangs can knock foes off their feet, while the micro-serrated edges of cutting Batarangs will slice a jumpline in half. Mini Batarangs have many sharp points and are thrown like Japanese shuriken.

GRAPNEL GUN

Batman uses a handheld grapnel gun to navigate Gotham City's rooftops. Its compressed CO_2 launcher fires a projectile—a grappling hook, Batarang, or wall-penetrating dart—attached to a reel of de-cel monofilament jumpline that can hold up to 400 lbs (181 kg). Once the projectile has latched onto its target, the reel pulls Batman up to his new vantage point in seconds. It is a definitive tool for Batman, allowing him to swing silently between Gotham City's towers. In emergencies, the explosive punch of the grapnel gun can also knock armored enemies off their feet.

PENETRATING DART

The grapnel gun assembly is often tipped with a wall-penetrating dart featuring a smart-acceleration drill bit. Upon impact, internal microcircuitry instantly detects the composition of the surrounding surface, then spins to secure firm anchorage in metal or masonry.

MICRO-DIAMOND DRILL BIT

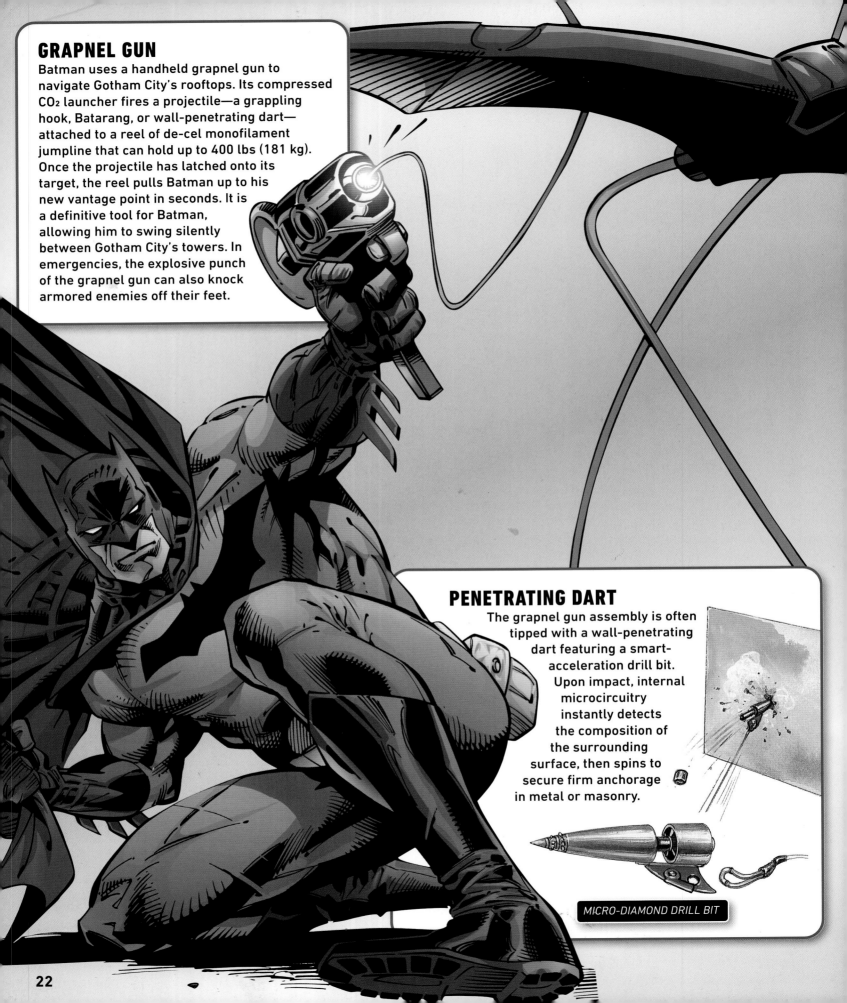

GADGETS

Batman is one of the smartest people on Earth and has both the tools and the training to deal with almost anything. His gadgets have been custom-built to his exact specifications.

HOLOGRAPHIC DISPLAY

Communication links in the Batsuit make it easy for Batman to tap directly into the Batcomputer on the go. While he used to have to tote around bulkier devices, today Batman is able to generate a holographic display projected directly from his armored wrist gauntlet. This "screen" responds to sensors on his opposing glove, enabling him to scroll or type at will.

CRIME SCENE KIT

Batman's detective work usually needs to be completed before the G.C.P.D.'s investigators arrive. A miniature crime scene analysis packet on his Utility Belt contains a fingerprinting kit, a DNA analyzer, several sterile sample bags, a chromatograph to identify substances within a testing sample, and a multi-spectrum environmental recorder.

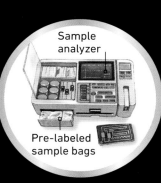

Sample analyzer

Pre-labeled sample bags

TOOL KIT

Drill bit engaged

Each tool in this tightly packed sleeve fits into a powered, universal drive unit inside the handle. Drill bits and tool points of various sizes are included, along with wire cutters or strippers and electronic lock pickers.

REBREATHER

The Dark Knight is often forced to operate underwater for significant amounts of time. His compact rebreather has been a staple of his Utility Belt for years. The oxygen it supplies has not only saved his life; it has also aided a drowning ally or innocent bystander.

GAS MASK

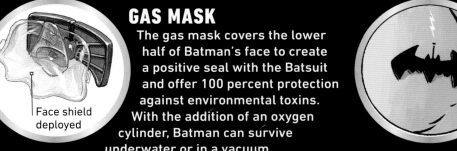

Face shield deployed

The gas mask covers the lower half of Batman's face to create a positive seal with the Batsuit and offer 100 percent protection against environmental toxins. With the addition of an oxygen cylinder, Batman can survive underwater or in a vacuum.

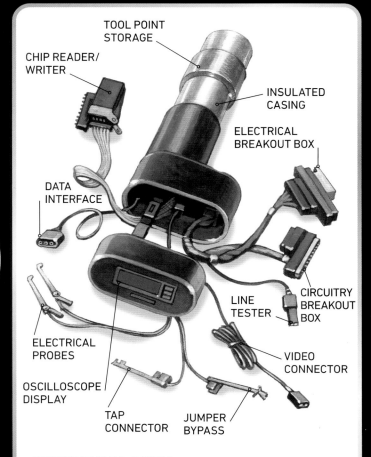

TOOL POINT STORAGE

CHIP READER/ WRITER

INSULATED CASING

ELECTRICAL BREAKOUT BOX

DATA INTERFACE

CIRCUITRY BREAKOUT BOX

LINE TESTER

ELECTRICAL PROBES

VIDEO CONNECTOR

OSCILLOSCOPE DISPLAY

TAP CONNECTOR

JUMPER BYPASS

UNIVERSAL TOOL

In the past, Batman used this piece of equipment to perform various electronic tasks. It had line taps, bypass jumpers, power and communication line analyzers, connectors for standard audio or visual and computing interfaces, and breakout boxes for linking with non-standard electrical configurations. When his universal tool couldn't get the job done, Batman directed the Batcomputer to hack into Gotham City's data grid.

BAT-TRACKER

Even if an enemy escapes an encounter with Batman, the Dark Knight has ways of catching up with his target. Key among those methods involves slipping a Bat-tracker on his unsuspecting foe. These tiny, self-adhering, bat-shaped devices broadcast the target's GPS to the Batcomputer's systems, allowing Batman to follow at his leisure.

THE BATCAVE

During daylight hours bats nest amid the stalactites.

Ceiling ports—quick-launch access for the Batplane.

The Joker's unmistakable calling card.

An information hub displays selected readouts.

The Batcave was also used as a garage. Various Batmobiles and vehicles built for specialized functions sat fueled and ready on a mechanized platform. The Batcave's concealed entrance connects to Gotham City's hidden network of tunnels, and the platform could rotate to move any vehicle into position. Batman and his partners are all trained mechanics.

The oversized 1947 penny was a prop used by the Penny Plunderer. Most of Batman's trophies date from the early days, back when his enemies were more likely to be theatrical than murderous.

Specialized Batsuits are positioned here for quick access. Batman has dozens of suits on display and many more stored out of sight. Among the is a case containing Jason Todd's Robin costume. It was originally put display to commemorate Jason's death, and even after Jason return Batman chose to leave the memor up as a reminder of his greatest failure to help an ally.

A trophy room houses museum pieces from the most famous cases of Batman's career. Because Gotham City's crooks have a taste for the extreme, many of these mementos are gigantic. A robotic tyrannosaurus rex, which can still be reactivated by Batman, is the only remaining relic from a villainous caper at Gotham City's Dinosaur Island amusement park.

An underground river links to Gotham City's waterways.

HIGH-TECH HEADQUARTERS

A natural cavern has always existed beneath Wayne Manor's grounds; it was once considered a holy place by the prehistoric Miagani tribe. After adopting the identity of Batman, Bruce Wayne recognized the cave's practicality as a secret base for his operations—not to mention the appropriateness of making a home among the true bats of Gotham City. While Batman currently chooses to operate out of several smaller "mini-caves" around Gotham City, the original Batcave remains the most impressive. It contains a trophy room, a chamber for combat training, and a garage for storing multiple Batmobiles.

The heart of the Batcave is the Batcomputer, a storehouse and advanced analyzer incorporati multiple hardwired supercomputers. A flexible user interface incorporates gestures, voice commands, and holographic floating panels. Batman can access data remotely through a heads-up display projected onto a contact lens through other computers in his direct network.

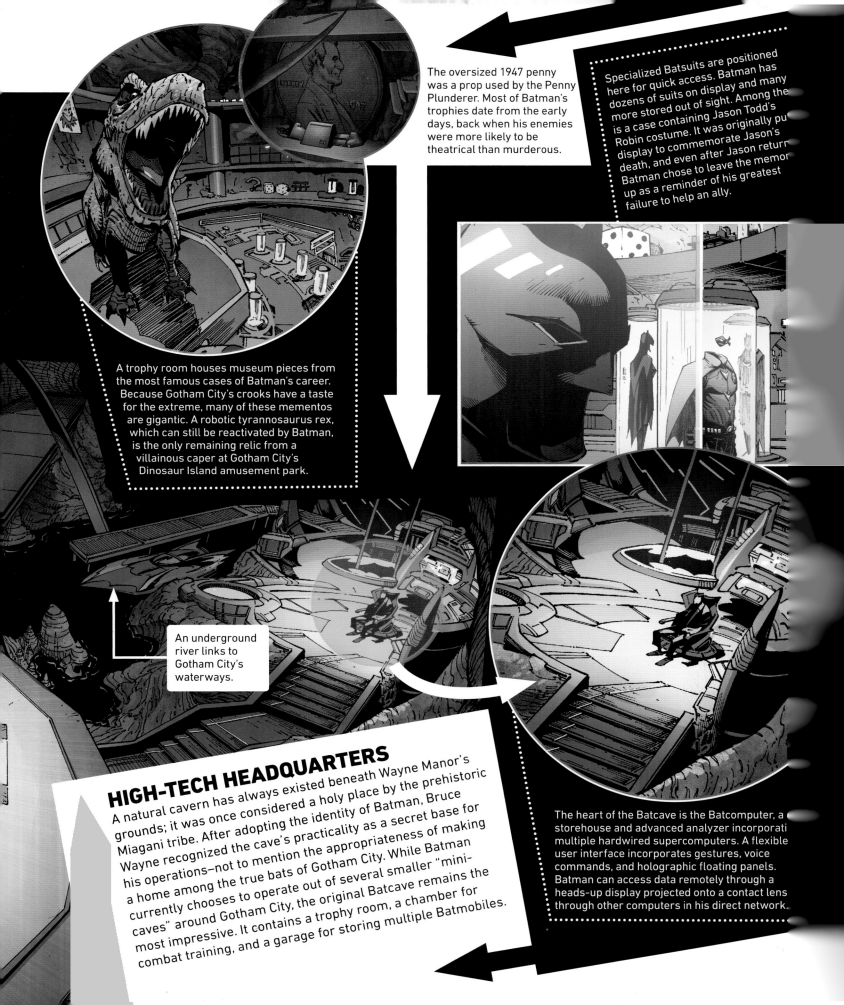

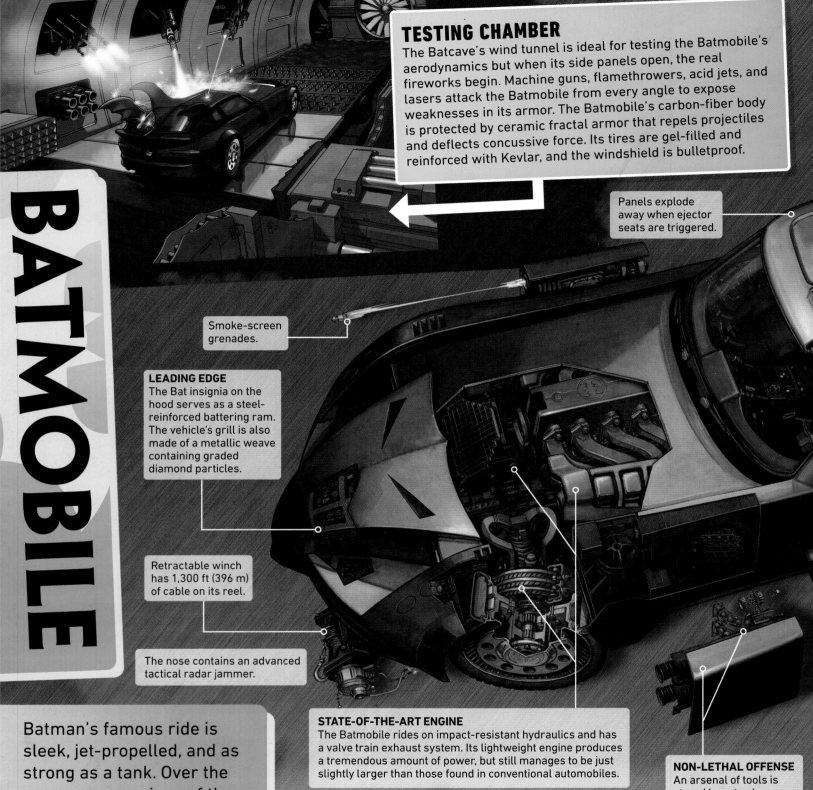

BATMOBILE

TESTING CHAMBER

The Batcave's wind tunnel is ideal for testing the Batmobile's aerodynamics but when its side panels open, the real fireworks begin. Machine guns, flamethrowers, acid jets, and lasers attack the Batmobile from every angle to expose weaknesses in its armor. The Batmobile's carbon-fiber body is protected by ceramic fractal armor that repels projectiles and deflects concussive force. Its tires are gel-filled and reinforced with Kevlar, and the windshield is bulletproof.

Panels explode away when ejector seats are triggered.

Smoke-screen grenades.

LEADING EDGE

The Bat insignia on the hood serves as a steel-reinforced battering ram. The vehicle's grill is also made of a metallic weave containing graded diamond particles.

Retractable winch has 1,300 ft (396 m) of cable on its reel.

The nose contains an advanced tactical radar jammer.

STATE-OF-THE-ART ENGINE

The Batmobile rides on impact-resistant hydraulics and has a valve train exhaust system. Its lightweight engine produces a tremendous amount of power, but still manages to be just slightly larger than those found in conventional automobiles.

NON-LETHAL OFFENSE

An arsenal of tools is stored here to slow down or deter foes without causing serious injury; retractable cannons can fire tear gas canisters, concussion grenades, tire-piercing caltrops, adhesive sprays, or Teflon lubricant slicks.

Batman's famous ride is sleek, jet-propelled, and as strong as a tank. Over the years, new versions of the Batmobile have regularly appeared. Nearly every design has featured an ominous, bat-winged profile to announce the arrival of the Dark Knight and strike fear in criminal hearts.

UNDER THE HOOD

The Batmobile is driven by a 1,200 horsepower jet turbine. Within the vehicle's nose is a sensor suite containing a landsat videomapper, a radar imager, and an infrared headlight mode, permitting Batman to engage in "blind driving" even when the Batmobile's windshield has been polarized for full opacity. A police-band radio monitors transmissions from the G.C.P.D., while omni-directional microphones controlled from the dashboard allow Batman to conduct remote surveillance when parked.

EJECTION SEAT
Both the driver and passenger seats can be ejected via dashboard buttons or voice commands. The ejector's solid-fuel rocket boost is extremely powerful—passengers are subjected to forces of up to 14 g.

A CO_2 launcher fires a reinforced grappling hook.

COMPUTER WORKSTATION
By sliding an armored panel out of the way, Batman can roll out a specialized computer for analyzing DNA samples and uploading data gathered via a satellite signal to the Batcomputer.

FIELD GEAR
Stores a defibrillator, forensic microscope, and crime scene kit.

GROUNDED JET
The Batmobile's jet turbine permits acceleration that is far beyond the capability of any conventional land vehicle. Equipped with high-flow air intake filters, the turbine also features an experimental quantum afterburner.

GETTING TRACTION
The wheels of the Batmobile are equipped with tri-aerated anti-lock disc brakes. Its gel-filled tires are auto-reinflating. When the tires are intentionally overinflated, embedded studs are pushed out for added grip on slippery surfaces.

GETTING TRACTION
A computerized pump feeds high-octane jet fuel from the main tank and twin auxiliary tanks. Cooling fins are installed to prevent the tanks from dangerously overheating.

KEY STATS
- **TOP SPEED:** 266 mph (428 kph)
- **LENGTH:** 16 ft (14.88m)
- **WIDTH:** 6.4 ft (1.95m)
- **HEIGHT:** 4.8 ft (1.46m)
- **ACCELERATION:** 0-60 mph in 2.4 seconds
- **UPPER TEMPERATURE LIMIT:** 1,100° Fahrenheit (593.3° Celsius)
- **LOWER TEMPERATURE LIMIT:** -230° Fahrenheit (-145.5° Celsius)

THE ECHO

Developed by Lucius Fox, the Echo is a small handheld device capable of interfacing with the Wayne Industries components in a standard car engine. It bypasses speed limitations while also creating a holo-interface that masks the car's true appearance, making it look and perform like a sleek Batmobile.

BATMOBILE DEVELOPMENT
1940'S
1950'S
1960'S
1970'S
1980'S
1990'S
2000'S
2010'S

BATMAN VEHICLES

The Batmobile might rule the streets, but Batman can't corral crime in all its forms until he covers land, air, and sea. Before he lost most of his funding, Batman employed a wide range of experimental vehicles, most manufactured at least in part by Wayne Industries. The Batplane and the Batboat allow the Dark Knight to keep pace with superpowered colleagues like Superman or Aquaman, while the Batcycle and other nimble rides provide the maneuverability the Batmobile lacks. Nearly every vehicle Batman has ever employed bears a blue or black color scheme.

BATPLANE
Batman maintains a squadron of Batplanes, from rapid interceptors to massive cargo carriers that sit in a secret hangar. Most Batplanes are capable of vertical takeoff and landing and bear dynamic camouflage to evade sensors. The Batplane has a highly advanced autopilot that responds to remote voice commands.

Wings are lined with anti-icing units.

BAT-GLIDER
Struts are braced with Kevlar for added tensile strength.

Batman can't fly like a real bat, but his glider provides the next best thing. This lightweight and responsive glider can be used for silent drifting between rooftops, or—when its twin engines are attached—for a single-person powered flight. In case of an unexpected landing in Gotham City Harbor, it is outfitted with an emergency flotation device. Without its engines, the glider is small enough to be stored in a shoulder-slung case.

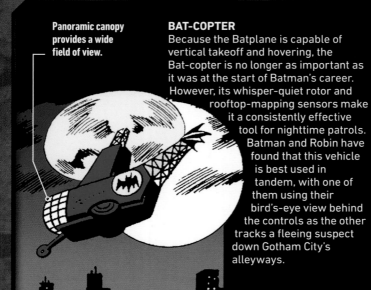

Panoramic canopy provides a wide field of view.

BAT-COPTER
Because the Batplane is capable of vertical takeoff and hovering, the Bat-copter is no longer as important as it was at the start of Batman's career. However, its whisper-quiet rotor and rooftop-mapping sensors make it a consistently effective tool for nighttime patrols. Batman and Robin have found that this vehicle is best used in tandem, with one of them using their bird's-eye view behind the controls as the other tracks a fleeing suspect down Gotham City's alleyways.

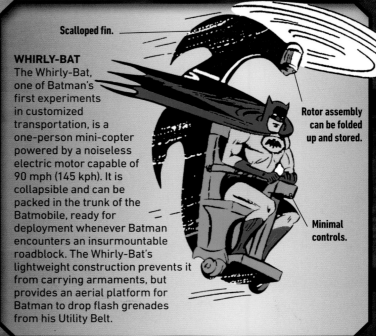

Scalloped fin.

WHIRLY-BAT
The Whirly-Bat, one of Batman's first experiments in customized transportation, is a one-person mini-copter powered by a noiseless electric motor capable of 90 mph (145 kph). It is collapsible and can be packed in the trunk of the Batmobile, ready for deployment whenever Batman encounters an insurmountable roadblock. The Whirly-Bat's lightweight construction prevents it from carrying armaments, but provides an aerial platform for Batman to drop flash grenades from his Utility Belt.

Rotor assembly can be folded up and stored.

Minimal controls.

BATCYCLE

The Batcycle can go places that the Batmobile can't. This custom-built street motorcycle has a 786cc liquid-cooled engine and a sleek profile for roaring through narrow gaps in traffic. The Batcycle's computer-controlled gyroscopic stability system helps it stay upright during high-speed chases. Though Batman presents a bigger target on the Batcycle, the vehicle's front cowling and windscreen are bulletproof. A variant of the Batcycle is the Bat-Pod, a small motorcycle that can be stored inside the Batmobile and ejected while the larger vehicle is still in motion.

Puncture-proof racing tires for road traction.

BATBOAT

The Batboat carries an arsenal of non-lethal weapons, including hull-puncturing homing torpedoes, controlled-explosion depth charges, and a harpoon gun. A pneumatic grapnel can latch onto other ships or serve as an anchor. Outrigger pods can turn the Batboat into a high-speed hydrofoil capable of speeds up to 150 mph (241 kmh). The Batboat is fully sealed and capable of submerging should Batman require a more clandestine mode of aquatic travel.

BAT-TRAIN

Not only has Batman used a Subway Rocket Batmobile to speed along Gotham City's subway tracks, he has also employed a Bat-Train for high-speed transport. While intended for a single passenger, the train car can also accommodate a guest or two, as was the case when Batman hauled the Super-Villain Deathstroke along with him on a recent mission.

BATSPAWN

During the height of his technological excess, Batman employed a drone army called Batspawn from his Wayne Industries factory located in the Gotham City neighborhood of Tricorner Yards. These self-propelled, unmanned, bat-shaped devices helped him survey the city like never before.

BAT-RAPTOR

As fast and maneuverable as his Batcycle, yet better shielded against small arms fire, the Bat-Raptor is capable of firing a variety of devices, from grappling hooks to an ejection seat.

ORIGIN

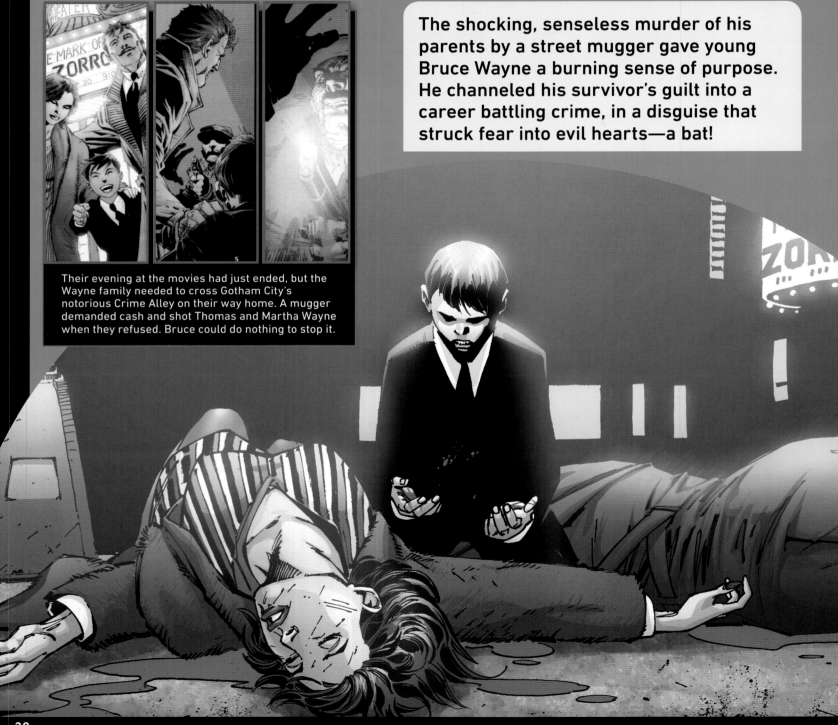

The shocking, senseless murder of his parents by a street mugger gave young Bruce Wayne a burning sense of purpose. He channeled his survivor's guilt into a career battling crime, in a disguise that struck fear into evil hearts—a bat!

Their evening at the movies had just ended, but the Wayne family needed to cross Gotham City's notorious Crime Alley on their way home. A mugger demanded cash and shot Thomas and Martha Wayne when they refused. Bruce could do nothing to stop it.

BECOMING THE BAT...

Haunted by what he had witnessed, and wracked with guilt over his inability to act, Bruce vowed that no one would suffer the same fate that he had. As heir to the Wayne family fortune, he had both power and privilege—yet those advantages didn't prevent Thomas and Martha Wayne from dying in a flash of gunpowder. Bruce knew he couldn't bring them back, but with the right resources at his disposal he could make the streets safe again.

He knew it wasn't enough to simply fund the police—not in dangerous and corrupt Gotham City. Instead, Bruce decided to take the fight directly to those who challenged law and order, avenging his parents every time he saved a life and every time he put a crook behind bars.

Bruce Wayne left Gotham City to undertake the training he would need to carry out his one-man campaign. He studied languages and psychology at Cambridge University and the Sorbonne. He meditated in the mystic Tibetan city of Nanda Parbat and lived among the Ghost Tribes of the Ten-Eyed Brotherhood in Africa. In Korea, he learned the art of the ninjutsu under Master Kirigi. From the world-class manhunter Henri Ducard he gained the secrets of tracking targets by the clues they left behind. Bruce absorbed every ounce of instruction, but remained troubled by the amoral stance of his tutors. Most of them cared only for the technique itself, and didn't concern themselves with how their students might apply it.

After years of globe trekking, Bruce had honed his body and mind to near-perfection. It was time to return home. Though he had become an expert martial artist and criminologist, Bruce dressed in simple street clothes on his first patrol. Unimpressed, the thugs fought back. Bruce knew he could tame the city only when his mere reputation was enough to demoralize his foes. He must be a frightening figure, someone who struck from the shadows. Inspired by a bat crashing through a window in Wayne Manor, Bruce seized on the notion of creating a mysterious "Batman" to strike fear in the hearts of the cowardly and the superstitious. Tales of the Batman spread. Soon, the swirling cape and pointed cowl were enough to frighten the guilty into confessing their darkest crimes.

LEAVING GOTHAM CITY

KIRIGI—NINJA MASTER

HENRI DUCARD

"I must be a creature of the night. Black, terrible—a bat!"

AN INDOMITABLE WILL

Batman does not possess superhuman powers, but his absolute determination and strength of will make him nearly unstoppable.

GENIUS INTELLECT

All of Batman's most amazing feats, from his combat mastery to his detective prowess, are the products of a brilliant mind. His unique mental gift is the ability to learn and retain the secrets of many disciplines simultaneously.

• TECHNICAL QUALIFICATIONS: Batman has considerable expertise in computer programming, electronics, and bomb disposal.

• LANGUAGES: Batman speaks dozens of languages, including Russian, French, German, Japanese, Cantonese, Turkish, Arabic, and Swahili. He also knows phrases in extraterrestrial tongues.

• MASTER TACTICIAN: Batman's most powerful weapon is his ability to read his enemies and anticipate their next moves. This gives him an edge in personal combat and planning strategic campaigns.

• ESCAPOLOGY: From the writings of Houdini and instruction from escape artist Mister Miracle and stage magician Zatara, Batman has learned to free himself from straightjackets, handcuffs, locked trunks, and other traps in seconds.

• PILOTING/DRIVING: Batman is an expert automobile, motorcycle, and hydrofoil driver. In the air, he can pilot jet fighters, helicopters, and even space shuttles.

• TRACKING/DETECTING: Batman is peerless at shadowing suspects, looking for clues, and tracing fugitives.

• DISGUISE: Batman can alter his voice, stance, and mannerisms, and mimic dozens of accents.

PSYCHOLOGY

Fear is what distinguishes Batman from other Super Heroes. Fear is why he adopted the identity of a bat, and why criminals often surrender at the mere sight of his swirling cape. Batman exploits his reputation to squeeze information out of underworld contacts, but he isn't above using force when necessary. Roughing up a suspect gets quick results, and suspending them from the top of a skyscraper with nothing more than a batrope around their feet is even better. Scare tactics like these have spread Batman's terrifying reputation far and wide.

MATCHES MALONE
This crook maintains a low profile in Gotham City's underworld. However, the real Matches Malone died years ago—and the current holder of that name is actually Batman in disguise! By assuming the identity of a preexisting villain whose backstory stands up to scrutiny, Batman has gained inside information on Black Mask, Two-Face, and other crime kingpins. "Matches" has a nondescript and easily forgettable appearance, with his only quirk being the matchstick that he constantly keeps between his teeth.

Batman's shift isn't over when he returns to his home base. These days, he usually functions out of several small satellite Batcaves around the city, rather than relying on a secret headquarters beneath Wayne Manor. But within each of these caves is a forensics laboratory that would be the envy of any police force. The Batcomputer can perform heavy data crunching or hack into protected public records, and Batman stays connected to its systems while he is out in the field so he can make on-the-spot analyses of his surroundings. For more thorough results, however, Batman insists on bringing samples back to one of his micro-caves and running tests there.

Thanks to his detection skills, Batman often discovers clues that previous investigators have missed.

CRIME-FIGHTING TECH
Batman possesses some of the most advanced investigative equipment in the world. The tools at Batman's disposal include:

- Fume/particulate analyzer
- Gunpowder and explosive residue analyzer
- Forensic microscope
- Chemical spectrometer
- Multiband light-source projector
- Latent print development chamber
- Tire track and footprint impression kits
- Indented writing restoration tools
- Serial number restoration gel
- Global G.P.S. tracking system
- Facial composite software
- Autopsy investigation tools
- Electronic surveillance and line tap detectors
- Narcotic reagents and chromatography test kits
- Fluorescent invisible detection powder

ALWAYS WATCHING...
The Batcomputer is connected to the internal networks of the C.I.A., Interpol, the covert operations agency Checkmate, and most of the world's governments. To gain a better perspective on global trouble spots, Batman designed and launched the Brother Eye surveillance satellite, but he destroyed it when it grew dangerously self-aware.

STAYING ON TOP

Batman's skills are legendary, but if he doesn't stay in top condition he'll quickly lose them. Gotham City's guardian maintains an exhausting daily regimen that keeps him ahead of the pack.

FIGHTING STYLE

Although Batman has endeavored to become an expert in every continent's top martial arts disciplines, he has chosen to combine his talents to create a highly personal combat style that comprises several core arts. The distance separating Batman from his opponent is what usually dictates which combination of abilities he will use first.

WEAPONIZED

Batman is skilled with all firearms, though he has sworn never to carry or use one. He is an expert with projectile weapons, such as bows, crossbows, and blow guns, as well as most types of martial arts weapons, such as swords, staffs, and fighting sticks.

"THE MOST DANGEROUS MAN ALIVE."

Batman patrols Gotham City nearly every night—at a minimum this provides an intense cardio and upper-body workout with rope swinging and parkour-style acrobatics. But patrolling doesn't provide the full workout he requires. The Dark Knight also engages in short but intense sessions that focus on building endurance, maintaining muscle, or practicing combat routines. Batman varies his schedule daily to give his body enough time to recover from the previous workout. These sessions are interspersed with restorative SWS (slow-wave sleep) naps throughout the day.

SPARRING

Former professional boxer Ted Grant, better known as Wildcat, taught Batman the sweet science of bare-knuckled pugilism. Batman toughens his fists by working a punching bag, and he also practices his footwork against Robin. Sparring, however, is one area that does not require much gym practice. Batman gets to test his skills by throwing punches at Gotham City's many crooks each night.

DIET

Batman eats high-protein, high-calorie foods to fuel his hard-working body. Batman isn't obsessive about diet and enjoys a business luncheon as Bruce Wayne. He never drinks alcohol, and secretly substitutes ginger ale for champagne at social functions.

- BREAKFAST: Oatmeal, a banana, two boiled eggs, orange juice or green tea.
- MID MORNING: Tuna, four rice cakes with peanut butter.
- LUNCH: Grilled chicken, jacket potato, steamed vegetables, vitamin and essential-oil supplements.
- AFTERNOON SNACK: Cottage cheese, oatmeal crackers, fruit.
- DINNER: Grilled chicken, fish or steak, steamed vegetables, rice or pasta.
- BEFORE BED: Protein shake.

PHYSICAL ATTRIBUTES

STRENGTH

Batman's body might be 210 lbs (95.3 kg) of toned muscle, but he doesn't prioritize weight training above an all-over approach to fitness. Matched with honed combat techniques, he is able to put maximum power behind each blow and knock out opponents twice his size. Because Batman often needs to carry others—be they rescued hostages or handcuffed crooks—his lifting strength is considerable.

ENDURANCE

Stamina is arguably Batman's secret weapon. Others may match him in strength or speed, but they often grow tired and drop their defenses. Batman's training includes runs and swims of up to an hour at a time. When he's on a mission, short meditative breaks allow him to refresh his body and mind.

REFLEXES

Batman's incredible reflexes are the result of the mental training he received in the monastery of Nanda Parbat and the ninjutsu skills taught by Master Kirigi. He's so fast he can snatch an arrow mid-flight.

AGILITY

Nightly patrols over Gotham City's rooftops require a gymnastic mix of leaping, tumbling, balancing, and rope swinging. Dick Grayson, who was a circus acrobat before he became Robin, has taught his mentor a thing or two about the high-wire arts. When Batman pairs agility with strength, he can take down targets with devastating force.

DURABILITY

Batman owns some of the most advanced medical equipment in the world courtesy of Wayne Biotech. In his career, Batman has been shot, stabbed, burned, and frostbitten. Killer Croc has snapped his ribs and Bane has broken his back. Batman originally relied on the help of Alfred Pennyworth for medical care, owing to Alfred's experience as a former battlefield medic. But now the Dark Knight no longer has that luxury, and often has to deal with his wounds himself.

He is a man of few words, but when Batman speaks, people listen. The Dark Knight has also spent time alone, pondering his motivation for his heroic crime-fighting mission. Those long hours have brought him a high level of self-awareness.

"I made a promise on the grave of my parents that I would rid this city of the evil that took their lives. I believe someday I will make good on that promise."

"I don't enjoy fear. But I've learned to respect it."

"I believe in Jim Gordon. I believe in Harvey Dent. "I believe in Gotham City."

"They say that when you kill a man you not only take away what he was, but all he will ever be."

"I hardly even knew my parents as people. But suddenly I knew the world. It was hard and cold and dark and lawless. Its face was fierce and bestial. The only face I had with which to glare back at it... was utterly inadequate."

"Criminals, by nature, are a cowardly and superstitious lot. To instill fear into their hearts, I became a bat."

"Deep down, Clark's essentially a good person... and deep down, I'm not."

"One day, there will be no pain, no loss, no crime. Because of me, because I fight. For you. One day, I will win."

"If detective work were easy, everyone would be doing it."

"Days. Months. Years, spent memorizing the finite ways there are to hurt and break a man."

"I chose this life. I know what I'm doing. And on any given day, I could stop doing it. Today, however, isn't that day."

"The first person I ever revealed my identity to was Dick Grayson. I wanted to make a difference in his life, the way, if my parents had lived, they would have made a difference in mine."

"He tried to use Gotham's legends against me. But I'm the only legend this city needs."

"Dick saw being Robin as a thrill. It's probably why he outgrew it. Jason saw Robin as a game. It's probably what got him killed."

"Think clean thoughts, chum."

"Batman and Robin will never die!"

"I was done playing nice... a long time ago!"

"Because Gotham isn't Batman. Gotham isn't the Owls. Gotham is... Gotham is all of us."

"Everyone thinks they know me. No one does."

"There are no good deaths. But there are good lives. Let's try to live one of those."

GREAT ESCAPES!

Batman's mind and body are honed to perfection. With the physical and mental working in synchronization, the Dark Knight can pick any lock and fight his way free from the strongest of snares.

When gangsters heard Batman describe an "inescapable" death trap he'd dreamed about, they built it for real—then took bets on whether he would survive! Batman jammed the machine gun as the chamber filled with water, and escaped through a hole in the wall.

"I've escaped from every conceivable deathtrap. Ten times. A dozen times."

— BATMAN

BATMAN VS. BODY TRAP

The Joker's goons fired strange webbing at Batman and Robin, which wrapped around their torsos and grew tighter as they struggled. Robin couldn't breathe and was fading fast. Batman entered a state of meditative calm to relax his muscles, sloughing off the constricting material and cutting Robin loose with a Batarang.

BATMAN VS. WOLVES

While working on the Mad Monk case, Batman found himself cornered by a pack of wolves. He hit them with a cloud of knockout gas and entangled one with a Batarang line, but another sank its fangs into his leg. Batman tried blasting the wolf with pepper spray and blinding it with his cape before he finally gained

BATMAN VS. BURIAL

Doctor Hurt and the agents of the Black Glove had beaten Batman, and as their final act of triumph, they buried him alive. Batman slowed his breathing and focused his muscle movements, which allowed him to break the coffin's lid and methodically make his way up through the loose layer of dirt that marked his shallow grave.

BATMAN VS. DROWNING

The Scarecrow flooded a Gotham City sewer tunnel, and Batman saved the mayor from the rising waters. In search of an exit, Batman swam through the passageways using his rebreather, and when it expired he pressed on with only the air in his lungs. Close to death, Batman at last found a hatch and escaped with the

BATMAN VS. SCORPION VENOM

During a swordfighters' duel with Rä's al Ghül, Batman stepped too close to a desert scorpion and it stung him on the heel. Left to die on the burning sands, Batman kept his strength up until Talia al Ghül could deliver an anti-venom antidote in the form of a kiss. Batman, exhausted but defiant, challenged Rä's al Ghül to a rematch.

BATMAN VS. ROLLER COASTER

Inside a Guatemalan cavern, The Joker tied Batman's arms and placed him on top of an amusement-park train—with an innocent victim lying directly in its path! Batman snatched a stalactite to cut his bonds, then hurled a Batarang at the engine's front wheels. His aim was perfect: The train jumped the track, sparing The Joker's hostage at the

BATMAN VS. THE G.C.P.D.

Trapped in the cellar of a condemned building and surrounded by a squad of hostile police officers, Batman used a blowgun to render several of them unconscious. To cover his escape, Batman summoned thousands of bats using an ultrasonic transmitter hidden in his boot.

BATMAN VS. SUPERMAN

Poison Ivy brainwashed Superman and turned him against Batman, but Batman reasoned that Superman wouldn't use deadly force against a friend. Batman subdued him with hypersonics, electrocution, and low-dosage Kryptonite. Catwoman broke Ivy's spell by putting Lois Lane

MORE GREAT ESCAPES

WEARING A MASK

Those who know Batman well agree that his true personality is that of the grim, unsmiling Dark Knight, while the Bruce Wayne in the newspaper headlines is merely a role. Bruce is a skilled actor, assuming other identities (such as the crook Matches Malone) when the need arises.

KEEPING SECRETS

His parents' murder is a matter of public record, so to preserve his anonymity, Batman crafted Bruce Wayne's personality to be the complete opposite of the terrifying Dark Knight. Bruce makes occasional appearances at Wayne Industries for interviews or to attract new investors, but leaves the daily running of the company to his employees so he can pursue his "playboy" lifestyle.

KEY DATA

FULL NAME Bruce Wayne

OCCUPATION Businessman, philanthropist

WEAPONS/POWERS/ABILITIES Genius intellect, wealthy with technological resources, powerful political connections, master detective, strategist, and martial artist

AFFILIATIONS Wayne Enterprises, Batman, Inc.

RELATIVES Thomas and Martha Wayne (parents, deceased); Dick Grayson (adopted son); Jason Todd (adopted son); Tim Drake (adopted son); Damian Wayne (biological son); Kate Kane (cousin)

FIRST APPEARANCE
Detective Comics #27 (May 1939)

"A brighter, better Gotham is just one dream away!"

BRUCE WAYNE

BRUCE WAYNE

Bruce is well-liked and knows when to turn on the charm. With a single speech he can win over a roomful of hostile investors.

Who is Bruce Wayne? Many would describe him as a bored playboy, heir to a rich fortune. None realize it is all an act. The death of his parents changed Bruce, and his true personality is indistinguishable from the deadly serious demeanor of the Batman.

Dick Grayson, Tim Drake, and Damian Wayne are seldom asked to appear in the intense public spotlight.

Bruce maintains his after-hours image as a nightclub-hopper by recklessly flashing his money— while carefully sipping a non-alcoholic drink.

Nobody would suspect the hands-on role Bruce has assumed to ensure that the loss he suffered is never experienced by others.

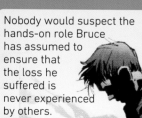

IN THE PUBLIC EYE

The fun-loving side of Bruce Wayne died years ago, after a mugger's bullets ended his parents' lives. However, Batman maintains the Bruce Wayne playboy façade at nightclubs, yacht races, and gallery openings, where the exploits of a handsome socialite get covered in the *Gotham Gazette*.

Alfred Pennyworth was Bruce Wayne's right-hand man. More like a father than a butler, Alfred was as loyal to Bruce as humanly possible.

Gotham City has seen significant change thanks to the Wayne Family over the years and its interest in city planning and development. As heir to his family's billions, Bruce Wayne has often been at the forefront of that endeavor. However, while Wayne Industries remains a fixture in Gotham City, Bruce Wayne's personal fortune has taken a turn for the worse. Due to illegal corporate machinations by none other than the infamous criminal called The Joker, Wayne has gone from billionaire to merely comfortably wealthy. He has since taken up residence in the neighborhood of Fort Graye, preferring to live life on a smaller scale as both Bruce Wayne and Batman.

Bruce has been romantically linked to a string of beautiful women over the years, including Vicki Vale, Silver St. Cloud, and Jezebel Jet. And while Batman recently flirted with the idea of marriage with his longtime romantic partner Catwoman, Bruce remains single. He is nonetheless a family man. Bruce has four sons, all of whom have filled the role of Robin. He legally adopted Dick Grayson, Tim Drake, and Jason Todd, while Damian Wayne is his biological son with his former lover Talia al Ghūl.

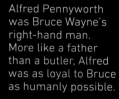

WAYNE MANOR

A STATELY HOME

The ancestral home of the Wayne family has stood on Gotham City's northern slope for generations, at the center of what is now the wealthy Crest Hill area of Bristol Township. While the mansion remains a private residence, Bruce Wayne sometimes opens its gates to welcome hundreds of partygoers to charity auctions and masquerade balls. Within Wayne Manor are treasures acquired through generations of wealth, including rare paintings, antique weapons, suits of armor, and historic documents dating back to Gotham City's founding. Beneath the manor lies the Batcave, accessed through a secret passage hidden behind a grandfather clock. The grounds of Wayne Manor also house garages, gardens, and stables.

HISTORY

Originally built for Bruce Wayne's ancestor Darius Wayne during the 1800s, the manor forms a distinctive "W" shape when viewed from above. The cave beneath the manor grounds has existed since prehistoric times, and was formerly sacred ground for the Miagani tribe and the location of a pirate's treasure stash. After Darius Wayne, the ownership of the manor remained in family hands. It passed to Alan Wayne in the early 20th century, and eventually to Thomas and Martha Wayne, then their son Bruce. After Bruce Wayne launched his career as Batman, he gave Wayne Manor a radical but largely invisible upgrade. The subterranean cavern became the high-tech Batcave, while the mansion received a state-of-the-art sensor web to keep Bruce Wayne alerted to unwelcome visitors. Wayne Manor went unoccupied for a brief time when Dick Grayson left for college, with Bruce temporarily relocating to a penthouse apartment in the city. After an earthquake rocked Wayne Manor and caused extensive damage to its foundations, Bruce rebuilt his home, adding new features to make it even more secure.

Bruce Wayne's childhood memories of Wayne Manor were mostly happy, but in one incident he fell into a pit connected to the subterranean network under the manor. The screeching bats he encountered left him shaken.

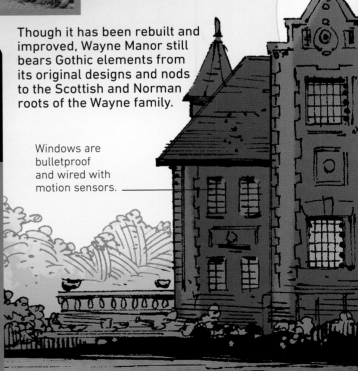

Though it has been rebuilt and improved, Wayne Manor still bears Gothic elements from its original designs and nods to the Scottish and Norman roots of the Wayne family.

Windows are bulletproof and wired with motion sensors.

The forefathers of the Wayne family are placed in chronological order in the portrait hall. They include witch hunter Nathaniel Wayne, Revolutionary War hero "Mad" Anthony Wayne, and Judge Solomon Wayne.

CATACLYSM

When a magnitude 7.6 earthquake shook Gotham City, it left Wayne Manor in ruins. Within the city limits, criminals ran wild as the government implemented a civilian evacuation and, subsequently, an armed blockade. Bruce Wayne was preoccupied with keeping the peace as Batman, but he invested in the swift reconstruction of the manor as a symbol of Gotham City's inevitable return.

SECURITY

Wayne Manor is the Batcave's first line of defense. Its systems are among the best in the world. Gargoyles and other ornamental statuary conceal radar sensors and heat-imaging scopes, and every inch of the grounds is bathed by motion sensors and biometric detectors that set off silent alarms when triggered. Non-aggressive deterrents include nausea-inducing sonic projectors, while more extreme measures against intruders include net traps and a taser charge that electrifies the entire lawn. Wayne Manor is shielded from electronic surveillance by an electromagnetic bubble.

- Proximity motion detectors
- Interior silent alarms
- HIAD (Human Identification At a Distance) sensors
- Voice-activated taser lawn

THE BATCAVE

A grandfather clock conceals the entrance to the Batcave. When its hands are turned to 10:48, the time of Thomas and Martha Wayne's deaths, a door behind it unlocks. The Batcave can also be reached via access vents or secret hatches in the sewer tunnels.

Radar and biometric sensors are concealed from view.

Retractable floodlights can turn night into day.

The mansion's foundations are reinforced against tectonic shocks.

Wayne Manor

Main level

Sub-levels 1–7

WAYNE INDUSTRIES

Wayne Industries is synonymous with Gotham City, and has been for decades. While Bruce Wayne has sat at its head since his return to Gotham City after years of studying abroad, he has recently stepped down from the family business. Now a millionaire rather than billionaire, a paid figurehead rather than the secret brains behind the operation, Bruce is content to leave the company in the hands of Lucius Fox, one of the few people in the world that he trusts implicitly.

AS OLD AS GOTHAM CITY

Traditions run deep in Gotham City. The Wayne family has made their home here since the 1600s, and by the 1800s, Solomon Wayne was helping to shape the city with a truly unique vision. Many Waynes took a direct interest in using their family fortune actively, including prominent figure Alan Wayne, but others—like Bruce's father Thomas, who was a highly skilled physician—chose to dedicate their lives to serving the community in other ways. This family history would inspire Bruce to prioritize, not just Gotham City as a whole, but also each individual who lives there.

LUCIUS FOX

Chosen by Wayne Industries' board as the new CEO of the transitioning company, Lucius Fox had already been steering Wayne Industries for years, even if his name wasn't atop the company's letterhead. The Batman half of Bruce Wayne's life nearly always took the bulk of Bruce's time and effort, leaving Fox to navigate the choppy waters of Gotham City's corporate boardrooms. Lucius is also a genius-level inventor, and before he ascended to CEO, many of his designs contributed to Batman's variety of weapons and vehicles. Lucius not only knows about Batman's double life, but his own family has begun to follow in the Dark Knight's footsteps, including his son Luke Fox, the Super Hero Batwing.

A VISION OF THE FUTURE
As a well-known public figure, Bruce Wayne attracts a lot of attention, which he uses for his advantage. At a press conference at Wayne Manor, he announced an ambitious plan for Wayne Industries. A holographic projection displayed his vision for a revitalized downtown business district.

A HANDS-OFF CEO
Bruce Wayne has a brilliant mind, but in order to maintain his schedule as Batman and his public mask as a lazy socialite, his appearances at Wayne Industries' offices are few and far between. Bruce draws a healthy salary from his company without charting the company's direction. He has long since placed his trust in Lucius Fox, so when the bulk of the Wayne fortune was transferred to Fox's family after The Joker stole the money during the so-called Joker War, Bruce saw this development as a way to get back to the basics of his life as a crime fighter.

GOTHAM CITY

Gotham City is a vibrant hub of industry and culture, whose citizens are protected by Batman's constant vigilance.

THE CITY'S HISTORY

A Puritan community founded in the early 1600s, Gotham City soon became linked with rumors of occult practices and witchcraft. This notorious reputation was not helped by its proximity to dens of murder such as Slaughter Swamp.

Gotham City's distinctive skyline took shape in the 1800s, when Judge Solomon Wayne led a Gothic Revival movement that gave the city a wealth of flying buttresses and gargoyles. These share space with Wayne Industries' shining edifices of glass and steel.

The city houses both the fantastically wealthy and the desperately poor. Tension between the two classes has led to incidents like the fatal mugging that orphaned young Bruce Wayne.

Gotham City's business district is a haven for boutiques and art galleries. This prosperity has lured both common crooks and Super-Villains. Arkham Asylum houses the criminally insane; other felons are confined to Blackgate Penitentiary, a maximum-security facility.

1 Wayne Manor	**7** Amusement Mile	Treatment	**20** Monolith Square	**28** Beacon Tower	**36** Gotham Gazette Offices
2 Gotham County Underwater R.R. Tubes	**8** Gotham Zoo	**15** Arkham Asylum	**21** Surh Complex	**29** Gotham Superior Courthouse	**37** City Hall
3 Robert Kane Memorial Bridge	**9** Gotham Botanical Garden	**16** Gotham Light & Power	**22** Ace Chemical	**30** Vincefinkel Bridge	**38** Cathedral Square
4 Cherry Hill Park	**10** Crime Alley	**17** Central Gotham R.R. Tubes	**23** Burnside Tunnel	**31** Vauxhall Centre	**39** Gotham Harbour
5 Knight's Dome Sporting Complex	**11** Kane Estate	**18** Gotham Water District Tunnel	**24** Robinson Park	**32** Wayne Industries	**40** Paris Island
6 Gotham Train Station	**12** New Trigate Bridge	**19** Gotham University	**25** Mercy Hospital	**33** Wayne Tower	**41** Blackgate Penitentiary
	13 Old Steam Tunnel		**26** Iceberg Lounge	**34** The Clock Tower	
	14 Gotham Sewerage		**27** South Gotham R.R. Tubes	**35** G.C.P.D. Headquarters	

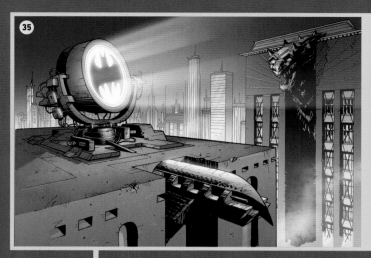

G.C.P.D. HEADQUARTERS

The downtown HQ of the Gotham City Police Department is called "Gotham Central" by the officers based there. Atop the building sits the Bat-Signal, which alerts Batman to emergencies. However close ties with Batman are not popular among the detectives of the Major Crimes Unit.

CRIME ALLEY

This street once carried the name Park Row, until the murders of Thomas and Martha Wayne, two of Gotham City's leading citizens. The G.C.P.D.'s failure to solve the case led to the street being nicknamed "Crime Alley," and contributed to the erosion of the public's confidence in the powers-that-be.

ARKHAM ASYLUM

This institution has become a second home for The Joker, Two-Face, and other mass murderers. Arkham's security is a public concern. Escapes by inmates are common. The facility has been destroyed and rebuilt more than once, each time quickly falling back into its old patterns.

GOTHAM CITY HARBOR

The harbor docks are scenes of constant activity, with traffic coming and going at all hours. The international import and export business is a huge part of the city's economy, but it also provides cover for extensive weapons smuggling and drug trafficking.

ROBIN

"If there's one thing I've always been sure of, it's that Batman will need a Robin, and Robin will need a Batman."

ALFRED PENNYWORTH

As the Dark Knight's squire, Robin fills a vital role in Batman's life. Many have worn the Robin costume in the years since Dick Grayson first used the name, and Batman and Robin continue to live up to their public nickname: the Dynamic Duo.

JASON TODD

Jason Todd first met Batman when he was caught trying to steal the Batmobile's tires—and their relationship has been a tempestuous one ever since. For a time, Jason adventured as the second Robin, but his rebellious nature made him a problematic partner for Batman. He met a brutal end when The Joker took his life in a time-bomb blast after a vicious beating. Jason later returned thanks in part to a dip in the life-renewing Lazarus Pit. As the Red Hood, Jason's life is a constant struggle between following Batman's example, and taking a crueler approach to crime fighting, one that often employs a lethal edge.

DICK GRAYSON

Dick Grayson proved that Batman's fight against crime didn't need to be a lonely one. Already a star acrobat as a child, Dick became an orphan the day a gangster sabotaged his parents' high-wire act—all because their employer, Haly's Circus, refused to pay protection money. Bruce Wayne took the boy into his home, and soon the two were a crime-fighting double act, with front-page headlines proclaiming the sensational exploits of the two Caped Crusaders. When he grew from a boy to a man, Dick found a new identity as Nightwing, but he left Batman with a firm belief in the power of a partner.

STEPHANIE BROWN

The daughter of second-rate crook Cluemaster, Stephanie Brown became a costumed hero to foil her father's criminal schemes. As Spoiler, Stephanie formed a close relationship with Tim Drake that put her into the Batman family's orbit. She briefly became the fourth Robin, and later seemingly died at the hands of gangster Black Mask. However, Stephanie survived, recuperating in Africa before returning to Gotham City. Stephanie has embraced her Spoiler identity once more, while also serving as one of Barbara Gordon's Batgirl agents.

DAMIAN WAYNE

Bruce Wayne didn't even know he had a son until he met ten-year-old Damian Wayne face-to-face. The child of Bruce and Talia al Ghūl, Damian grew up in the care of the League of Assassins and received genetic augmentation to make him the perfect fighting machine. Batman took Damian under his wing to curb his violent impulses. During a period when Bruce was believed to be dead, Dick Grayson took over as Batman and made Damian the new Robin. Now that Bruce has returned, the pairing of Batman and Robin is truly a family act.

TIM DRAKE

Tim Drake figured out the secret: Batman and Robin's real identities! Following the death of Jason Todd, Tim grew so concerned that the increasingly unhinged and withdrawn Dark Knight needed a new squire that he volunteered to become the third Robin. Later, when Captain Boomerang murdered Tim's father and made him an orphan, Tim found a new home in Wayne Manor as Bruce Wayne's adopted son. As Robin, Tim led the Teen Titans and proved himself in combat and as a detective. He has since gone solo as Red Robin, now that Damian Wayne has assumed his former role.

ALFRED PENNYWORTH

For years, visitors to Wayne Manor were more likely to meet Alfred Pennyworth than the actual man of the house, Bruce Wayne. The Wayne family's butler secretly provided support for Batman's crime-fighting operation; tragically, that role would ultimately cost Alfred his life.

Food, drink, and medicines were some of the necessities Batman would likely have neglected if Alfred hadn't brought them to the Batcave.

Of all the Robins Alfred mentored, Batman's son Damian Wayne tested Alfred's patience the most.

DECADES OF SERVICE

Alfred made sure Batman's costume was clean and in fighting shape night after night.

Alfred had been there since the beginning. After Bruce lost his mother and father in a tragic mugging, the loyal butler became his surrogate father. He was involved in the legal wrangling that prevented Bruce from being placed with other relatives or in foster care. As a young boy and then as Batman, the Dark Knight trusted Alfred with his life, even though it was Alfred who would be tasked with making that particular sacrifice.

A trained field medic, chef, and actor, Alfred possessed many skills that helped aid the Batman in his war on crime. He stitched Batman's wounds, repaired his uniform, prepared his meals, and kept Wayne Manor—as well as the massive Batcave beneath it—clean and free from as much guano as he could manage. Alfred's dry wit often softened the Dark Knight's more extreme impulses, and he kept Batman grounded by reminding him of the bonds that truly matter.

While Alfred died at the hands of the Super-Villain Bane, his legacy lives on in the mentorship between Batman and his many Robins. Alfred left his own personal fortune to Dick Grayson, ensuring that this original Robin and current Nightwing could now blaze his own trail independent of Gotham City.

For Bruce Wayne's public duties, Alfred ensured Bruce always made a good impression.

One of Alfred's primary duties at Wayne Manor was to convince curious Gothamites that nothing was amiss, despite Bruce Wayne's frequent absences.

Other than Batman, Oracle, and perhaps Tim Drake, no one knew more about the Batcave's complex computer systems and vehicle pool than Alfred.

Restocking a Utility Belt with smoke grenades or stitching a torn glove were all in a day's work for Alfred. He was always on hand for repairs at the end of Batman's long evenings of crime fighting.

KEY DATA

FULL NAME Alfred Pennyworth

OCCUPATION Butler, mechanic, surgeon, repairman

WEAPONS/POWERS/ABILITIES Armed and unarmed combat training, skilled actor

AFFILIATIONS Outsiders, Batman Inc.

RELATIVES Jarvis Pennyworth (father, deceased), Julia Pennyworth (daughter), Wilfred Pennyworth (brother), Daphne Pennyworth (niece)

FIRST APPEARANCE *Batman* #16 (April–May 1943)

RAISING A SON

Bruce became an orphan while still a boy, and Alfred stepped in to become his father figure. When Batman was believed killed during the events of the *Final Crisis*, Alfred faced the terrible task of burying Bruce's body and saying goodbye to the man he had loved as a son.

Alfred was at all times impeccably dressed, honoring the butler tradition embraced by his father, Jarvis Pennyworth.

Batman's gear is what keeps him alive and his identity secret, so he trusted few with its care other than Alfred.

Alfred's fingerprints, voice pattern, and retinal scans granted him secure access to Batman's equipment in Wayne Manor and the Batcave.

CLEAR-HEADED CALM

Nothing rattled Alfred. The multitalented butler could repair Batman's vehicles, deal with armed intruders in the Batcave, or treat Batman's wounds. He even doubled for Batman when necessary.

JULIA PENNYWORTH

Following her father into the British military, Julia Pennyworth served with the Special Reconnaissance Regiment. She lent her talents to Batman's fight as Penny-Two, advising Batman in the field. She is also close to Batwoman, taking her place on occasion.

COMMISSIONER GORDON

"I've got a friend coming who might be able to help. Should be here any minute."

COMMISSIONER GORDON

If Batman is Gotham City's strength, Jim Gordon is its soul. The former commissioner of the Gotham City Police Department is Batman's ally in the war against crime, one who served as a rare person of integrity within a justice system notorious for its corruption.

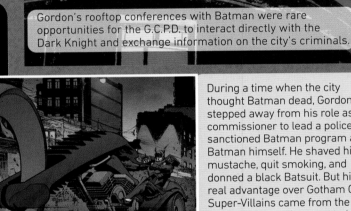

Gordon's rooftop conferences with Batman were rare opportunities for the G.C.P.D. to interact directly with the Dark Knight and exchange information on the city's criminals.

Gordon is an ordinary man in a city of many maniacs.

MAKING A DIFFERENCE

James Gordon thought he had seen everything during his time on the Chicago police force until his transfer to Gotham City. Afflicted with the triple curse of street crime, institutional rot, and a slew of costumed Super-Villains, Gotham City needed a champion. It got two. As Gordon fought for reform within a crooked police department, a vigilante dressed as a bat emerged to battle the villains the police wouldn't touch. After a rocky start, Batman and Gordon became staunch allies, and a Bat-Signal was installed on the roof of G.C.P.D. headquarters so Gordon could always get in contact with the Dark Knight.

James Gordon eventually rose through the ranks to the position of Commissioner, a role in which he served with little interruption over the years. However, when The Batman Who Laughs—a hybrid of Batman and The Joker from a dark dimension—corrupted Gordon with dark metal, he was forced to do the villain's bidding and could no longer serve as head of the police force. Since cured, Gordon has thus far refused to return to the G.C.P.D., preferring to continue his campaign against injustice without Gotham City's official permission.

When tempted to kill The Joker, Gordon held back—and helped convince Batman to do the same.

During a time when the city thought Batman dead, Gordon stepped away from his role as commissioner to lead a police-sanctioned Batman program as Batman himself. He shaved his mustache, quit smoking, and donned a black Batsuit. But his real advantage over Gotham City's Super-Villains came from the high-tech armor he operated, a metal Batsuit dubbed the Rookie.

When infected by The Batman Who Laughs' dark metal, Gordon simply called himself the Commissioner. He followed the twisted Batman's orders without question or qualms of conscience. He was eventually freed from The Batman Who Laughs' malign influence by Lex Luthor, of all people.

Gordon's only son, James Jr., grew up to become a serial killer, forcing his father to arrest him and send him to Arkham Asylum. James eventually killed himself when he proved unable to control his inner demons.

TAKING A STAND

You can always count on James Gordon to do the *right* thing, not the popular thing. This has earned him Batman's respect, but also attracted the scorn of politicians who prefer the old Gotham City ways of quiet bribery. Gordon's enemies always know where to find him, making his courage even more remarkable.

Gordon toyed with dying his hair red for a while to appear as he did when he first joined the police force. His recent retirement has seen him embrace his proper age and gray hair.

HAZARDOUS DUTY

Gordon has been shot, beaten, stabbed, and kidnapped during his career, but he shows no signs of slowing down. He continues to dedicate his lifetime of experience to the cause of justice.

KEY DATA

FULL NAME James W. Gordon

OCCUPATION Police Commissioner

WEAPONS/ POWERS/ ABILITIES
Weapons training, unarmed combat training, logical detective mind

AFFILIATIONS Barbara Kean Gordon (first wife), Sarah Essen Gordon (second wife, deceased), Barbara Gordon (daughter), James Gordon Jr. (son, deceased), Roger C. Gordon (brother, deceased), Thelma A. Gordon (sister-in-law, deceased)

FIRST APPEARANCE
Detective Comics #27 (May 1939)

GOTHAM CITY POLICE DEPARTMENT

GOTHAM CITY GUARDIANS

Batman can't be everywhere at once. The men and women of the Gotham City Police Department attempt to keep the peace in their hometown by dealing with everything from purse-snatchings to Super-Villain rampages. Once riddled with corruption, the G.C.P.D. cleaned up its act under the leadership of Police Commissioner James Gordon. Now the men and women of the G.C.P.D. fight to continue Gordon's legacy under the command of one of his prize pupils, Commissioner Renee Montoya.

EVERYDAY DANGER

When a crime is believed to have been committed by a Super-Villain, the case is usually kicked up to the Major Crimes Unit. Though their roster has shifted over the years and some have fallen in the line of duty, the team's detectives continue to put their lives on the line, as well as dealing with the day-to-day frustrations of paperwork and red tape.

JAMES GORDON

Gordon battled his way to the top of the G.C.P.D., opposed by a crooked mayor and a corrupt cop culture bred by his predecessor, Commissioner Loeb. As commissioner, Gordon brought in a crew of handpicked detectives. He also forged strong ties with Batman. Because the Dark Knight was an unsanctioned vigilante, a non-city employee was assigned the task of switching on a rooftop Bat-Signal to summon Batman. Gordon is no longer with the police force, but this is not the first time he has stepped away, only to return when his city needed him most.

COMMISSIONER RENEE MONTOYA
Renee Montoya has been a devoted detective for years. While she took a break from her duties as a cop to become the faceless costumed hero called The Question, she has since returned to the G.C.P.D. and has recently been awarded the position of Commissioner.

HARVEY BULLOCK
Infamously fond of cigars and donuts, Harvey Bullock is a sloppy dresser but an excellent cop. He is fiercely loyal to James Gordon, and eventually even briefly took over the role of commissioner when Gordon was infected by The Batman Who Laughs.

COMMISSIONER MICHAEL AKINS
Michael Akins took over as police commissioner during another stint when James Gordon was away from the job. Akins was uncomfortable with the close link between his department and the secret crime-fighting activities of the Dark Knight.

DETECTIVE CRISPUS ALLEN
Crispus Allen was a dogged perfectionist who insisted on bringing every case he was assigned to a conclusion. Killed by a corrupt officer named Jim Corrigan, Allen eventually became the supernatural hero called The Spectre, but has since passed on from that role.

CAPTAIN MAGGIE SAWYER
Captain Sawyer first headed the Special Crimes Unit (S.C.U.) in Metropolis, tasked with containing the public threat posed by Superman's foes. She became Gotham City's police commissioner while Gordon briefly took time off to serve as the city's official Batman. She has since returned to Metropolis to continue her police work there.

SIMON SAINT AND THE MAGISTRATE
Simon Saint is the wealthy head of Saint Industries, a corrupt company that has resorted to criminal means in an attempt to see a future where the Gotham City Police Department is replaced by a private security force called the Magistrate.

JASON BARD
A private investigator known for his on-again/off-again romances with Barbara Gordon, Jason originally clashed with the Gordon family, and briefly served as police commissioner through less than honorable means.

SERGEANT HARVEY HAINER
During Batman's earliest adventures, the Bat-Signal at police headquarters was activated by Sergeant Harvey Hainer, whose bad eyesight didn't prevent him from acting nobly to help the Dark Knight's cause.

COMMISSIONER SARAH ESSEN GORDON
James Gordon's second wife and his brief successor as commissioner, Sarah Essen Gordon was shot and killed by The Joker near the end of the disastrous event known as *No Man's Land*.

DETECTIVE MCGONIGLE
Alongside James Gordon, Detective McGonigle was one of the first Gotham City Police Department members established in Gotham City during Batman's early career. Unlike Gordon, he wasn't very fond of the Dark Knight.

MAYOR CHRISTOPHER NAKANO
Like several other Gotham City Mayors before him, Mayor Nakano doesn't approve of Batman. As a former officer in the G.C.P.D., Nakano has pledged to take the power out of the hands of vigilantes.

FRIENDS & ALLIES

Batman has plenty of enemies, but help is never far away. From famous faces to top-secret operatives, everyone has a place in Batman's network.

WONDER WOMAN

No mere Super Hero, Diana is the daughter of Queen Hippolyta from the mystical land of Themyscira—known as Paradise Island by outsiders—where the all-female Amazons maintain a proud warrior culture. After leaving her home and arriving in Man's World, Diana took the name Wonder Woman. Alongside Superman and Batman, Wonder Woman is the third member of a trinity that unofficially leads the Super Hero community.

SUPERMAN

The last son of the dying world of Krypton, Superman grew up in the care of a kindly Kansas couple as mild-mannered Clark Kent. He eventually left small-town life in favor of the big city of Metropolis and a career as a *Daily Planet* reporter. The Man of Steel is one of Batman's oldest and closest friends despite their differing approaches to crime fighting. While Batman may be the cynical brains behind the Justice League of America, it is Superman who is the team's optimistic public face. Both heroes are inspirations to the many others who have followed in their wake.

BARBARA GORDON/ORACLE

The daughter of former Gotham City Police Commissioner James Gordon, Barbara Gordon carved her own unique path as the most iconic Batgirl. Shot by The Joker and forced to rely on a wheelchair, Babs transitioned into Oracle, an information broker for the Super Hero set. While she has since regained the use of her legs, Barbara has decided to wear her cape and cowl only sparingly, choosing to use her technical expertise to organize her own team of Batgirls from behind her computer screen.

CATWOMAN

Originally making her mark on Gotham City as the town's most notorious cat burglar, Selina Kyle is not one to be so easily classified. Selina shares a longstanding romantic relationship with Batman, knowing not just his secret identity, but nearly everything about him. She often joins forces with the Dark Knight to fight off some of the city's more dangerous criminals, but is most active on her own, providing protection and a safe haven for the teenage thieves of the Gotham City neighborhood known as Alleytown.

BATWOMAN

Kate Kane is Bruce Wayne's cousin on his mother's side, and stubbornness must indeed run in the family. A former army brat who was thrown out of the service due to her sexual orientation, Kate was trained by her father and his special ops cronies. After a firsthand encounter introduced her to the Dark Knight, Kate was inspired to don her own Batsuit as Batwoman, using her family fortune to fund her nocturnal heroics. She recently led the field team for a group of Batman's inner circle, until she and Batman butted heads one too many times.

AZRAEL

The centuries-old Order of Saint Dumas selected Jean-Paul Valley to become their avenging angel Azrael, submitting him to psychological conditioning and sending him out to assassinate the wicked. Jean-Paul reformed under Batman's influence, and even took Batman's place after Bane broke the hero's back. But he eventually went too far, becoming overly violent, and Batman had to reclaim his role by force. Jean-Paul later took his fight to the cosmos for a time, serving with the space-faring team dubbed Justice League Odyssey.

THE HUNTRESS

The current Huntress emerged from the aftermath of a mob hit, when a young Helena Bertinelli swore revenge on the rival family that had gunned down her own. Trained in the ways of fighting and marksmanship, Bertinelli joined the super-spy organization Spyral. For a time, she served alongside Dick Grayson, before she went her own way as the vigilante Huntress. She has gone on to become a frequent ally to Batman, as well as a member of the Birds of Prey.

BATWING

Luke Fox is one of Lucius Fox's two sons, and shares his father's brilliance in the laboratory as well as Batman's natural aptitude for the fighting arts. A former MMA boxer, Luke took up the mantle of the hero Batwing, wearing a hi-tech suit that makes even Batman's Batsuit seem obsolete by comparison. Luke has meshed extremely well with the other heroes of Gotham City, but he can't seem to get along with his own brother, Tim "Jace" Fox.

DR. LESLIE THOMPKINS

Dr. Leslie Thompkins is a regular fixture in Gotham City's Crime Alley, where her humanitarian efforts are the district's sole bright spot. She runs a free clinic that provides treatment for the homeless, inspired by the long-ago murders of Thomas and Martha Wayne and the orphaned boy she comforted on that day. Leslie eventually learned of Bruce Wayne's Batman career, and counsels him against giving in to the darker side of his nature, while constantly worrying that she has not been a good enough role model for him.

SPOILER/BATGIRL

Raised by the second-string villain Cluemaster, Stephanie Brown set out to sabotage her father's crimes as the masked hero Spoiler. She caught the attention of Tim Drake and soon found herself running with Batman's crew, even becoming the fourth person to take on the role of Robin. Black Mask seemingly murdered Stephanie, but she survived and secretly recuperated in Africa under the care of Dr. Leslie Thompkins. Stephanie has since returned to her Spoiler identity, working as one of Oracle's Batgirls.

ORPHAN/BATGIRL

Cassandra Cain is an orphan in title only. In reality, she's the daughter of assassin Lady Shiva and David Cain, the original killer who bore the Orphan moniker. Taught body language in order to communicate, Cassandra is a natural fighter, able to predict her opponent's next move from their slightest gesture. While she has the potential to be the best martial artist in the world as she serves as one of Oracle's Batgirls, Orphan struggles to fit into civilian life after such a traumatic upbringing.

THE SIGNAL

Duke Thomas has played a part in Batman's career since the fabled "Zero Year" that saw The Riddler take over Gotham City while the Dark Knight was just a novice hero. After his parents were afflicted with Joker Venom during one of Batman's battles with The Joker, Duke's life become even more bizarre when Batman took him under his wing. While Duke was briefly part of an unofficial group of Robins, he embraced his light and shadow powers to become the Super Hero known as The Signal.

KATANA

Katana (Tatsu Yamashiro) seemingly lost her husband Maseo when he was stabbed by her magical sword called the Soultaker. However, she has since successfully mastered that formidable weapon as well as multiple martial arts disciplines, and continues to communicate with her beloved Maseo as long as his spirit remains trapped inside her blade. Learning to curb her deadly techniques as a former assassin, Katana has joined several incarnations of Batman's Outsiders, forming a tight bond with several of that team's other founders.

BLACK LIGHTNING

An Olympic-level athlete with the power to unleash electrical bolts, Jefferson Pierce won fame as the costumed hero Black Lightning. At Batman's request he was one of the founding members of the Outsiders, using his metahuman abilities, leadership skills, and martial arts prowess to their fullest extent. Black Lightning currently leads the latest incarnation of the Outsiders, and is constantly challenging the Dark Knight to see the world from another point of view.

HARLEY QUINN

Known to the world as simply The Joker's ex-girlfriend, the zany vigilante called Harley Quinn is trying her best to change that perception. As psychologist Dr. Harleen Quinzel, she first encountered The Joker, while working at Arkham Asylum. She fell in love with the killer and helped him escape custody. After spending way too long with "Mr. J," Harley realized the error of her ways and is now trying to help clean up a town that distrusts her.

BLUEBIRD

Harper Row grew up on the tough streets of the Gotham City neighborhood called the Narrows. But when given the opportunity, she not only caught the attention of Batman, but also of Bruce Wayne. Having helped the Dark Knight on a few missions, Harper lent her tech-expertise as a member of his inner circle, calling herself Bluebird. She works with Dr. Leslie Thompkins, helping the city's impoverished any way she can.

BLACK CANARY

Dinah Lance is a founding member of the Birds of Prey. An expert martial artist, she has the superpowered ability to vocalize a concussive, ultrasonic Canary Cry. Black Canary and fellow Justice League member Green Arrow are frequently a passionate item, although both of them are so stubborn that their relationship is often on the rocks. Black Canary has always been an ally of Batman's, even though her responsibilities to the Birds of Prey come first.

CREEPER

Jack Ryder earned minor celebrity status as a controversial talk-show host, but he really embraces the bizarre when he dons the appearance of the Creeper, a laughing, yellow-and-red figure more manic than perhaps any other hero in Gotham City. Though unpredictable, the Creeper is one of the good guys, and has joined forces with both the Outlaws and the Outsiders at different points in his career. Just the same, Batman relies on him only when other options are unavailable.

GHOST-MAKER

The mysterious man called Ghost-Maker went through nearly the exact same rigorous training as Batman, forging himself into an incredibly efficient crime fighter, albeit often

embracing deadly force along the way. He and Batman have competed with each other since they were teenagers, their rivalry became dire when Ghost-Maker emerged in Gotham City. However, Batman nonetheless appealed to Ghost-Maker's rational side, and the Dark Knight managed to recruit him into his inner circle, convincing the vigilante to only use non-lethal force while in his city.

GOTHAM GIRL

Claire Clover and her brother Hank used their family's wealth to literally buy superpowers. But gaining Superman-like abilities came with a high cost. Every time she and her brother used their powers,

they came closer to an early death. As Gotham and Gotham Girl, they helped clean up Gotham City, but Hank died when he expended too much energy. While she suffered a mental breakdown thanks to the villainous Psycho-Pirate's influence, Gotham Girl eventually regained her sanity. Batman then gave her Platinum Kryptonite, a radioactive rock that allowed her to retain her powers without their deadly side effects.

THE *FLASHPOINT* EFFECT
The timeline-shaking events of *Flashpoint* reset the Justice League's origins, bringing its seven core members together during an invasion by Darkseid and the Fourth World armies of Apokolips. Batman helped lead the counterattack, reigning in the team's loose cannons and directing newcomers.

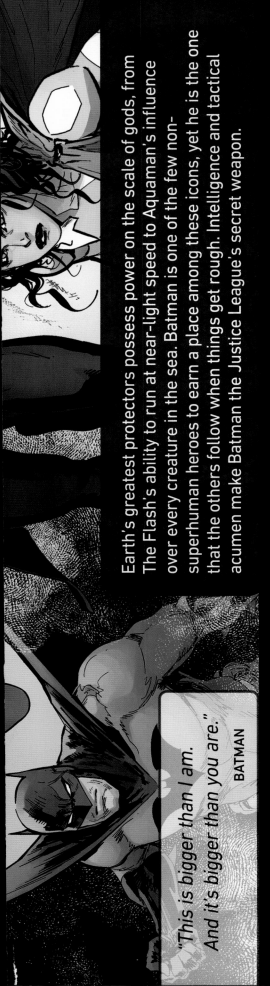

"This is bigger than I am.
And it's bigger than you are."

BATMAN

Earth's greatest protectors possess power on the scale of gods, from The Flash's ability to run at near-light speed to Aquaman's influence over every creature in the sea. Batman is one of the few non-superhuman heroes to earn a place among these icons, yet he is the one that the others follow when things get rough. Intelligence and tactical acumen make Batman the Justice League's secret weapon.

JUSTICE LEAGUE

JUSTICE LEAGUE OF AMERICA

When its members fight as one, the Justice League of America is almost invincible. But Earth has plenty of Super-Villains, and they have often ganged up in the hope of tearing apart the team. To face one incarnation of the Justice League of America, The Joker, Lex Luthor, and The Cheetah led Injustice League Unlimited, with membership largely consisting of villains hoping to take shots at their lifelong enemies. Gorilla Grodd joined to take a swing at The Flash, and the alien bounty hunter Fatality turned her anger toward Green Lantern.

JLA

A fresh alien assault, this time from the shapeshifting, extraterrestrial White Martians, put the new incarnation of the JLA on the map. The team consisted of Batman, Superman, Wonder Woman, Aquaman, the Martian Manhunter, and the next-generation versions of The Flash and Green Lantern. With his colleagues captured, Batman stood alone against the White Martian invaders and used their one weakness—fire—to topple their takeover bid. The team later expanded, adding a few other bat-allies, including Oracle and The Huntress.

JUSTICE LEAGUE INTERNATIONAL

Soon after the businessman Maxwell Lord organized a Justice League of his own, Batman found himself working alongside the likes of an arrogant Green Lantern named Guy Gardner and the less-than-serious team of Booster Gold and Blue Beetle. Known for off-the-wall antics as much as they were for saving the world from a variety of Earth-shattering threats, this incarnation of the Justice League also included the Super Heroes Fire and Ice, as well as the team's cookie-loving level head, Martian Manhunter.

ORIGINAL LEAGUE

Prior to several continuity-altering events, the Justice League of America originally pulled together to thwart the extraterrestrial Appellaxians and the space-going echinoderm called Starro. Fighting alongside fellow founding members Superman, Wonder Woman, The Flash, Green Lantern, Aquaman, and the Martian Manhunter, Batman provided the team with hi-tech gear and the computing resources of the Batcave. The Justice League operated from a hidden cavern in Happy Harbor, Rhode Island, before relocating to a space station in planetary orbit.

TEAM PLAYERS

Batman might act like a solo agent, but he has always been willing to enlist help from others, from Robin to the Batman Family. The most famous Super Hero squads on the planet have featured Batman on their rosters, and many teams only came into existence under his authority.

JUSTICE SOCIETY OF AMERICA

Before the original *Crisis on Infinite Earths* and on an alternate world called Earth-2, Batman and Superman spent World War II as reserve members of the Justice Society of America. Alongside Golden Age heroes like Sandman, Hourman, The Spectre, and Doctor Fate—as well as the original versions of Green Lantern, Hawkman, The Flash, and The Atom—the Justice Society of America battled the Axis powers as the Justice Battalion alongside the American armed forces and on the orders of President Franklin D. Roosevelt himself. Earth-2 was erased after *Crisis*, but returned most notably following the *Flashpoint* event, revealing strikingly different, modern costumes for its heroes.

BATMEN OF ALL NATIONS

As soon as the Dark Knight had made his mark in Gotham City, a number of global heroes followed his lead. France's Musketeer, Italy's Legionary, Argentina's Gaucho, Australia's Ranger, England's Knight and Squire, and the Native American Man-of-Bats all counted themselves within the loosely affiliated group Batmen of All Nations. The heroes first assembled to learn detection skills and tips from Batman. They regrouped many years later on an island, where the mysterious Doctor Hurt tested them with a series of potentially deadly traps.

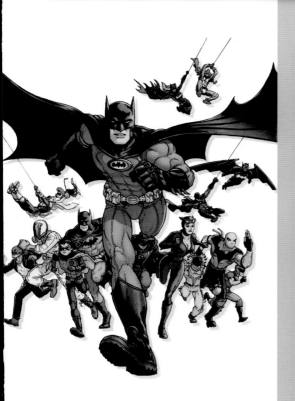

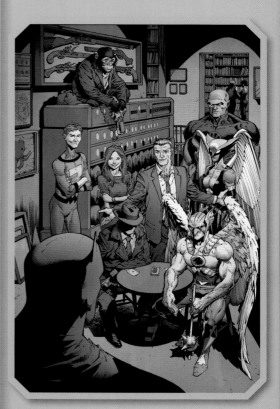

BATMAN INCORPORATED

With the Batmen of All Nations providing the template, the Dark Knight built his own international team, country by country. Batman, Incorporated has brought "Batman franchises" to many nations, including Japan, France, Russia, and the Democratic Republic of Congo.

THE OUTSIDERS

The first team created solely to serve Batman's interests, the Outsiders are covert agents who handle jobs that fall outside the range of public Super Hero institutions such as the Justice League of America. Batman has reinvented the group a few times over the years, and it has even formed without him, as its founders—Metamorpho, Black Lightning, Katana, Geo-Force, and Halo—have become a tight-knit group of friends.

THE GUILD OF DETECTION

After solving a mystery that took him nearly his entire career to crack, Batman realized he'd been following clues planted by the secret members of a highly exclusive club called the Guild of Detection. Determined to solve life's great mysteries, the group includes the likes of Hawkman, The Question, Detective Chimp, Elongated Man, and Golden Age tough guy Slam Bradley.

CATWOMAN

Bruce Wayne's Batman identity is much closer to his "true" personality than the manufactured playboy exterior he wears in public—and therefore Catwoman might be the woman who knows him best of all. The two have shared a flirtatious attraction ever since they debuted as Gotham City vigilantes. Catwoman is a thief, but since her crimes seldom harm the truly needy, Batman is willing to overlook her outlaw status. The two were nearly married, but opted instead to take some time apart in order to figure out how they fit into each other's life.

VICKI VALE

Vicki Vale was a photojournalist for the *Gotham Gazette* when she briefly dated Bruce Wayne. She has had a varied career over the years, often switching from print to television, and has recently been reporting for Gotham 4 News. Her investigations often lead her back to Batman, and on more than one occasion, she has been sure that Bruce Wayne and Batman are one and the same. However, she has never gone public with this information, revealing either a loyalty to her former boyfriend, or lingering doubts about truly proving his dark secret.

BATMAN'S LOVE LIFE

Batman keeps himself at an emotional distance from even his closest friends, making the passionate connection of romance a rare thing indeed. Yet several women have grown close to Bruce Wayne over the years, and a few of them have successfully penetrated his defenses and learned to love Batman, too.

JEZEBEL JET

As a supermodel, Jezebel Jet had a celebrity status equal to Bruce Wayne's. After she won Bruce's trust, he opened up to her about every detail of his life, even giving her a tour of the Batcave. However, Jezebel planted doubts in Bruce's mind about his sanity, and was finally revealed to be an undercover agent of Doctor Hurt's evil Black Glove organization. A vengeful Talia al Ghūl later targeted Jezebel for elimination.

SASHA BORDEAUX

Sasha Bordeaux worked for Bruce Wayne as his bodyguard, which put her in a position to uncover his secret Batman identity. She also fell in love with him, but a budding romance between Sasha and Bruce was cut short when both were held as suspects in the murder of Vesper Fairchild—another of Bruce Wayne's love interests. Eventually cleared of all charges, Sasha accepted a high-ranking position within the counterinsurgency team Checkmate, receiving a new identity and cybernetic implants.

VESPER FAIRCHILD

Radio host Vesper Fairchild met Bruce Wayne when he was a guest on her talk show, and the two became an item. Vesper later pursued a career as an investigative journalist, but when her work brought her too close to discovering his alter ego, Bruce cut Vesper out of his life. Soon after, Bruce discovered Vesper dead on the floor of Wayne Manor. The G.C.P.D. arrested Bruce as the primary murder suspect and it took months for Batman's operatives to identify the real killer.

JULIE MADISON

One of Bruce Wayne's first loves, Julie Madison met Bruce Wayne while she was still in school. When Batman was mistaken for dead and James Gordon briefly took up the role, Bruce used his time away from his Dark Knight identity to embrace his personal life. He and Julie rekindled their relationship and even worked together at the Lucius Fox Center for Gotham Youth. But when Bruce returned to the Batman mantle, he had to sacrifice his peaceful life with Julie once more.

SHONDRA KINSOLVING

Gifted with superhuman empathic and healing abilities, Shondra Kinsolving was a physical therapist who took on Bruce Wayne as a patient. Bruce had been suffering from exhaustion, and he and Shondra grew close during their sessions. Their romance was interrupted when Shondra's brother exploited her abilities for evil and she experienced a mental breakdown. Shondra recovered, but she moved on without Bruce Wayne.

TALIA AL GHŪL

As the head of killing organization the League of Assassins, Talia al Ghūl is without a doubt Batman's deadliest paramour. A liaison between the two resulted in the birth of a son, Damian Wayne—though Talia initially kept the boy's existence a secret from his father. She then brought Damian into Bruce's life and attempted to use him as a pawn to gain leverage over her "beloved." Talia's ambition is even greater than that of her father, Rā's al Ghūl, and she will settle for nothing less than world domination.

SILVER ST. CLOUD

Silver St. Cloud, a socialite and high-class Gotham City event coordinator, quickly learned Bruce Wayne's secret identity—but the truth split them apart. Ultimately, Silver couldn't bear living with the knowledge that every night Bruce faced death as Batman, and she broke off their romance. She returned much later to renew their connection, but experienced a brutal attack at the hands of the costumed assassin Onomatopoeia.

SUPER SANITY

Some psychologists at Arkham Asylum believe The Joker's madness may be a coping mechanism, allowing him to reinvent himself to fit the changing times. Over the years, The Joker has ranged from a harmless trickster to a deranged mass murderer.

It's no dye—The Joker's hair was left permanently green by his chemical bath! The same fluid made his skin turn ghastly white.

It is possible that, over the years, three different individuals have become The Joker, each taking a turn to match wits with the Batman. This might explain the Clown Prince of Crime's ever-changing style and level of viciousness.

Flowers tucked into The Joker's lapel are not just for decoration—they are often disguised acid squirters or gas sprayers.

The Joker's distinctive, comedic look is made up of a purple jacket with tails, a clashing yellow shirt, and a knotted green tie.

HOME AGAIN

The Joker's stays in Arkham Asylum do nothing to rehabilitate him. Instead, he seems to treat them as temporary vacations that enable him to regain his strength in preparation for his next outrage.

KEY DATA

REAL NAME Unknown

OCCUPATION Professional criminal

WEAPONS/ POWERS/ ABILITIES
Electrified joy buzzer, acid-squirting flower, exploding cigar, "bang"-flag harpoon gun, unarmed combat skills, brilliant criminal mind

AFFILIATIONS Injustice League, Black Glove, Legion of Doom, Red Hood Gang, Injustice Gang

RELATIVES None confirmed

FIRST APPEARANCE
Batman #1 (Spring 1940)

The Joker rarely misses a chance to get violent. The pointed toes of his shoes sometimes conceal pop-out knife blades.

"I'm not mad at all. I'm just differently sane."

THE JOKER

THE JOKER

Gotham City seems to breed theatrical villains, but The Joker has a killer act to top them all. The Clown Prince of Crime is Batman's archenemy. Never locked up for long, The Joker is always eager to spread his menacing mix of mirth and mayhem.

Batman often pays visits to Arkham Asylum in order to conduct interrogations.

The Joker and Harley Quinn used to be the underworld's most dysfunctional couple, but Harley has since moved on from the twisted psychopath.

GETTING THE JOKE

Colorful and chaotic where Batman is dark and driven, The Joker is the perfect foe for someone who has dedicated his life to keeping Gotham City's madness at bay.

Some say The Joker was once just an ordinary guy who felt forced to turn to crime to provide for his pregnant wife.

No one knows The Joker's origin or even his real name. Some claim he started out as a failed stand-up comedian driven to desperation by the death of his wife. While robbing a chemical plant as the criminal Red Hood, he fled from Batman and tumbled into a bubbling vat. When he emerged his skin was chalk-white, his hair shocking green, and his sanity a thing of the past. It is also theorized that The Joker was originally a much less tragic figure. Some believe he was a hitman, while others claim he was a career criminal who led the notorious Red Hood Gang willingly and quite shrewdly. The truth may never be known, as The Joker enjoys weaving his own faux origin stories whenever the opportunity arises.

The Joker escapes from Arkham Asylum with ease. His crimes are grandiose and imaginative, and usually involve fun items given deadly twists—an acid-squirting flower, for example, or an amusement park that he has transformed into a giant death trap.

Nearly everyone close to Batman has suffered from The Joker's evil. He beat Jason Todd, the second Robin, to death (although he would later be resurrected). He shot Barbara Gordon in the spine, sidelining her Batgirl career for years. And he murdered Sarah Essen, the wife of Police Commissioner James Gordon. Every crime hurts Batman, but he refuses to cross the line that separates him from killers like The Joker.

Feared by Gotham City's fellow criminals, The Joker is loved by just one—his delusional sidekick Punchline. With Batman as his straight man, The Joker has vowed to keep the people of Gotham City laughing—even if it kills them!

Joker Venom leaves its victims with a ghoulish grin, announcing The Joker's involvement.

The decaying infrastructure of Gotham City's Amusement Mile is The Joker's favorite haunt.

The Joker's murders are sometimes cruelly personal. He coldly shot Sarah Essen, wife of Commissioner Gordon.

The Joker is a deadly combatant when armed with knives or razors—something that often surprises Batman.

ROGUES GALLERY

TWO-FACE

Harvey Dent was an idealistic Gotham City district attorney until a criminal scarred half of his face with acid. The trauma caused him to become Two-Face, who viewed the world through the polar opposites of order and chaos. Two-Face's crimes always involve the number two, and he makes important decisions by flipping a scarred silver dollar and choosing the path of good or evil based on which side lands faceup. Attempts have been made to repair his facial scarring, but none of these have cured his insanity; although he has briefly returned to his Dent persona, he has ended up simply disfiguring one side of his face and becoming Two-Face once again.

MR. FREEZE

Dr. Victor Fries could have been a world-class scientist if his wife Nora hadn't contracted a terminal disease. Victor attempted to freeze her in cryogenic stasis until a cure was found, but in the process, Victor experienced an accident that changed his body chemistry so that he could no longer survive outside a sub-zero environment. He became the Super-Villain Mr. Freeze, wearing a life-sustaining cryo-suit and armed with his deadly freeze gun. He eventually found a cure for Nora's illness, but the process turned her into Mrs. Freeze, forcing her to suffer the same physical aversion to heat as her husband.

THE RIDDLER

Edward Nygma (sometimes spelled Nigma) is better known as The Riddler. He considers himself the second-best detective in the world, after Batman himself. He earned his reputation by staging robberies and leaving the clues in plain sight. In so doing, he dared the police to catch him—and proved himself their intellectual superior when they could not. This compulsion has resulted in him being repeatedly imprisoned in Arkham Asylum. Batman is the only person able to solve The Riddler's puzzles, and sometimes the two of them work together to solve perplexing cases. The Riddler has also been associated with the Secret Society of Super-Villains.

When it comes to crime, Gotham City is like no other place on Earth. Ever since Batman took down the Falcone family and other traditional criminal kingpins, a growing legion of colorful Super-Villains have filled the gap. Many of the worst offenders are also mentally unstable, ensuring that Arkham Asylum does a brisk business. Whether Batman is dealing with an obsessive mastermind, a costumed lawbreaker, or a mutated freak of nature, the Dark Knight always has his hands full.

THE PENGUIN

Mocked as a child for his short stature and beak-like nose, Oswald Cobblepot embraced the nickname "Penguin" when he made his mark in Gotham City's criminal underworld. Known to the public as the owner of the Iceberg Lounge nightclub, The Penguin secretly has a hand in gambling, gunrunning, stolen goods, and other illicit industries. He is also a former member of the Injustice League. The Penguin is obsessed with birds and is rarely seen without an umbrella. Unlike many of the Dark Knight's adversaries, The Penguin is sane and has the impeccable manners of a gentleman. He is a useful source of information, providing Batman with tips that enable him to foil the plots of The Penguin's rivals.

POISON IVY

A close encounter with biological toxins transformed biochemist Pamela Isley into the plant/human hybrid known as Poison Ivy. She can control plants with her thoughts and can turn humans into mind-numbed slaves by infecting them with spores. Poison Ivy's goal is to protect the natural world from those who would harm it, but her methods are too extreme for Batman. She has spent much of her life imprisoned in Arkham Asylum for the criminally insane, and has been a member of the Gotham City Sirens, the Injustice League, Injustice Gang, the Secret Society of Super-Villains, and the Suicide Squad. Her only human friend is Harley Quinn, but lately she has even forsaken that relationship in favor of the Green, calling herself Queen Ivy.

RĀ'S AL GHŪL

Also known as the Demon's Head, Rā's al Ghūl is the founder of the League of Assassins. His avowed aim is to restore the Earth's ecological balance by killing most of the planet's inhabitants. His favored method of assault on the world's population is the use of a biological weapon, such as a genetically engineered virus. He has lived for centuries as a result of periodic immersions in the Lazarus Pits, pools of rejuvenating chemicals that restore the dying to life. Rā's al Ghūl is an expert swordsman and an accomplished martial artist. He is also the father of Talia al Ghūl, and the grandfather of the fifth Robin, Damian Wayne (Talia's son with Batman).

BANE

Bane grew up inside the walls of a prison on the island nation of Santa Prisca. Serving time for his own father's acts of rebellion against the island's corrupt government, Bane was brutalized by his experience. His aggression made him a perfect test subject for the experimental Venom steroid. With tubes pumping Venom directly into his bloodstream, he gained vastly increased physical strength and broke out of the prison. Fascinated by Batman, Bane set his sights on challenging and defeating him. He hatched a plot that only ended when he broke Batman's back. Although Batman eventually recovered, Bane remains one of his most intimidating foes, made more so when he killed Batman's longtime butler, Alfred Pennyworth. Bane supposedly died during a recent gas attack at Arkham Asylum, but he has been presumed dead in the past only to return even stronger than before.

ROGUES GALLERY

SCARECROW

Dr. Jonathan Crane is trained in the psychology of fear, a subject he learned well during an unhappy childhood that was dominated by playground bullies. As an adult he studied phobias in a clinical setting, and developed a gas to activate the fear centers in the brains of its victims. Dressing up in rags and calling himself the Scarecrow, Crane forces the people of Gotham City to face their worst nightmares. His fear toxin makes his victims hallucinate, so that they believe that their worst phobias have come to life. The Scarecrow can also resort to physical combat, using a style called "violent dancing," based partly on boxing and the crane style of kung fu.

KILLER CROC

Killer Croc was born Waylon Jones, a child afflicted with a strange, progressive condition that triggered the emergence of primitive evolutionary traits in his genetic code. Over time he grew to resemble a massive crocodile, developing pebbly skin, a tooth-filled snout, and a tough protective hide. Taking the name Killer Croc after finding work wrestling alligators, he realized his superhuman strength could help him become a powerful, wealthy figure in Gotham City's crime scene. Prone to fits of bestial rage, Croc has been known to walk his own path, proving himself heroic with the Gotham City Monsters, yet slipping back into crime whenever the opportunity arises.

CLAYFACE

Many Clayfaces have taken shape over the years, and nearly all of them exhibit the ability to reshape their muddy, protoplasmic bodies into a variety of forms. The most active Clayface is Basil Karlo, a former actor whose face was scarred in a car crash, causing him to turn to an experimental drug called Renu. Its facial mud allowed him to reform his features at will, but an overdose caused his entire body to take on a dripping, mud-like appearance. Clayface can now alter his full form to appear as anyone or nearly anything, often forming clothing out of his very clay. While Basil attempted to reform his wicked ways as part of Batwoman and Red Robin's team of Gotham City heroes, his exterior has proven far easier to reshape than his criminal mind.

HUSH

The bandages covering his face hide the fact that Hush is Tommy Elliot, Bruce Wayne's friend since childhood. As a boy, Tommy attempted to murder his wealthy parents by cutting the brake lines in their car. His father perished in the crash, but Thomas Wayne intervened to save Tommy's mother. Furious with the Wayne family for ruining his plot to inherit the Elliot family's fortune, Tommy swore revenge. He grew up to become a gifted neurologist and plastic surgeon, but the desire for vengeance remained. As the devious criminal Hush, he is a master strategist and manipulator, consumed by a desire to kill Batman and ruin the life of his boyhood friend, Bruce Wayne.

"Big scary Batman, what scares you? Let's find out."

SCARECROW

BLACK MASK

At a young age, Roman Sionis murdered his parents by setting their mansion on fire. Inheriting the Sionis family cosmetics fortune, he carved an ebony mask out of his father's coffin and became the villain Black Mask, a major player in Gotham City's organized crime scene. Leading the False Face Society, Black Mask formed a hatred for both Bruce Wayne and Batman, nearly murdered Spoiler through torture, and found the time to start a war with Catwoman as well. Thanks to the machinations of Metropolis criminal Lex Luthor, Black Mask now has the ability to change his appearance at will, a trick he employed when attempting to pose as Ted Kord, the hero also known as Blue Beetle.

TALON

In Gotham City, an old nursery rhyme warns of the "Court of Owls." However, few realize that the term refers to a secret society that controls the city. As an assassin for the Court of Owls, William Cobb was just one of many Talons used to eliminate the Court's enemies. Enhanced and kept in an inert status until needed, the Talons are brutally efficient, and have fought dozens of heroes over the years, from western bounty hunter Jonah Hex to Batman. Cobb is one of the group's most notorious agents, and also happens to be Dick Grayson's ancestor. After several clashes with the Batman Family, Cobb was freed from Arkham Asylum to serve on Amanda Waller's clandestine government task force the Suicide Squad.

KILLER MOTH

One of Gotham City's more bizarre villains, Killer Moth modeled himself on Batman—instead of a bat, he used the image of a moth as the theme for his criminal persona. The Secret Society of Super-Villains member wears a winged suit and carries a cocoon gun capable of immobilizing his targets. Barbara Gordon trounced Killer Moth in one of her first outings as Batgirl, and the villain's defeats have only grown more numerous since then. Killer Moth has employed many different looks over the years, and was even briefly transformed into the hulking monster Charaxes. Following various reality-altering crises, he has since returned to the look and persona similar to the one he originally adopted.

THE BATMAN WHO LAUGHS

Below our own Multiverse lies a Dark Multiverse full of twisted nightmare realms that are usually temporary, and always tragic. From one such reality, Earth −22, Bruce Wayne broke The Joker's neck, killing him during a moment of rage. This act caused Wayne to be infected by a new strain of The Joker's nanotoxin, one that eventually corrupted his own personality with The Joker's. Still possessing Bruce's brilliant mind but tainted by The Joker's ruthless madness, he became known as The Batman Who Laughs. Thanks to the powerful entity Barbatos, and later Perpetua, The Batman Who Laughs not only traveled to Batman's Earth, he later reformed all of reality itself, ascending to his final form as the Darkest Knight.

FLASHPOINT BATMAN

In an alternate reality, Bruce Wayne's parents never died. Instead, Thomas and Martha Wayne tragically lost their son that night in Crime Alley. The pain eventually drove Martha Wayne mad, and she became her reality's Joker. Thomas Wayne became Batman, launching a deadly quest for revenge. Thomas eventually learned of a world where Bruce Wayne lived and became Batman. Working with the Super-Villain Bane, he attempted to manipulate his son of that world into dropping the cape and cowl, but failed thanks to his cruel methods. Bruce proved himself the true Batman while Thomas learned the price of teaming with criminals.

ROGUES GALLERY

SOLOMON GRUNDY

The supernatural menace Solomon Grundy came into being more than a century ago, after the body of Cyrus Gold sank into the murk of Slaughter Swamp and emerged as a shambling, undead monster. Possessing tremendous strength and unable to feel pain, Solomon Grundy is a nearly unstoppable bundle of animal instincts with almost no guiding intelligence. Each time he is destroyed, a new incarnation is reborn in the swamp, making Solomon Grundy effectively immortal.

DAVID CAIN

One of the world's most notorious assassins, David Cain is also known as Orphan, a name his daughter later adopted after his apparent demise. That daughter is Cassandra Cain, whom Cain sired with the even deadlier assassin Lady Shiva. Cain trained Cassandra in the art of combat, forcing her to use body language to communicate rather than speech. Cassandra rebelled against her father, and eventually joined Batman's forces, becoming the new Orphan, one of Barbara Gordon's Batgirls.

CALCULATOR

Noah Kuttler began his career by attempting to steal treasures while dressed in a computerized battle suit that resembled a giant pocket calculator. He found a better outlet for his mathematical genius by becoming an information source for the Super-Villain community, the evil opposite to Oracle. For the right price, the Calculator will hack into security cameras or disable alarm systems. A computer expert, his untraceable activities have helped hundreds of villains escape justice.

CALENDAR MAN

Julian Day's obsession with dates caused him to refashion himself as the costumed criminal Calendar Man. His crimes are oriented around equinoxes or obscure anniversaries, but Batman is always able to deduce his theme and send him back to Arkham Asylum. The Calendar Man is imprisoned in a glass-walled cell in Arkham's basement, where he is sometimes consulted as an expert resource on the methods used by other criminals.

CATMAN

Big-game trapper Thomas Blake set his sights on a new quarry when he grew bored with hunting. Adopting a cat theme, he set himself up as the costumed criminal Catman. Though he never earned much respect in Gotham City, Catman got a fresh start as a member of the Secret Six alongside Deadshot and other lesser-known villains. Catman possesses an honorable streak and has a deep respect for endangered jungle cats.

BLACK SPIDER

More than one villain has adopted the name Black Spider over the years. The moniker has also been used by gangster Johnny LaMonica and criminal Derrick Coe. However the original Black Spider was Eric Needham, who wore a purple and orange suit and used lethal force to deal with drug dealers. Needham was presumed dead for a time, and it remains to be seen if he really is the current possessor of the Black Spider identity.

CAVALIER

When Mortimer Drake first assumed the swashbuckling identity of the Cavalier, he wore a costume that resembled that of a 17th-century musketeer. The Cavalier was one of the Dark Knight's less dangerous foes, since he held fast to a personal code of honor that included chivalry toward women. He even helped Dr. Leslie Thompkins for a time with her clinic. However, his redemption seems to have been cut short, as he was killed during a mission with the Suicide Squad.

LADY SHIVA

Lady Shiva, originally Sandra Wu-San, is one of the world's most gifted martial artists. A child prodigy in unarmed combat, her fury was inspired by the death of her sister. She has been associated with both the League of Assassins and the League of Shadows, and eventually bore a daughter with David Cain named Cassandra. Shiva and Cassandra have a strained relationship due to Cassandra's allegiance to Batman and Oracle. The two were briefly reunited when Shiva allied with the Outsiders.

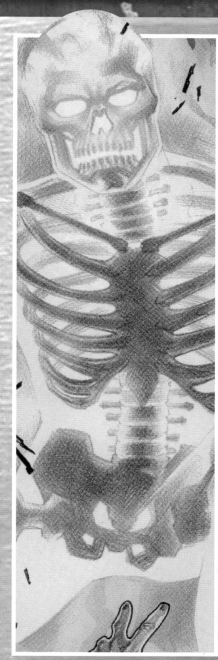

DEADSHOT

Marksman, Floyd Lawton claimed that he never missed. As Deadshot, he was in demand as a mercenary and hired killer. His protective battle suit was equipped with wrist-mounted guns and a targeting eyepiece. He fought Batman, but was more successful as a member of villainous teams, including the Suicide Squad and the Secret Six. Deadshot claimed not to care if he lived or died, a theory tested in real time when he was seemingly murdered by Black Mask.

DR. HURT

Dr. Simon Hurt's real name is Thomas Wayne, but he is not Bruce's father—he is a distant ancestor kept alive by mystical means. A brilliant scientist and mastermind, Hurt has been the head of both the Club of Villains and the Black Glove organization. He has set his sights on Bruce Wayne for decades, eventually concocting a plan that nearly resulted in the death of Batman, all to serve Thomas' dark god, the bat-like demon Barbatos.

DR. PHOSPHORUS

Dr. Alex Sartorius suffered a terrible fate when a nuclear reactor accident riddled his body with tiny radioactive particles. Burning with a fire that could never be extinguished, he adopted the name Doctor Phosphorous and shared his pain with innocent victims. Doctor Phosphorous constantly leaks toxic radiation and can kill with a single touch. At Arkham Asylum, the administrators constructed a special radiation-proof cell solely for his use.

ROGUES GALLERY

FIREFLY

The man most closely associated with the Firefly title, Garfield Lynns is a villain with a simple motivation—to make the world burn. He became the Firefly to provide an outlet for his pyromaniac urges, and many of his crimes of arson are motivated by nothing more than the desire to set something on fire. Firefly's suit gives him limited protection against extreme temperatures and also allows him to fly. His primary weapons are flamethrowers and incendiary grenades.

FLAMINGO

The mob enforcer known as the Flamingo is dangerously unstable. The same gangsters who keep him on their payroll also removed parts of his brain, leaving him without a moral conscience but with all his lethal skills intact. The Flamingo especially relishes torturing innocent victims and has earned notoriety as "The Eater of Faces." He also has a taste for fast motorcycles and flashy clothes, and can easily be found by following the trail of bodies he leaves behind.

HUGO STRANGE

Gifted psychiatrist Hugo Strange's obsession with Batman led him down the path of villainy. Some time ago, Strange deduced that Bruce Wayne was his target's secret identity but chose to keep the knowledge to himself. Multitalented, his skills at genetic engineering have enabled him to raise an army of mindless creatures he calls "Monster Men." Despite his crimes, Strange is considered a valued member of society, a misconception Hugo plans to exploit to the full.

KGBEAST

An elite division of the Russian KGB transformed Anatoli Knyazev into an unstoppable killing machine nicknamed the KGBeast. A crack shot, he was surgically enhanced with cybernetic implants that made him unnaturally strong. The KGBeast carried out assassinations on the orders of his Russian masters, which put him into conflict with Batman. One of his fiercest battles with the Dark Knight occurred after the Beast shot Nightwing in the head, nearly killing Dick Grayson and causing the hero to suffer severe memory loss.

JERVIS TETCH

A lifelong obsession with Lewis Carroll's *Alice in Wonderland* led Jervis Tetch to model his Super-Villain persona after the book's Mad Hatter character. Possessing a remarkable gift for microelectronics and an understanding of hypnotism, the Mad Hatter learned how to entrance others by fitting them with hats that contained tiny mind-control devices. His crimes invariably draw upon classic storybook themes, and he sometimes teams up with a group known as the Wonderland Gang.

MAXIE ZEUS

Once a mild-mannered Ancient Greek history teacher, Maxie Zeus mysteriously developed extreme delusions of grandeur and became convinced that he was the Greek god Zeus in human form. Highly intelligent, he has successfully positioned himself as a Gotham City crime boss, despite his penchant for togas and histrionics. Like the god whose name he shares, Zeus carries weapons shaped like lightning bolts that can zap opponents and unbelievers with lethal jolts of electricity.

MAN-BAT

Scientist Kirk Langstrom's study of bats went horribly wrong when an experimental serum transformed him into a half-bat, half-human monster. Like a true bat, Man-Bat can fly and sense his surroundings through echolocation. For a time, his animal instincts overrode his intellect and soon he was terrorizing Gotham City every night until sunrise. However, Langstrom eventually learned to control his Man-Bat side, and often remained in a bat-headed humanoid form. His intellect made him a valued member of Justice League Dark.

MISTER ZSASZ

The Arkham Asylum inmate with the strongest desire to kill others is probably Victor—known as Mister—Zsasz. This serial killer cuts a fresh notch in his skin to mark the death of each victim. Born into wealth, he lost it all and convinced himself that life had no meaning. To Mister Zsasz, killing is his gift to the world as he "liberates" his victims from their futile lives while injecting some fleeting excitement into his own existence. Mister Zsasz is an expert fighter when armed with knives or razors.

PROFESSOR PYG

A mask-wearing scientist/artist with a pig obsession, Professor Pyg started out as ringmaster of the traveling Circus of Strange. His villainous cast captured spectators and turned them into subjects for Pyg's gruesome experiments. Professor Pyg's sadistic surgery is used to create Dollotrons—lobotomized victims with blank masks permanently grafted to their faces. Pyg also harbors more general ambitions: His fondest wish is to infect Gotham City's population with a highly dangerous, mind-altering virus.

VENTRILOQUIST

Meek, soft-spoken Arnold Wesker rapidly inspired fear and respect as a Gotham City crime boss when he channeled his repressed rage through his gangster puppet, Scarface. Wesker lets Scarface handle the dirty work, executing mob snitches with a miniature Tommy gun cradled in Scarface's wooden arms. Wesker has been active in recent years, working for Batman during a suicide mission, and then serving as the "Alfred" to Thomas Wayne's corrupt version of the Dark Knight during Thomas's partnership with Bane.

PUNCHLINE

Obsessed with serial killers and The Joker in particular, Alexis Kaye was a student at Snyder College, an institution 40 miles (64 km) north of Gotham City. While there, she developed a hit list of fellow students and, in order to impress The Joker, exposed the dean of the college to a paralyzing version of Joker Venom. The ploy worked, and she soon became The Joker's new moll, and a fan-favorite of misguided Gothamites who mistook her for one of the Clown Prince of Crime's true victims.

ANARKY

Lonnie Machin has been bucking the system for most of his young life. As Anarky, he has had repeated clashes with the Dark Knight and Red Robin, believing that the needs of the people should come before the law and order of an organized government system. While he purports to want only the best for Gotham City and its citizens, Anarky is constantly breaking the law, whether in company with other criminals while armed with his taser staff, or hacking online under the codename of Moneyspider.

DEATHSTROKE

Slade Wilson went from elite soldier to mercenary for hire, thanks to the help of an experimental military serum that enhanced his speed, endurance, strength, and overall efficiency. Initially facing Dick Grayson and the Teen Titans on multiple occasions, Wilson would also develop a rivalry with Batman over the years, and has proven himself the Dark Knight's near equal. Named after the sword he uses on most of his ruthless missions, Slade Wilson is now better known to the world as Deathstroke.

KITE MAN

Charles Brown got his start in the world of Gotham City crime while working on various hi-tech projects, such as improving the aerodynamics of the Jokermobile. Brown became a low-level henchman, used as an informant on both sides of the underground Super-Villain clash dubbed the War of Jokes and Riddles. However, he was eventually pushed too far and began to use his knowledge of wind patterns to become Kite Man—one of the less fearsome members of Batman's ever-expanding Rogues Gallery.

TIMELINE

Batman's life has been constantly altered due to cosmic crises and events. He soldiers on, his past a patchwork of different realities that tell the troubled story of the life of the Dark Knight.

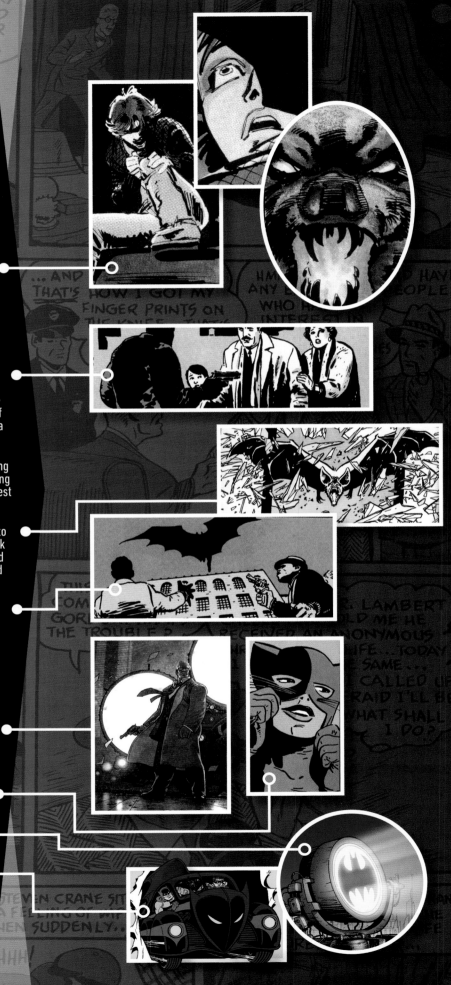

- Bruce Wayne is born to Martha Wayne and Dr. Thomas Wayne. He is their only child and is heir to a family fortune going back generations to the founding of Gotham City.

- Bruce grows up in Wayne Manor, attended to by Alfred Pennyworth, the family butler. His best childhood friend is Thomas "Tommy" Elliot.

- At an early age, Bruce falls into a concealed pit in the grounds of Wayne Manor and lands in a huge underground cave filled with bats.

- Dr. Thomas Wayne dresses as a costumed character he calls "the Batman" for a masquerade ball, and defeats a gang of hoodlums when they crash the party.

- After taking Bruce to a movie, Thomas and Martha Wayne are shot and killed by a mugger while walking though Park Row. The gunman, a thug named Joe Chill, escapes and the case is never officially resolved. Leslie Thompkins is one of the first people to arrive at the murder scene and comforts a traumatized Bruce.

- Bruce grows up in the care of Alfred Pennyworth. The young Wayne leaves Gotham City to travel the world, studying criminology and forensics while training under the greatest martial arts masters.

- Years later, Bruce Wayne returns to Gotham City. He vows to battle wrongdoers and prevent crimes like the one that took his parents' lives. In an early outing, he nearly dies and retreats home. There he sees a bat in his father's study and takes it as an omen.

- Now determined to strike fear into the hearts of criminals as the Batman, Bruce develops his costume and weapons and eventually renovates the cavern beneath Wayne Manor into his secret headquarters, the Batcave.

- In his first adventures, Batman battles corrupt cops, crooked politicians, and the mobsters that control Gotham City's underworld.

- James Gordon, a new face on the Gotham City police force, finds himself allying with Batman against the corruption that has taken root within the G.C.P.D. under the leadership of Commissioner Loeb.

- Selina Kyle is inspired by Batman's example and begins her career as Catwoman.

- The Gotham City Police Department places a Bat-Signal on the roof to alert Batman to emergencies.

- Batman develops a sleek armored car he calls the Batmobile, later employing a variety of diferent models.

- Batman battles a mysterious figure called the Red Hood who falls into a vat of chemicals during their skirmish.

- Batman encounters Superman for the first time, and the two eventually develop an uneasy friendship.

- Batman matches wits with a variety of strange new criminals including Professor Hugo Strange, the Mad Monk, Clayface, Dr. Death, The Riddler, Poison Ivy, The Penguin, Scarecrow, Solomon Grundy, and most notoriously, The Joker.

- To combat these new threats, Batman continues to develop vehicles including the Batcycle, Bat-Gyro, and Batboat.

- Jervis Tetch, Calendar Man, and Mr. Freeze are among the new villains that continue to plague Gotham City.

- Batman teams up with James Gordon and district attorney Harvey Dent to take down the notorious Falcone crime family. In the process they find themselves on the trail of a serial killer known as Holiday.

- Harvey Dent is splashed with acid by a criminal. The left side of his face suffers severe scarring, and Harvey becomes the double-sided villain Two-Face.

- Batman investigates the identity of the Hangman killer and once again crosses paths with the Falcone crime family.

- The murderous Reaper returns to stalk the streets of Gotham City.

- After his trapeze-artist parents are slain by gangster Boss Zucco, Dick Grayson joins the Dark Knight's crime-fighting crusade by taking on the role of Robin, the Boy Wonder.

- Batman welcomes new members into his war on crime, and soon attracts an entire Batman Family. Ace the Bat-Hound is his canine partner, while former circus acrobat Kathy Kane becomes the original Batwoman. Later, Betty Kane becomes the first Bat-Girl.

- Among the newest crop of Gotham City villains to sprout up are Killer Moth, Catman, and Kite Man.

- Batman teams with not just Superman, but also Wonder Woman, The Flash, Green Lantern, Aquaman, and Martian Manhunter to form the Justice League of America.

- Matt Hagen becomes the monstrously malleable Clayface II. Other new villains include Blockbuster, Cluemaster, and the Wrath.

- Robin helps found the Teen Titans alongside other Super Hero sidekicks.

- Barbara Gordon puts on the cape and cowl to become Gotham City's latest hero—Batgirl! She soon fights not just Killer Moth, but also the pyromaniac Firefly.

- Dick Grayson leaves the Batcave to fly solo as Robin and attend Hudson University. As a result, Bruce Wayne and Alfred Pennyworth relocate their main base of operations to the rooftop penthouse of the Wayne Foundation building in the heart of Gotham City. A new Batcave is established beneath the Wayne Foundation's skyscraper.

TIMELINE

• Man-Bat, Talia al Ghūl, Rā's al Ghūl, Rupert Thorne, Black Spider, Dr. Phosphorus, Lady Shiva, and a third Clayface prove to be new thorns in Batman's side. Meanwhile, an obscure villain called Deadshot reinvents himself into a deadly assassin.

• Platinum-haired Silver St. Cloud becomes Bruce Wayne's latest romantic interest, though their relationship is short-lived.

• Lucius Fox becomes Bruce Wayne's business manager and accepts responsibility for running the day-to-day business operations of Wayne Industries.

• Gangster Maxie Zeus surfaces in Gotham City, as does Killer Croc. Later, Black Mask also takes a swing at becoming a crime boss.

• Batman quits the Justice League of America and assembles his own team of Super Heroes, the Outsiders, whose members include Katana, Metamorpho, Geo-Force, Halo, and Black Lightning.

• Jason Todd officially debuts as the second Robin while Dick Grayson changes his name to Nightwing.

• Multiple realities are merged into one during the epic event known as *Crisis on Infinite Earths*. In the aftermath, some elements from Batman's history are rewritten as a new, unified timeline takes effect.

• The Ventriloquist and his puppet Scarface, the Russian assassin called the KGBeast, and other new threats emerge including the Ratcatcher and cult leader Deacon Blackfire.

• The Joker shoots and paralyzes Barbara Gordon, and kidnaps Commissioner Gordon so he can subject him to psychological torture.

• Jason Todd goes in search of his real mother, but is killed by The Joker.

• Tim Drake officially joins Batman's crusade as the third Robin.

• No longer able to use her legs after The Joker's attack, Barbara Gordon takes on a new role as the all-seeing information broker Oracle.

• The political activist vigilante Anarky, martial artist King Snake, and deranged serial killer Mister Zsasz enter the Dark Knight's Rogues Gallery.

• Stephanie Brown, aka the Spoiler, becomes a vigilante to thwart her father, the Cluemaster.

• The villain called Bane breaks Batman's back, leaving him paralyzed. Bruce Wayne is forced to relinquish the mantle of Batman to newcomer Jean-Paul Valley (Azrael). Jean-Paul Valley adopts a formidable suit of Bat-armor to defeat Bane.

• Now recovered from Bane's injury, Bruce Wayne reclaims the title of Batman from Jean-Paul Valley. Before returning

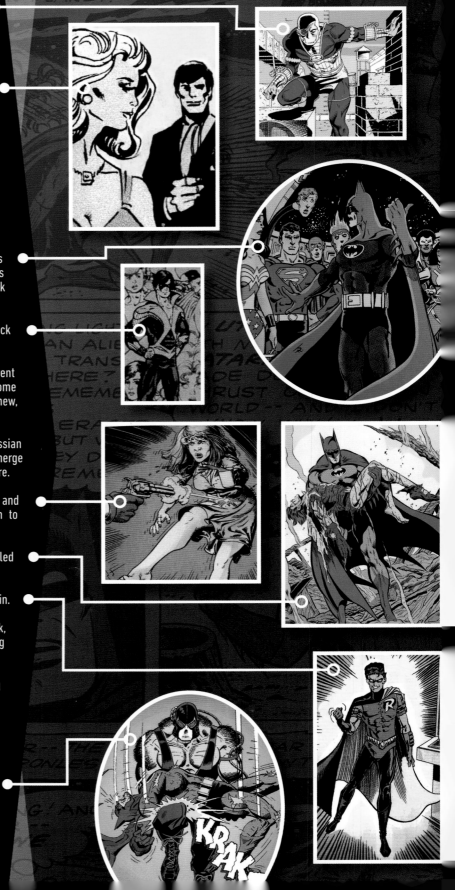

- A plague hits Gotham City, soon followed by a powerful earthquake. Its citizens evacuate and the city becomes a No Man's Land, ruled by criminal fiefdoms and protected by Batman and his agents.

- Martial arts prodigy Cassandra Cain inherits the mantle of Batgirl from Barbara Gordon; Harley Quinn becomes The Joker's sidekick.

- The Joker murders James Gordon's second wife, Sarah Essen-Gordon. Gotham City is reopened to the rest of the world soon after.

- Bruce Wayne's former paramour Vesper Fairchild is found murdered. Bruce and his bodyguard Sasha Bordeaux are held as suspects but eventually cleared of all charges.

- Bruce Wayne's boyhood friend Tommy Elliot appears as the bandaged villain Hush, launching an elaborate plot against Batman that involves nearly every member of the Dark Knight's Rogues Gallery.

- Heeding Batman's call, Stephanie Brown becomes the fourth Robin. After being fired from the position, she is captured by Black Mask and nearly killed.

- Tim Drake's father is killed by The Flash villain Captain Boomerang, leaving Tim an orphan.

- Batman develops the Brother Eye surveillance satellite but realizes that his construction has become self-aware. Brother Eye turns thousands of innocent victims into malevolent OMAC agents.

- Jason Todd, restored to life after his murder at the hands of The Joker, assumes the vigilante identity of the Red Hood.

- After surviving the event dubbed *Infinite Crisis*, Batman decides to take time off to retrace the path that led to his transformation into the Dark Knight. It is a quest that spans the better part of a year, but helps him shed some of his darkness at the hands of the mysterious Ten-Eyed Men.

- With Batman away from Gotham City, Harvey Dent tries— and fails—to become the city's protector, Kate Kane becomes the new Batwoman, and former Gotham City police detective Renee Montoya becomes the new Question.

- Bruce Wayne returns to Gotham City and officially adopts Tim Drake as his legal son.

- A new Ventriloquist and Scarface arrive on the scene for a time, as do villains Humpty Dumpty and Roxy Rocket.

- Bruce Wayne learns he has a biological son, Damian Wayne, as a result of a long-ago liaison with Talia al Ghūl.

- Stephanie Brown resurfaces as Spoiler, revealing to Tim

- Doctor Hurt implements a plan to take down Batman, orchestrating a grand conspiracy with his Club of Villains and ally Jezebel Jett.

- At the end of the universe-shaking *Final Crisis* event, the New God Darkseid apparently annihilates Batman with his Omega Sanction beams.

- Ex-cop Michael Washington Lane becomes the new Azrael, picking up where Jean-Paul Valley left off.

- A new Dynamic Duo emerges, with Dick Grayson as Batman and Damian Wayne as Robin. At first their partnership seems rocky, but they put aside their differences long enough to defeat the schemes of the psychotic Professor Pyg.

- Tim Drake takes up the identity of Red Robin while Stephanie Brown becomes the newest Batgirl.

- The Green Lantern Corps faces its biggest challenge during the *Blackest Night* crisis. Black Lantern rings bring the corpses of dead heroes to life, including what is believed to be the body of Batman, but this Black Lantern Batman proves to be a clone.

- Sent into the past by Darkseid's power during the *Final Crisis* event, Batman embarks on a journey through time and eventually returns to the present day.

- Speaking to the news media, Bruce Wayne reveals that he has secretly funded Batman's activities for years, and announces the formation of a new global Super Hero team: Batman Incorporated.

- Reality is altered during the *Flashpoint* event, and Dr. Thomas Wayne fights crime as Batman. The Flash restores the timeline; Batman now has a new "Zero Year" origin and the Justice League consists of Batman, Superman, Wonder Woman, Aquaman, Cyborg, The Flash, and Green Lantern.

- The Batman and Robin pairing becomes a father/son team when Dick Grayson returns to the role of Nightwing. Barbara Gordon, now recovered from her paralysis, once again takes up the mantle of Batgirl.

- Batman faces the threat of Gotham City's oldest secret society, the Court of Owls, and dozens of assassins called Talons.

- The Red Hood takes command of a new team of international operatives called the Outlaws. Meanwhile, Red Robin focuses on leading the Teen Titans.

- Damian Wayne is killed by the villainous Heretic under the command of Talia al Ghūl. Batman later resurrects his son, thanks to a trip to the planet Apokolips and an artifact called the Chaos Shard.

- Batman and The Joker "die" after a violent fight in the Batcave, only to return thanks to a mysterious metal called Dionesium. When he returns, Bruce Wayne has lost all memory of his past life as Batman.

James Gordon steps away from his job as commissioner to become a G.C.P.D.-sanctioned Batman in an armored Batsuit called the Rookie. Meanwhile, his daughter Barbara sets up a new life for herself in the borough of Burnside.

• Dick Grayson becomes an agent for the secret operatives called Spyral after he is presumed dead by the world. He serves with Helena Bertinelli.

• Duke Thomas becomes an unofficial Robin in a group of underground crime fighters named We Are Robin.

• Bruce Wayne uses a hi-tech device to restore his memories as Batman and returns just in time to help defeat a new villain, Mister Bloom.

• Parts of past continuity are restored in a *Rebirth* across the DC universe due to the manipulation of cosmic forces. After which, Dick Grayson becomes Nightwing again and Helena Bertinelli becomes The Huntress.

• Batman meets Gotham and Gotham Girl, and angers longtime villain Bane during a mission to Santa Prisca.

• The Batman Who Laughs emerges while Batman and the Justice League learn of the Dark Multiverse and the bat-like demon Barbatos' invasion of Earth. Afterward, Duke Thomas adopts the identity of the Signal.

• Batman and Catwoman decide to get married, but Selina ends up leaving the Dark Knight at the altar.

• Bane takes over Gotham City with the help of the Batman from the *Flashpoint* reality, Thomas Wayne. A misguided Gotham Girl becomes Thomas Wayne's "Robin."

• Bane kills Alfred in front of Damian Wayne's eyes. Batman eventually stops both Bane and his alternate universe father, Thomas.

• The Joker is the next to claim Gotham City as his own, doing so with a gang of clowns and by stealing the Wayne fortune in his so-called Joker War.

• New faces Punchline, Ghost-Maker, and Clownhunter appear in Gotham City, causing plenty of challenges for the Dark Knight.

• The Justice League faces off against the mother of the Multiverse, Perpetua, and her chosen right-hand man, The Batman Who Laughs. While they defeat the villains, The cosmos is once again altered, causing the heroes to remember all of their past adventures from a variety of timelines. Some heroes and villains are brought back to life during this *Infinite Frontier*.

• Barbara Gordon returns to the job of Oracle, as Stephanie Brown and Cassandra Cain become her Batgirls.

• With his fortune handed over to the Fox family, Bruce Wayne lives on a smaller scale, operating out of a brownstone in the neighborhood of Fort Graye with a garage-like Batcave beneath. He adopts a back-to-basics approach to cleaning up Gotham City.

GOLDEN AGE
'30s & '40s

Amid economic depression and worldwide war, Batman emerged as a new kind of popular star: the comic book Super Hero.

By creating Superman and then Batman, DC inaugurated the Golden Age of Comics. Suddenly, newsstands blossomed with brightly colored covers advertising the exploits of Super Heroes and readers snapped them up by the millions. Under the guidance of Harry Donenfeld and Jack Liebowitz, DC built up a roster of all-stars that extended to Maxwell C. Gaines' All-American line and its own Wonder Woman, Green Lantern, and The Flash.

The collaborative efforts of writer Bill Finger and artist Bob Kane brought Batman to life in the pages of *Detective Comics* #27. After establishing himself as the lead figure in *Detective Comics*, the Dark Knight was rewarded for his staying power when he became the title's permanent cover feature and the star of a second comic book all of his own.

Batman received a sidekick, Robin, the Boy Wonder, and employed a butler named Alfred. He also attracted a Rogues Gallery that included The Joker, Catwoman, The Penguin, The Riddler, Mad Hatter, and Hugo Strange.

Though Bob Kane received sole credit on most Batman stories of the Golden Age, Bill Finger and Kane's assistant Jerry Robinson played critical roles in spreading the Dark Knight's popularity. By the close of the 1940s, artists Dick Sprang, Lew Sayre Schwartz, and Jim Mooney were also mainstays on the Batman comic books.

OVERLEAF
Detective Comics #31 (September 1939):
Bob Kane's iconic cover featuring the Monk would be the inspiration for dozens of homage covers.

SEPTEMBER, 1939

No. 31

Detective COMICS

10¢

64 PAGES OF Thrill-Packed ACTION

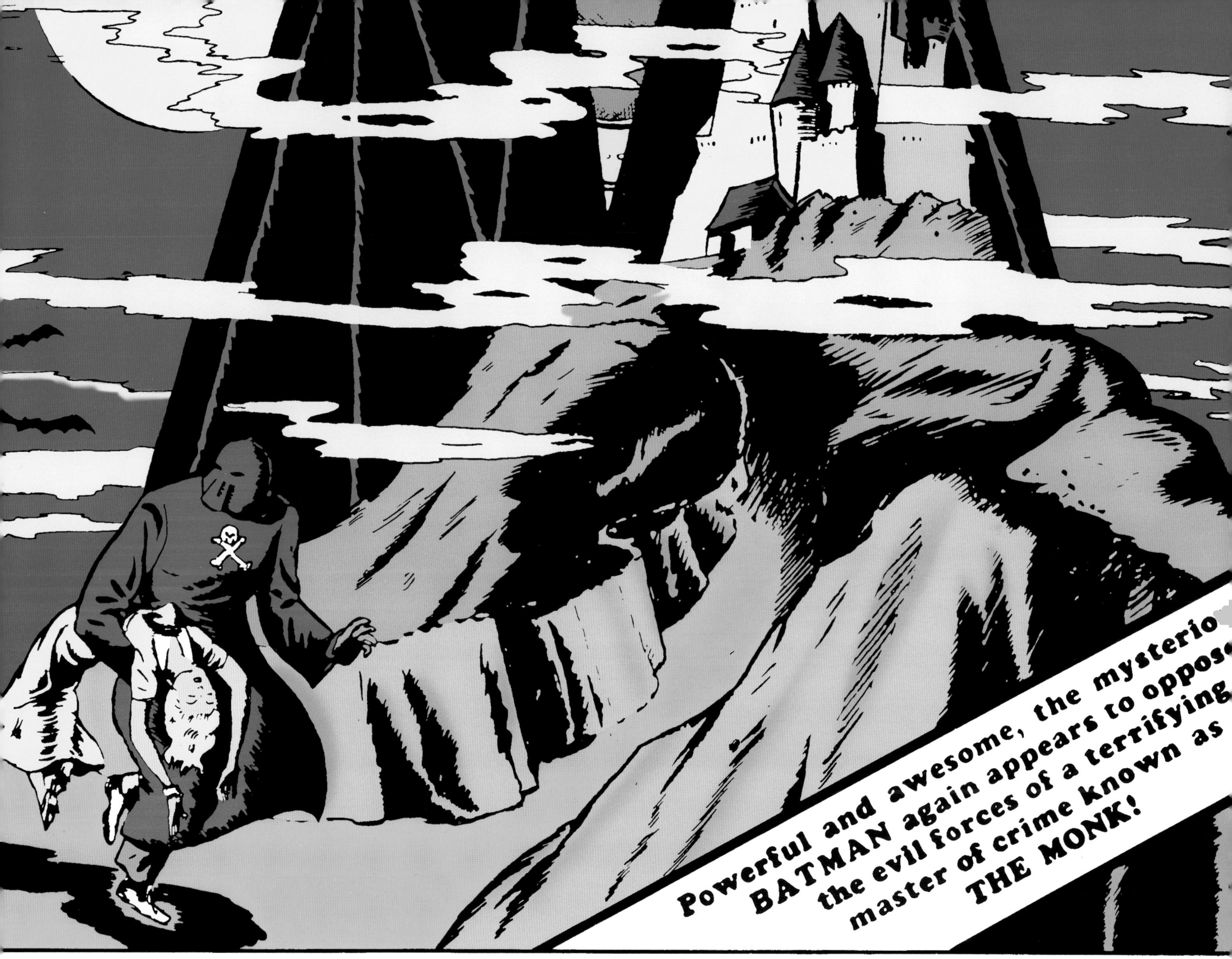
Powerful and awesome, the mysterio
BATMAN again appears to oppos
the evil forces of a terrifying
master of crime known as
THE MONK!

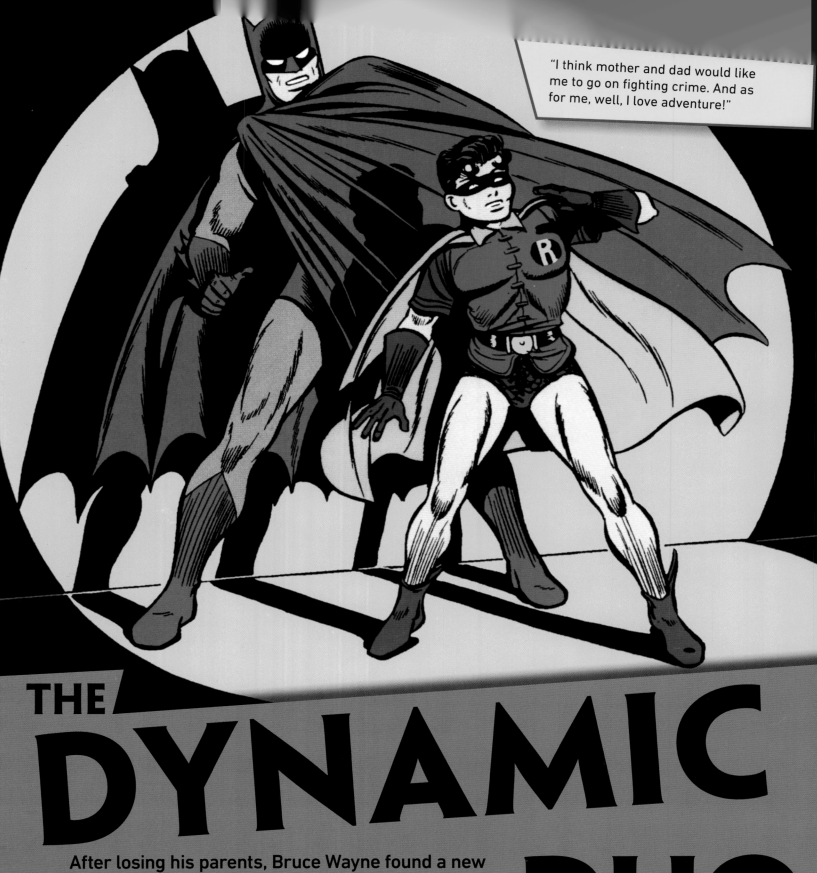

"I think mother and dad would like me to go on fighting crime. And as for me, well, I love adventure!"

THE DYNAMIC DUO

After losing his parents, Bruce Wayne found a new purpose as a crime fighter. When circus acrobat Dick Grayson suffered a similar tragedy, Bruce gave him the same chance. Gotham City's crooks soon learned to fear the one-two punch of Batman and Robin!

THE FLYING GRAYSONS

TRAGEDY UNDER THE BIG TOP

Boss Zucco was one of the gangsters bleeding Gotham dry when Batman began his career. Zucco's goons tried to extort Haly's Circus for "protection" money but the owner stood firm, knowing that the Flying Graysons—husband and wife acrobats John and Mary with their young son Dick—would wow a sell-out crowd with their outstanding aerial act. But as punishment for defying him, Boss Zucco chose to set an example for others by targeting the star performers.

With a bright costume that evoked both the Robin Hood legend and the red-breasted bird, Robin injected a sense of fun into Batman's grim mission.

Zucco's men made one last demand for a cut of Haly's profits, but left empty handed.

At that evening's performance, a sabotaged rope snapped. In front of a packed crowd, John and Mary Grayson fell to their deaths.

Bruce Wayne had seen it all. Remembering his own childhood loss, he arranged for the orphaned boy to become his legal ward.

After intense training in boxing, acrobatics, jujutsu, and criminology, Dick Grayson became Robin—Batman's new partner!

"...And swear that we two will fight together against crime and corruption and never to swerve from the path of righteousness!"

SWINGING INTO ACTION

With his small size and his costume recalling colors of the circus, Robin didn't inspire fear in thugs like Batman did. But he exploited the overconfidence of bigger and clumsier foes, outmaneuvering them with his high-wire expertise. And with Batman's training under his belt, he could punch far above his weight. After gaining experience against Catwoman, The Penguin, and other costumed crooks, Robin started taking on solo missions.

During one of their first adventures, Batman and Robin thwarted The Joker's ghastly crimes.

#1
BATMAN

"You played your last hand, Joker!"

BATMAN

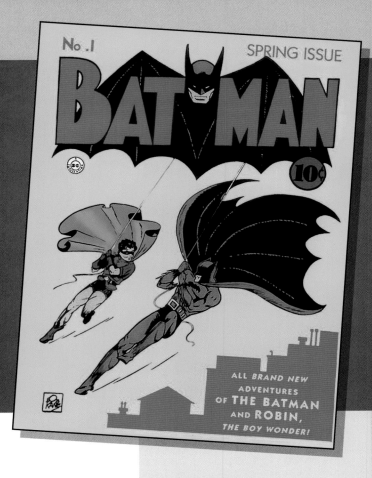

MAIN CHARACTERS: Batman; Robin; The Joker; the Cat (Catwoman)
SUPPORTING CHARACTERS: Commissioner Gordon; Henry Claridge;
Jay Wilde; Brute Nelson; Chief Chalmers; Mrs. Martha Travers
LOCATIONS: Claridge mansion, Brute Nelson's headquarters,
The Joker's hideout, the Drake Museum, the Travers' yacht

BACKGROUND

With *Detective Comics'* new Batsuited hero providing a huge boost in sales during 1939, DC had few qualms about giving the Batman his own solo title the following year. *Batman #1* opened with a concise two-page origin story adapted from a similar piece in *Detective Comics* #33. As well as recapping Batman's origins for the uninitiated, *Batman #1* also had an equally important contribution to make to the Dark Knight's comic-book canon—the introduction of the murderous Joker and the sultry "Cat"—later to be dubbed Catwoman. The Joker starred in two different stories within this issue, while Catwoman and another new threat, Hugo Strange's Monster Men, took up the remaining two tales. Originally, The Joker was intended to die in his second feature, but editor Whitney Ellsworth had the story amended to ensure the villain's survival, realizing the potential that the Clown Prince of Crime had to offer.

PUBLICATION DATE
Spring 1940

EDITOR-IN-CHIEF
Whitney Ellsworth

COVER ARTIST
Bob Kane

WRITER
Bill Finger

PENCILER
Bob Kane

INKER
Jerry Robinson

LETTERER
Jerry Robinson

The Stories...

Terror grips Gotham City as a new criminal, The Joker, announces via radio broadcast that he will kill a wealthy man named Henry Claridge at midnight and steal his heirloom diamond.

The police try to protect the target, but at 12 o'clock he falls dead with a ghastly smile on his face **(1)**. The Joker names more victims, including Jay Wilde, owner of the Ronkers Ruby, and additional police officers are deployed as bodyguards. Their precautions prove useless as The Joker uses blowguns and slow-acting poisons to turn Wilde **(2)** and later victims into grinning corpses while he steals their gems.

The gangster Brute Nelson, head of Gotham City's crime scene, is irritated by The Joker's success. He vows to get even **(3)**, but The Joker arrives at Nelson's front door to kill him and claim the mantle of Gotham City's crime kingpin. Batman interrupts The Joker's coup d'état, but the clown-like criminal escaps. Robin tracks The Joker to his hideout, but is captured by his grinning adversary. Batman attempts to rescue the Boy Wonder **(4)**, but the maniacal criminal unleashes a volley of bullets. This time it is The Joker's turn to be surprised, as Batman is wearing a bulletproof vest beneath his costume. Soon, The Joker is behind bars **(5)**. However, he will escape again in the issue's final story, after two brief interludes, the first starring Hugo Strange and the next starring the new threat of the Cat.

The tale featuring the Cat (later Selina Kyle, aka Catwoman) begins when Mrs. Martha Travers, a wealthy heiress, hosts a party on her yacht **(1)**, Dick Grayson goes undercover as a steward to keep an eye on her valuable necklace. Dick intercepts a mysterious note signed by "the Cat," but is unable to stop the necklace from being stolen. A boat full of gangsters then approaches the yacht **(2)**. The mobsters are unable to find the necklace, but when they try to shoot a man for protecting his wife, Dick steps in to help but is knocked overboard. He uses this opportunity to suit up as Robin, and before long the Boy Wonder has defeated the crooks **(3)**, with help from Batman.

Meanwhile, a fire alarm interrupts a masquerade party taking place on the yacht **(4)**. An old woman is revealed to be the Cat in disguise **(5)** when her quick moves prove she isn't as frail as she seems **(6)**. Batman recovers the stolen necklace but is entranced by her feminine charms **(7)**. The Cat jumps overboard to freedom, and the Dark Knight jostles the Boy Wonder when he tries to stop her. Robin protests, but Batman is smitten by the Cat's "lovely eyes."

BATMAN AND THE JOKER

Without Batman, The Joker wouldn't exist. In his original and most frequently recounted origin story, the Clown Prince of Crime gained his chalky complexion and shocking green hair after falling into a bubbling vat while fleeing from Batman during a burglary. Driven to madness by the experience, the no-name hoodlum became Gotham City's most infamous mass murderer, who has never stopped plotting his revenge. Batman and The Joker have altered their looks and methods over the years, but they still represent opposite extremes of order and chaos.

In his first showdown with the Dark Knight, The Joker demonstrated surprising strength in physical combat. But when Batman proved to be his superior, The Joker soon resorted to knives and guns.

CIRCUS OF CRIME

The Joker's features forever mark him as a clown. During one early caper, he dressed as a jester and recruited acrobats and a strongman to form a traveling circus. Giving performances at the homes of wealthy Gothamites, The Joker was in the perfect position to scope the mansions and plan after-hours robberies. Batman and Robin deduced the plot, unmasked the circus's madcap mastermind, and made short work of The Joker's carnival crew.

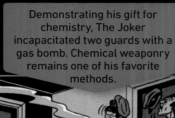

Demonstrating his gift for chemistry, The Joker incapacitated two guards with a gas bomb. Chemical weaponry remains one of his favorite methods.

JOKERMOBILES

Though he would deny it, The Joker has often patterned himself after the object of his obsession. In one adventure he made his own Utility Belt, and once the Batmobile hit the streets it wasn't long before a Jokermobile followed. With his leering face emblazoned on the vehicle's hood, The Joker cut an unmistakable path through the city traffic.

Not to be outdone by the Batplane, the Jokergyro was capable of vertical ascent, taking TheJoker high above Gotham City.

COMEDY OF TEARS

The Joker seemed to have become a tragedian when his thefts of autographed objects caused misery among Gotham City's citizens. His goal seemed to be to make people cry, while at the same time using the stolen signatures to forge official documents and gain access to millions of dollars in valuables. In a dramatic sequence of events, Batman and Robin tracked the villain to a movie set, where they traded blows atop an artificial cliff as a studio cameraman captured their moves on film.

Continuing the chase many miles from Gotham City's gray skyline, The Joker made his getaway across a sun-baked beach in a most unusual choice of vehicle—a sand sailboat, with Batman in hot pursuit.

After crashing his plane, The Joker came around with no memory of his criminal past. Calling himself "Ed Smith," he surrendered his stolen loot and was rewarded for his honesty, while a baffled Dynamic Duo tried to deduce his hidden agenda. When his amnesia faded, The Joker quickly returned to his wily ways!

CLAYFACE

Once, Basil Karlo was a horror-film star. But when a director passed him over in favor of a younger leading man, Karlo vowed revenge. Making himself over as the ghoulish Clayface, he wreaked havoc on the movie set until Batman and Robin brought down the curtain.

CATWOMAN

Selina Kyle's love of jewels spurred her to become a high-stakes cat burglar. Whether breaking into a penthouse apartment or raiding a luxury yacht, Catwoman was a constant headache for the G.C.P.D. She and Batman have engaged in opposites-attract flirtation ever since their first meeting.

THE PENGUIN

Batman refused to believe that oddball Oswald Cobblepot could be a master criminal until he swiped two priceless paintings from an art museum by hiding them in his umbrella. Cobblepot then shot a mobster and took over his gang, renaming himself The Penguin. He carried an impressive array of umbrellas capable of spraying stun gas or squirting acid.

ENTER THE VILLAINS

Is Batman to blame for the riot of colorful characters who commit crimes in Gotham City? Maybe not, but it's hard to escape the conclusion that many of them would not be in their current roles if the Dark Knight hadn't paved the way. Catwoman was one of the first to emulate Batman and don a costume, and soon the city exploded with thieves laying claim to nicknames and crime gimmicks. Before long, Batman had an entire Gallery of Rogues!

JERVIS TETCH

Tetch chose to pattern his Mad Hatter soubriquet after the *Alice in Wonderland* character. Initially he focused on nabbing treasures like the Gotham City Yacht Club's trophy, but in time he expanded his racket to include mind-controlling targets through microelectronics. This greatly increased his ranking among the most wanted criminals of Gotham City.

THE RIDDLER

Edward Nigma (later Nygma), aka The Riddler, valued intellectual challenges more than ill-gotten gains. When the G.C.P.D. failed to solve his puzzles, The Riddler realized that only the World's Greatest Detective could be his peer. The Riddler left clues for Batman to decipher, deploying wordplay and larger-than-life death traps.

TWO-FACE

After Harvey Dent (originally named Harvey Kent) suffered the physical and psychological scarring that transformed him into Two-Face, he based every decision on the flip of a coin. At first, this obsession led to equal amounts of good and bad actions—Two-Face might rob a bank one day, and donate the loot to charity the next. Some Gothamites hailed him as a hero, but in time his evil side grew to be the stronger.

SCARECROW

Professor Jonathan Crane taught a course on the psychology of fear, before realizing that terror could be used as a weapon for gaining power and riches. He dressed in a scarecrow costume to frighten his victims, and if that didn't work he shot them with a handgun. As the legend of the Scarecrow grew, Crane began to employ his trademark hallucinatory fear gas to ensure he gave his victims nightmares.

KEY ISSUE

#16
BATMAN

"I have known since last night that you were the Batman and Robin—but I saw no reason to mention it till now!"

ALFRED BEAGLE

MAIN CHARACTERS: Batman, Robin, Alfred Beagle
SUPPORTING CHARACTERS: Gaston LeDuc, Manuel Stiletti, Pablo, Thomas
LOCATIONS: Gotham City pier, Wayne Manor, the Batcave, abandoned Gotham City theater

BACKGROUND

Where would Batman be without Alfred? The unflappable British butler was Batman's confidant, helpmate, emergency surgeon, and father figure. However, Alfred started out in comics as a rotund comic-relief character who arrived on the boat from England to provide readers with laughs. "Here Comes Alfred," one of several stories packed into *Batman* #16, not only introduced the character as a proper gentleman (the son of a butler named Jarvis, no less), it also had him discover Batman and Robin's secret identities, granting Alfred unique influence in their exploits. As the Dynamic Duo became a trio, Alfred (given the last name Beagle, later becoming Pennyworth) linked Batman's double life of nocturnal vigilantism and the public façade required of a wealthy and well-known man of leisure. Within a year of his debut, Alfred received a thinner, mustachioed makeover as a result of his appearance in the 1943 *Batman* movie serials, and later, a new backstory as a guiding presence in Batman's life since childhood.

PUBLICATION DATE
April–May 1943

EDITOR
Whitney Ellsworth

COVER ARTIST
Jerry Robinson

WRITER
Don Cameron

PENCILER
Bob Kane

INKER
Jerry Robinson

LETTERER
Jerry Robinson

The Story...

Batman and Robin don't think they need a butler, but when Alfred discovers their secret identities, he becomes the only person who can save them from a gang of international crooks.

Alfred Beagle fancies himself an amateur detective and he is casting a suspicious eye on his fellow passenger Gaston LeDuc **(1)** when a gang of thugs led by Manuel Stiletti attempt to steal his suitcase **(2)**. Batman and Robin rush to break up the would-be robbery **(3)** but turn down Alfred's offer to help track the crooks when they make a fast getaway.

Back at Wayne Manor, Bruce Wayne and Dick Grayson **(4)** are astonished when Alfred knocks on their door. However, Alfred has not deduced their identities, but instead announces his intention to serve as the Wayne household's butler, as his father did before him. Bruce remembers Alfred's father from the past and doesn't have the heart to turn Alfred away.

As night falls, Alfred reads a news story about the exiled Duke of Dorian, who has fled an invasion in his homeland, and recognizes him as his shipmate Gaston LeDuc **(5)**. Meanwhile, the Stiletti gang track Alfred down to Wayne Manor. The gang try again to nab his luggage, but Batman and Robin foil the act once more. Alfred then goes to check on Bruce and Dick, and stumbles across a hidden tunnel that leads to the Batcave. Alfred is awed to find he is working for Gotham City's most famous crime fighters! **(6)**.

Batman and Robin follow the Stiletti gang to an abandoned theater, where the gang capture them. The villains suspend the duo high above the theater's stage **(7)** then drive across town to find Gaston LeDuc. It turns out that Alfred's suitcase provides coded clues—sent by the crooks' overseas accomplice—which lead them to LeDuc's location. LeDuc is indeed the exiled Duke of Dorian and he is carrying the priceless crown jewels of his homeland—something the Stiletti gang are keen to get their hands on.

The gang take the Duke of Dorian prisoner and return to the theater only to discover that Alfred has picked up Batman and Robin's trail and freed the crime fighters. The crooks are collared and the crown jewels returned to their rightful guardian **(8)**.

The next evening, as Alfred attends to his duties at Wayne Manor, he spots the Bat-Signal in the night sky. Without a word, he brings Bruce Wayne and Dick Grayson their Batman and Robin costumes, each of them impeccably cleaned and pressed **(9)**. With their

WORLD'S FINEST

Among the first Super Heroes to emerge onto the global stage, Batman and Superman have set the tone for all the heroes who have followed. Though their approaches couldn't be more different—Batman is a secretive Gotham City vigilante, while Superman is the reassuring public face of Metropolis—the two forged a close bond very early in their careers. This bond of trust even extends to their secret identities, allowing Bruce Wayne and Clark Kent to visit one another as professional colleagues. When World War II broke out in 1939, the world needed the two Super Hero friends more than ever.

The U.S.'s true heroes in the fight against the Axis powers were the members of its military forces. Batman, Robin, and Superman never failed to salute the Army, Navy, Marines, and Air Force for their service and sacrifice. During the war, the three Super Heroes usually remained stateside, where they boosted morale and busted enemy spy rings.

LIFE DURING WARTIME

As the Golden Age took hold, bank robberies in Gotham City soon took a back seat to the movements of a tyrant's armies in Europe. When Hitler's tanks rolled into Poland, Batman and Superman got ready to do their part in defending international freedom against the Axis powers of Nazi Germany and its allies. In 1940, even before the United States entered into the war, the two heroes aided their country's allies by capturing Nazi saboteurs in besieged Great Britain. Other heroes joined their cause, and soon their numbers had swelled to the point where a Super Hero strike force could arise. Batman and Superman signed on as reserve members of the Justice Society of America, serving alongside the Green Lantern, The Atom, and The Flash.

In the 1980s, it was revealed that, following Japan's attack on Pearl Harbor in 1941, Batman and Superman joined a second Super Hero team, the All-Star Squadron, comprised of dozens of Golden Age heroes. These adventures, as well as nearly all of Batman's exploits from the 1940s, were retroactively said to occur on the parallel world of Earth-2, a planet where Batman and Superman were not only allies, but also close friends.

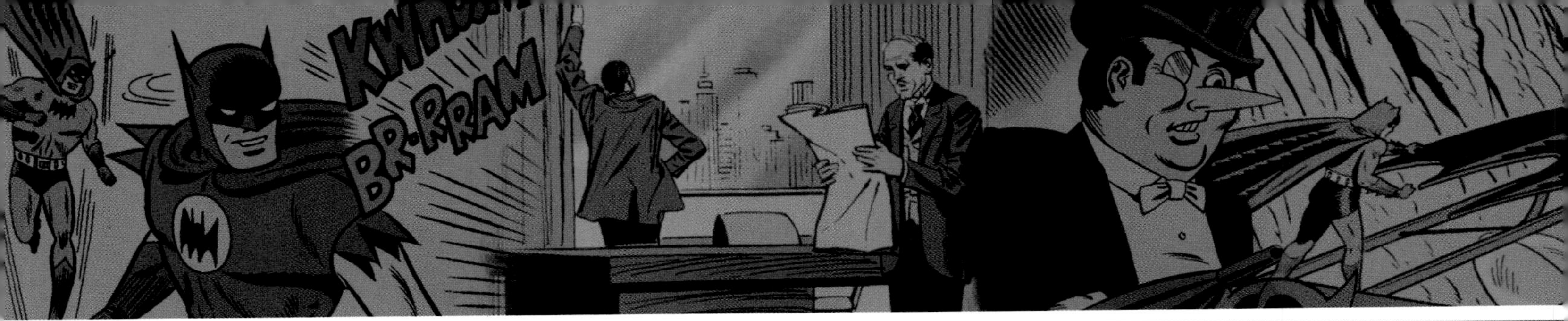
BR-RRAM

SILVER AGE

'50s & '60s

Batman found new fame in the Silver Age of Comics—but the popularity may have cost him his edge.

By the 1950s, masked vigilantes had become passé. But Batman was one of the few Super Heroes who never went out of style. While other Super Hero titles folded, replaced by comics starring cops, cowboys, funny animals, and lovelorn teens, Batman remained in print—but he did change dramatically all the same.

Under the leadership of DC editor Jack Schiff, Batman became an unlikely sci-fi star. His adventures now featured aliens, robots, and radioactive freaks, and he regularly teamed up with Superman in *World's Finest Comics*.

The evolution of the Dark Knight also affected his supporting cast. Kathy Kane arrived on the scene as the first Batwoman, with her niece Betty Kane as Bat-Girl. These female counterparts to Batman and Robin rounded out what became known as the Batman Family, which also included the crime-fighting dog Ace the Bat-Hound.

This tonal shift wasn't merely a sign of shifting public tastes. Psychologist Fredric Wertham's alarmist essays on a purported link between comic books and juvenile delinquency prompted Senate hearings and the creation of the self-regulatory Comics Code Authority. Prohibiting comic books containing "gore, sexual innuendo, or excessive violence," the CCA effectively quashed anything that might be considered envelope-pushing.

When *Batman* sales declined, editor Julius Schwartz was brought in to give the series a more modern, realistic new look spearheaded by artist Carmine Infantino. Stripped of the science-fiction elements and extended Batman family, the revamped series was a critical success, and Schwartz prepared to take the character back to his dark roots as the 1960s abated.

OVERLEAF
Batman #171 (May1965):
The Riddler was reintroduced in a comic said to have inspired the style of the classic Batman *TV show of 1966.*

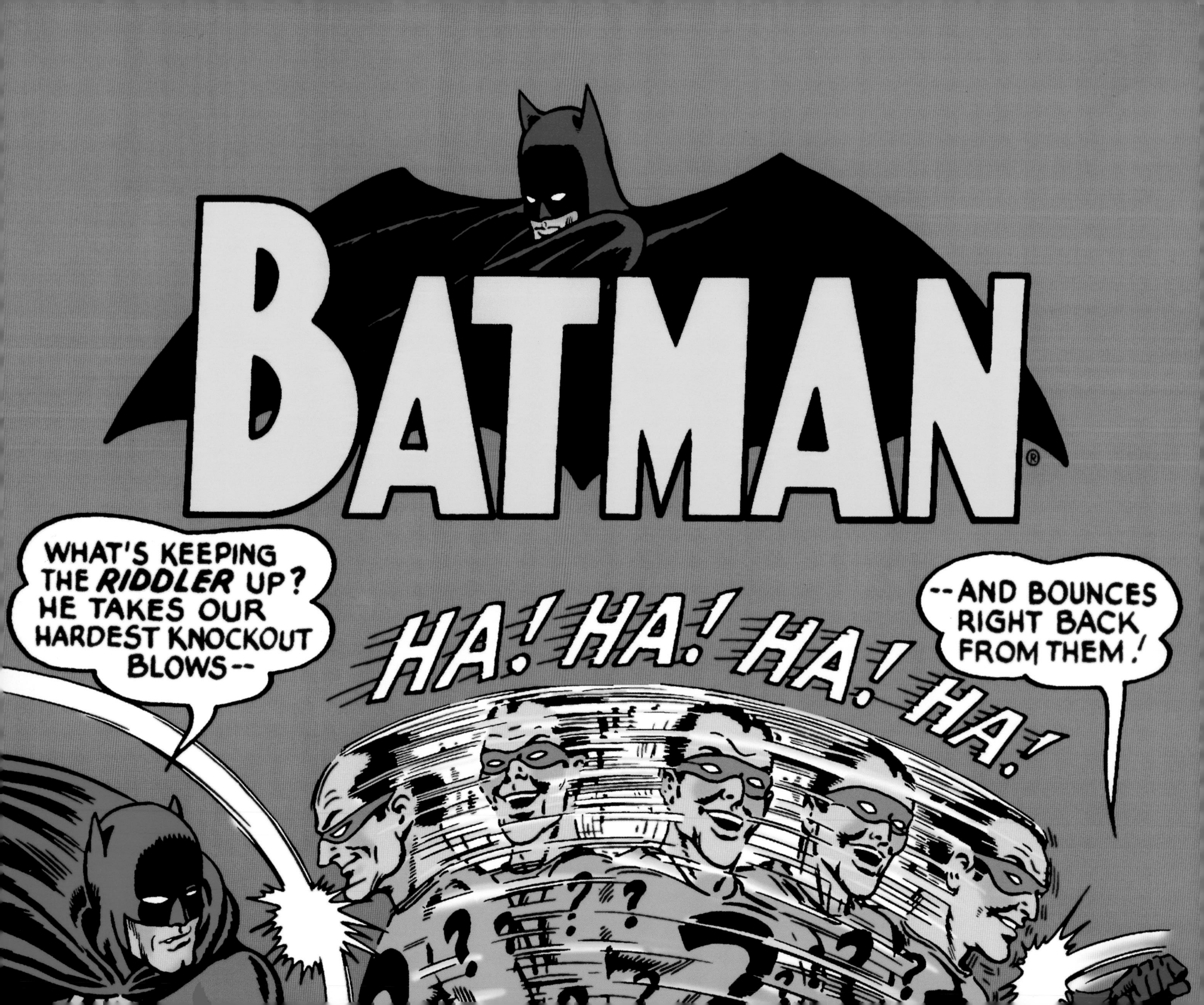
BATMAN®
WHAT'S KEEPING THE RIDDLER UP? HE TAKES OUR HARDEST KNOCKOUT BLOWS--
HA! HA! HA! HA!
--AND BOUNCES RIGHT BACK FROM THEM!

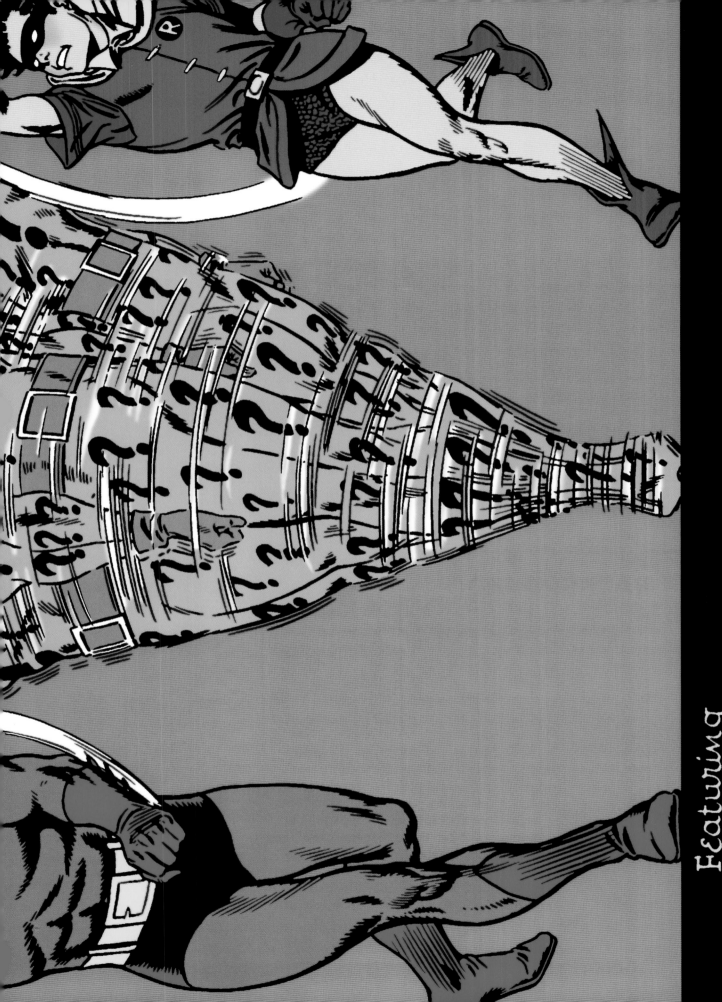

Featuring "REMARKABLE RUSE of the RIDDLER!"

#113
BATMAN

"That's because I'm the Batman of Zur-En-Arrh! Through a powerful telescope I've observed your every action!"

Batman of Zur-En-Arrh

MAIN CHARACTERS: Batman, Batman of Zur-En-Arrh (Tlano)
SUPPORTING CHARACTERS: Robin
LOCATIONS: Wayne Manor, replica Batcave of Zur-En-Arrh, capital city of Zur-En-Arrh

BACKGROUND

By the late 1950s, DC had a host of comics on the shelves that spanned every genre from the Wild West to romance. Nonetheless, the company's only ironclad superstars were Batman and Superman. The Man of Steel had arrived first, and now he was leading the way into a new era of sci-fi strangeness, one that also impacted Batman's series.

In "Batman—The Superman of Planet X," that strangeness is on full display. The story brings Batman to an alien world where he possesses abilities far beyond those of mortal men. Although firmly a product of its time, this story was remembered fondly by writer Grant Morrison, who layered many elements into his 2008 saga "Batman R.I.P.," in which Batman's memories of Zur-En-Arrh were reimagined as delusions created by Bruce's strained psyche. This issue also featured two other exciting tales, one introducing the villain False Face, who would also go on to appear in the 1966 *Batman* TV show.

PUBLICATION DATE
February 1958

EDITOR
Jack Schiff

COVER ARTIST
Sheldon Moldoff

WRITER
Ed Herron

PENCILER
Dick Sprang

INKER
Charles Paris

LETTERER
Milton Snapinn

The Story...

On the alien world of Zur-En-Arrh, Batman becomes a superpowered defender and an inspiration to millions of extraterrestrials.

In the middle of the night, Batman is seized by a sudden need to suit up **(1)** and take off in the Batplane. While airborne, a blinding light **(2)** transports him halfway across the galaxy! There, a man in a modified Batsuit greets him **(3)**. The man says that Batman has been teleported to the planet Zur-En-Arrh, where the population is kept safe thanks to the example that Batman himself has set. His host, a scientist named Tlano, explains that he has watched the Dark Knight's escapades through a telescope. In time, he chose to model himself after his idol, becoming the Batman of Zur-En-Arrh.

The extraterrestrial hero gives Batman a tour of his replica Batcave, which houses an atomic-powered Batmobile, a rocket-shaped Batplane, and a remarkable piece of equipment called the Bat-radia **(4)**. Using Tlano's futuristic science, the Bat-radia can stall the getaway vehicles of fleeing crooks and create many other amazing effects.

However, when invaders interrupt the tour by advancing on Zur-En-Arrh's capital city, Tlano draws a ray-gun and fires it at Batman's chest. The shots bounce harmlessly away **(5)**. Just as Superman gained amazing abilities when exposed to Earth's yellow sun and lower gravity, so Batman finds that he possesses similar powers on Zur-En-Arrh. An astonished Dark Knight verifies that he can now bend girders with his bare hands **(6)** and even fly **(7)**.

Batman leaps into action against the invading forces, using a chunk of metal to swat aside deadly nuclear orbs **(8)**. The invaders retaliate with their best soldiers, but they crumple beneath Batman's mighty fists. Switching tactics, the warriors suddenly vanish! Batman retreats to the duplicate Batcave where he learns that the invaders have deployed giant robots to wreak havoc in the capital city **(9)**.

The Dark Knight discovers that the robots also possess invisibility fields, but Tlano uses the Bat-radia to turn the robots visible. Rushing to the scene in his Batplane, Tlano issues a molecular shower from the Bat-radia that overloads the robots' stealth screens. The enemy's secret weapons are exposed for a counterattack by Batman **(10)**. Thanks to his new powers, he fashions a gigantic lasso and ensnares the robots, tossing them to the ground as the invaders flee to their ships.

With Zur-En-Arrh safe from invasion, Batman accepts a souvenir from Tlano. The Bat-radia of Zur-En-Arrh will make a fine addition to the Batcave's trophy room.

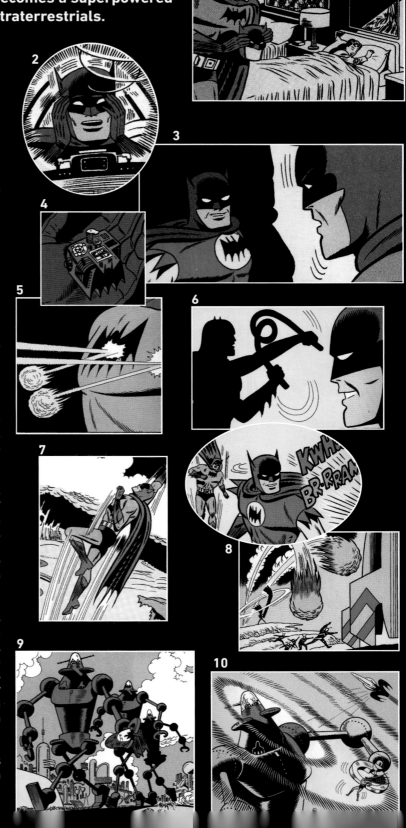

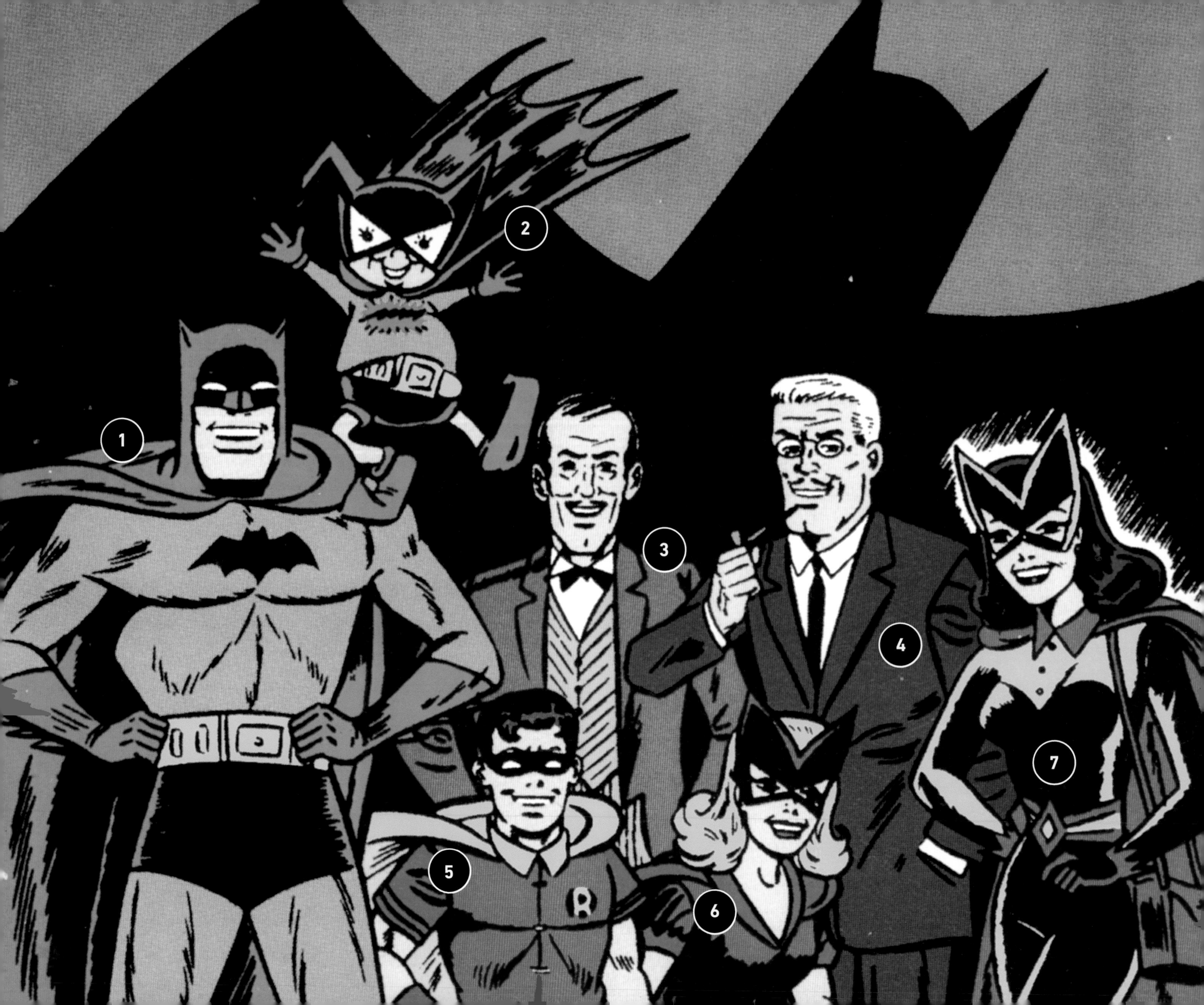
1
2
3
4
5
6
7

THE BATMAN FAMILY

After emerging as Gotham City's champion, Batman rapidly became an inspiration to many others. Before long he had gathered around him a group of allies so fiercely loyal that they became known as the Batman Family. Robin was the first, but before long circus performer Kathy Kane and her niece Betty followed his example to become the original Batwoman and Bat-Girl. Commissioner Gordon of the Gotham City Police Department had already been welcomed into the fold, as had Alfred Pennyworth—perhaps the Dark Knight's most trusted ally. More unusual members of the

1 BATMAN
2 BAT-MITE
3 ALFRED
4 COMMISSIONER GORDON
5 ROBIN
6 BAT-GIRL (BETTY KANE)
7 BATWOMAN (KATHY KANE)
8 ACE THE BAT-HOUND

DETECTIVE COMICS

ISSUE #327

"It's a risky business—but when has that stopped us?"

BATMAN

MAIN CHARACTERS: Batman, Robin, Frank Fenton, Smiler
(Roland Meacham
SUPPORTING CHARACTERS: Linda Greene, a Rare Chemical Company
employee, James "Jimmy" Packer, various underground criminals, an
unnamed Gotham City Police Department captain
LOCATIONS: Gotham Village, Jefferson Square Park, a Gotham Village
café, a Gotham City penthouse apartment, the Batcave, the Rare Chemical Company,
122 Suburban Avenue, a Gotham Village home, Sub-Gotham Village

BACKGROUND

Unlike most characters in comics, Batman can be said to have had two
unique Silver Ages. The first was under the stewardship of editor Jack
Schiff, who attempted to mimic the success of the Superman titles by
pitting a Batman "family" against sci-fi threats. The second age began
with *Detective Comics* #327, the first "New Look" Batman under the editor
responsible for revitalizing The Flash, Julius Schwartz.

This Batman had a yellow oval around his famous Bat-
Symbol, fought street criminals or Super-Villains with his
detective skills, and partnered with a teenaged Robin.

It was this more down-to-earth era that would serve as
the prime inspiration for the smash hit *Batman* TV
series of 1966.

While this issue featured an Elongated Man backup
story that complimented its detective theme, the main
tale included a major misstep, one Schwartz would be
sure not to repeat. Batman used a gun to hold off the
villains at the story's end, an act usually forbidden by
The Dark Knight's crime-fighting code.

PUBLICATION DATE
May 1964

EDITOR
Julius Schwartz

COVER ARTIST
Carmine Infantino and Joe Giella

WRITER
John Broome

PENCILER
Carmine Infantino

INKER
Joe Giella

The Story...

When touring the area known as Gotham Village, Batman and Robin uncover a mystery that reveals a secret criminal society living beneath the city streets.

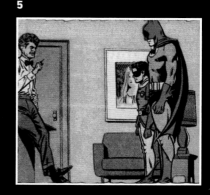

As Bruce Wayne and Dick Grayson are strolling through picturesque, bohemian Gotham Village **(1)**, they encounter a distraught young woman named Linda Greene. Linda fears that her fiancé, James Packer, is mixed up in a criminal plot. She produces a map of Gotham Village he has dropped. The map is marked with an X in a circle, a symbol the Dynamic Duo recognize **(2)**.

Batman and Robin were recently chasing a jewelry thief when an explosion knocked them unconscious **(3)**. When they awoke, Batman's cowl had a circled X on it; the same symbol was also visible on Robin's forehead **(4)**. The symbols faded, but Batman deduced that they had been made by a phosphorus isotope, an item that was only sold at the Rare Chemical Company on Gotham City's Morrow Street.

Following the sales record of the chemical back to the apartment of one Frank Fenton, the Dynamic Duo found they were literally frozen in Fenton's presence, unable to stop him from packing up his stolen jewelry and leaving **(5)**. Once the paralysis wore off, Batman and Robin returned to the Batcave to devise a plan of action.

Back in the present, Batman and Robin track down Linda's fiancé Jimmy. They see him enter a house at the spot marked on the map. Inside, a staircase leads to a cavern **(6)**, the hideout for crooks called Sub-Gotham Village **(7)**. Its amenities include a bar, a movie theater, and a "travel bureau" for planning escapes. Finding Fenton with Sub-Gotham's organizer, Smiler, Batman and Robin easily break Fenton's paralysis trance this time around and best the lawbreakers **(8)**. Batman uncharacteristically holds them at bay with a criminal's gun **(9)**.

The police arrive and Batman unmasks Smiler, revealing Roland Meacham, chairman of the committee to preserve Gotham Village. Batman reveals that he and Robin used concealed lead lining on their foreheads to prevent Fenton's unique handheld device from sending a signal to their forehead brands and freezing their motor functions **(10)**. Batman learns that Jimmy isn't in Smiler's gang, but was trying to stop the criminals, which later comes as a relief to Jimmy's fiancée.

THE SILVER AGE

THE BATPLANE

THE WHIRLY-BAT

Daylight illuminated Batman's shadowy world during this era, as new friends joined his quest and Gotham City welcomed him with open arms. The villains of the Rogues Gallery gave him a break, too. Even The Joker abandoned mass murder and embraced harmless theatrical crimes. For a while, Gotham City became a magnet for otherworldly weirdness with various aliens paying visits. However, these sci-fi exploits soon gave way to detective stories and Super-Villain hijinks. This period wouldn't last, but it was a lighthearted and unexpected diversion.

BAT-GADGETS AND GIZMOS
Batman increased his daytime visibility, patrolling Gotham City in vehicles of all shapes and sizes. New, sleek designs for the Batplane took wing as Batman deployed his latest technology. The Whirly-Bat gave Batman a whole new vantage point on crime fighting, and the Batmobile evolved into a near-tank with a steel-reinforced bat-symbol that doubled as a battering ram.

A crash in the old Batmobile broke Batman's leg but gave him a great excuse to bring in a sleek new vehicle.

BATMOBILE

FAMILY LIFE
Introduced in the first half of Batman's Silver Age period, Kathy Kane and Betty Kane didn't remain in the roles of Batwoman and Bat-Girl for long. With Ace the Bat-Hound rounding out his odd family unit, Batman received newfound public praise and earned law-enforcement legitimacy as a deputized officer of the G.C.P.D. The Batman Family welcomed its final member when a tiny extra-dimensional being with reality-shaping powers took the name Bat-Mite. As the "New Look" Batman came to fruition, these heroes would be relegated to relative obscurity, while Barbara Gordon became the new Batgirl, gaining an iconic status never achieved by previous bat-themed, female Super Heroes.

Bat-Mite meant well, but often underestimated his strength. After blessing Bat-Girl with temporary superpowers to help her win Robin's heart, Bat-Mite discovered that his meddling only placed her in jeopardy.

As Robin grew in strength and experience, he started flying solo without Batman to back him up. While routing the criminals who sought to exploit a teachers' strike, the Boy Wonder succeeded in disarming one thug with a flying kick.

FREAKY FOES

As Gotham City experienced an outbreak of sci-fi weirdness, citizens grew used to bizarre threats, such as huge mechanical men. These "all hands on deck" emergencies required the contributions of each member of Batman's band of crime fighters. When the strangeness subsided and Gotham City returned to its former level of menace, the Bat Family shed most of its members.

With perfect timing and a winning smile, Kathy Kane swung into action as the original Batwoman. A romance with her male counterpart seemed on the cards, but the sparks between Batman and Batwoman never ignited.

POISON IVY
In her debut as Poison Ivy, brilliant botanist Pamela Isley proved her supremacy over Gotham City's other female criminals by tricking them into fighting each other. She also managed to plant her poison kiss on Batman before inviting him to join her in a life of crime!

CLAYFACE
The new Clayface was treasure hunter Matt Hagen, who possessed the bizarre ability to mold his claylike body into anything he imagined. Batman and Robin fought him in bird, snake, and dragon forms.

THE JOKER
The Clown Prince of Crime claimed to have discovered Batman's secret identity. His boast proved hollow, and in the end it was Batman who unmasked The Joker's circus disguise.

SCARECROW
Jonathan Crane unleashed a fresh batch of nightmare-inducing fear gas when he returned as the Scarecrow. Crane's belief in the power of terror was his undoing. He didn't expect Batman and Robin to break his psychological hold; however they did just that—and then located his hideout by tracking fallen pieces of straw.

Deep in the grip of Scarecrow's fear gas, Batman and Robin needed a pep talk from Alfred to snap them back to reality.

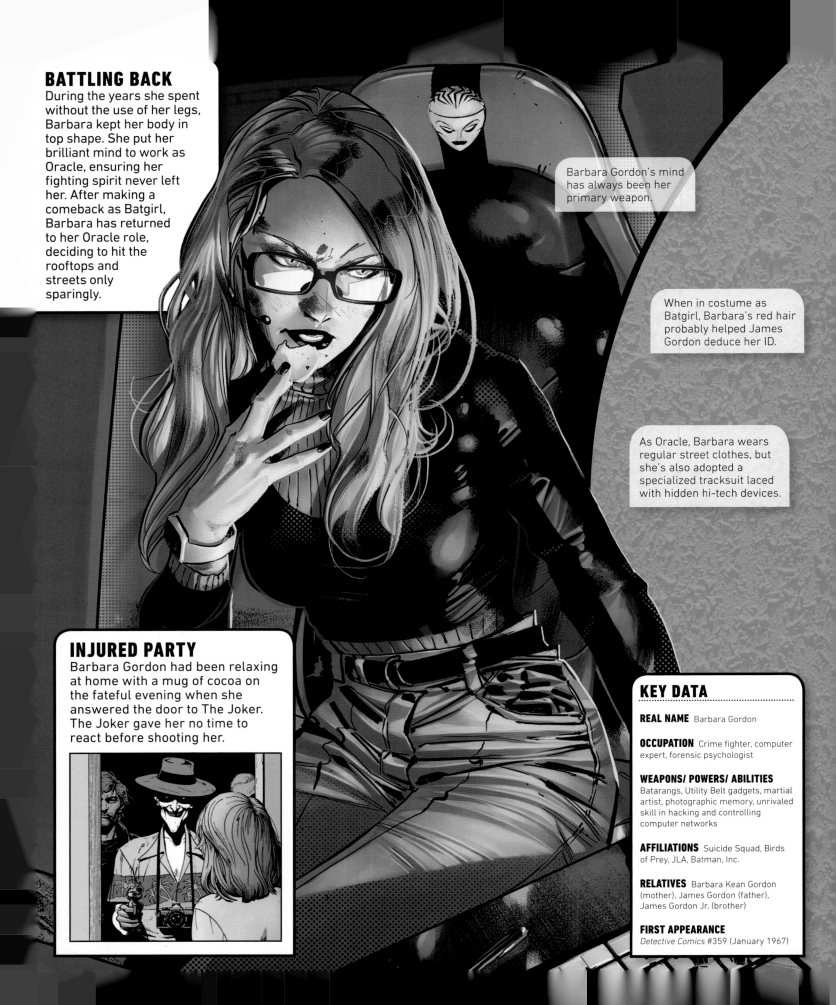

BATTLING BACK

During the years she spent without the use of her legs, Barbara kept her body in top shape. She put her brilliant mind to work as Oracle, ensuring her fighting spirit never left her. After making a comeback as Batgirl, Barbara has returned to her Oracle role, deciding to hit the rooftops and streets only sparingly.

Barbara Gordon's mind has always been her primary weapon.

When in costume as Batgirl, Barbara's red hair probably helped James Gordon deduce her ID.

As Oracle, Barbara wears regular street clothes, but she's also adopted a specialized tracksuit laced with hidden hi-tech devices.

INJURED PARTY

Barbara Gordon had been relaxing at home with a mug of cocoa on the fateful evening when she answered the door to The Joker. The Joker gave her no time to react before shooting her.

KEY DATA

REAL NAME Barbara Gordon

OCCUPATION Crime fighter, computer expert, forensic psychologist

WEAPONS/ POWERS/ ABILITIES Batarangs, Utility Belt gadgets, martial artist, photographic memory, unrivaled skill in hacking and controlling computer networks

AFFILIATIONS Suicide Squad, Birds of Prey, JLA, Batman, Inc.

RELATIVES Barbara Kean Gordon (mother), James Gordon (father), James Gordon Jr. (brother)

FIRST APPEARANCE *Detective Comics* #359 (January 1967)

BARBARA GORDON

> *"Feeling a creep crumble beneath my feet? I didn't even know how much I missed it."*
>
> BATGIRL

Following her "million-dollar debut," Barbara Gordon quickly became Gotham City's most memorable Batgirl. While she excels against street criminals and Super-Villains alike, Barbara's true talent and passion remain behind a keyboard as the information guru Oracle.

Years of unarmed combat training enabled Batgirl to take on enemies many times her size and weight.

NEVER GIVE IN

Gordon was proud of his daughter's inner strength.

The daughter of Gotham City Police Commissioner James Gordon, Barbara Gordon followed her father into crime fighting in a way he never expected! Inspired by the Dynamic Duo, Barbara invented the identity of Batgirl in her teenage years and snuck out every night to battle villains like Killer Moth. Her father never knew the truth, and Barbara always made it home in time to pursue her studies.

Barbara's costumed capers came to a sudden end when The Joker shot her during a raid to kidnap Commissioner Gordon. Left without the use of her legs, Barbara tapped her near-photographic memory in a new career as the mysterious Oracle. With her ability to hack into surveillance cameras and unlock classified military databases, Oracle became an indispensible asset to Super Heroes around the globe. As Oracle, Barbara briefly served with the covert government strike team Suicide Squad and later built a state-of-the-art headquarters inside a Gotham City clocktower. She also recruited Black Canary as her primary field operative, eventually teaming her with The Huntress as the three of them informally became known as the crime-fighting team Birds of Prey.

While she later regained the use of her legs through a hi-tech implant and set out as Batgirl once more, Barbara has decided she best serves Gotham City as a computer operative, and works with Batgirls Cassandra Cain (Orphan) and Stephanie Brown (Spoiler) when she's not supplying information to Batman himself.

Stephanie Brown became Batgirl for a time following a brief turn as Robin.

Cassandra Cain used her martial-arts upbringing to become a silent, terrifying Batgirl.

Batgirl has a close—but competitive—relationship with Nightwing, whom she has known since she was a teenager.

After she regained her ability to walk, Batgirl opted instead to sprint, protecting the Gotham City borough of Burnside.

Her third costume change since her return to the cape and cowl, Batgirl's most recent Batsuit paid homage to her original look and featured a hidden backpack underneath her cape for quick changes on the go.

BRONZE AGE

'70s–MID '80s

Times were changing, and so was Batman. The hero reclaimed his relevance during an artistic explosion.

The end of the 1960s brought seismic cultural changes. With anti-war protests on the evening news and psychedelic rock on the radio dial, the comics of the Silver Age seemed hopelessly square. The solution, argued a new wave of comics writers and artists, was to restore relevance to the medium.

The results were mixed. At DC, writer Denny O'Neil and artist Neal Adams collaborated on titles like *Green Lantern*. The stories looked gorgeous, with an unprecedented realism in capturing the human form, while the writing acknowledged the hero's fallibility and wove in contemporary problems like pollution and drug abuse. But readers didn't respond with the sales figures that the comics arguably deserved.

Things were better on *Batman*. There, O'Neil and Adams restored an edge of menace to the Dark Knight's Rogues Gallery, letting classic villains like The Joker and Two-Face show their murderous sides once more. Editor Julius Schwartz even sent Robin away to college—a clear sign that comics were growing up.

Creators such as Steve Englehart, Marshall Rogers, Dick Giordano, Len Wein, Frank Robbins, Irv Novick, Jim Aparo, and Mike W. Barr took Batman through the era, as DC head Jenette Kahn brought the company into an age of experimentation. Among the new titles released at the time were *Batman Family* (which ran for 20 issues), *Batman and the Outsiders* (32 issues), and *The Joker* (which only lasted nine).

OVERLEAF
Limited Collector's Edition #C-51(August 1977): No villain encapsulates the threats faced by the globetrotting Batman of the 1970s better than Rā's al Ghūl.

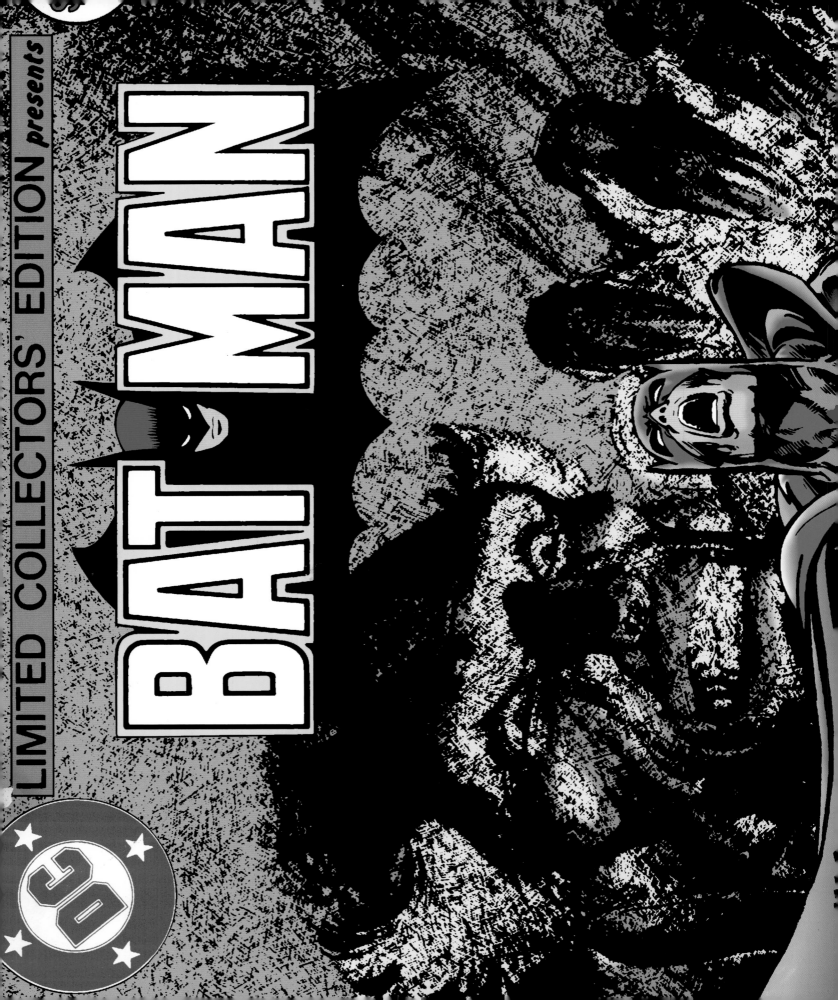

LIMITED COLLECTORS' EDITION *presents*

BAT·MAN
BAT·MAN

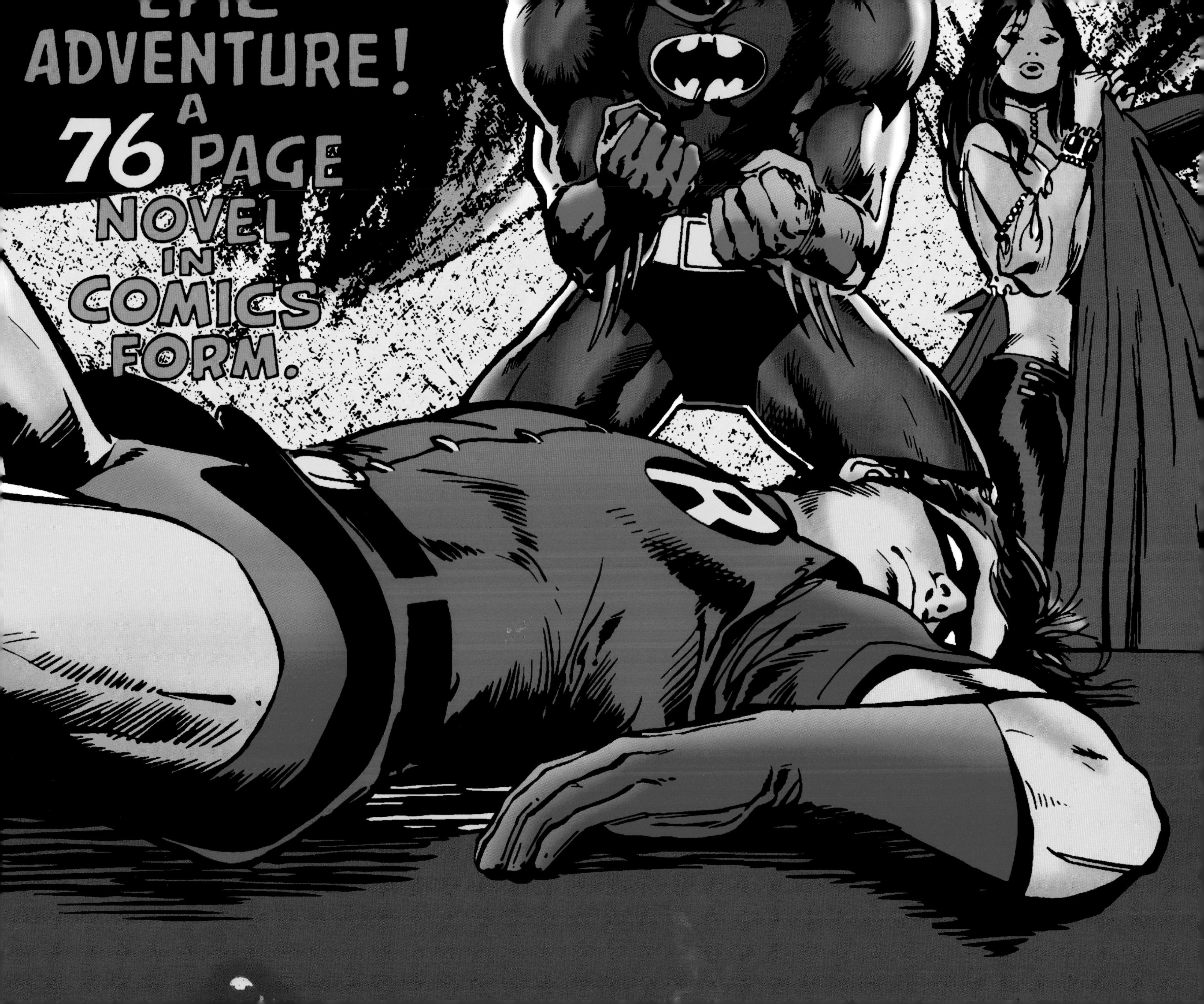
ADVENTURE!
A
76 PAGE
NOVEL
IN
COMICS
FORM.

BATMAN'S EVOLUTION

Not even a Super Hero like Batman can halt the passage of time, and this was a period when great changes were afoot for the Dark Knight.

"Didn't think I'd take it this hard."

His bags packed, Dick Grayson took one last look at Wayne Manor—his home ever since the murder at the circus that left him an orphan.

LEAVING THE NEST
Dick Grayson had grown out of his Boy Wonder role, and needed to choose a future that wasn't defined by Batman. He elected to attend Hudson University to pursue a degree. A gloomy Bruce Wayne and Alfred Pennyworth took in their now-quiet surroundings, then resolved to make their own break from the past. They abandoned Wayne Manor in favor of a downtown skyscraper where Batman could operate closer to the action.

Dick tried to keep his emotions in check during his farewells, but he did allow a single tear to fall as he rode away toward a new life.

Bruce could see no reason to remain at his family's ancestral home. He and Alfred left for central Gotham City.

*"Take a last look Alfred...
Then seal up the Batcave...FOREVER!"*

THE PENTHOUSE

WAYNE FOUNDATION

BATMAN'S PENTHOUSE
After Robin went off to college, Batman and Alfred relocated to a penthouse apartment in the heart of Gotham City. Perched atop the Wayne Foundation Building, headquarters of the charitable arm of Wayne Enterprises, the penthouse served as a luxurious home for Bruce Wayne, while the building's sub-basements and its makeshift Batcave concealed the Batmobile, Batplane, and other tools needed to carry out the Dark Knight's war on crime. Its location also put Batman within easy reach of the areas of the city he patrolled by night. Alfred had doubts about the move, but they vanished when he saw how energized Bruce had become.

Bruce Wayne found a new way to do good through Victims, Inc., but some problems could only be solved by Batman.

ONE BULLET TOO MANY

Recognizing that the police and courts were often incapable of delivering justice, Bruce Wayne announced the creation of the Victims Incorporated Program (VIP). Victims, Inc. would aid those who had fallen through the cracks of the system, like Dr. Fielding, a woman whose husband's killer had gone unpunished due to sloppy investigative work. Bruce gave the woman an interest-free loan to help keep her practice afloat, while Batman tried to identify the killer.

Bruce took a tough-love approach with Dr. Fielding, urging her to stop mourning her husband and try to avenge him. It didn't go smoothly.

Batman spread word that Dr. Fielding was ready to testify against her husband's killer. The crook got to her first and tried to silence her.

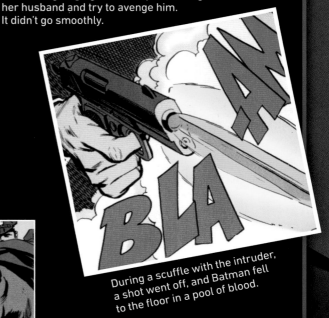

During a scuffle with the intruder, a shot went off, and Batman fell to the floor in a pool of blood.

The bullet, lodged in Batman's shoulder, proved to be the key to cracking the case —it could identify the gunman.

After removing the bullet, Batman ran it through a ballistics database and found the culprit.

#251
BATMAN

"Without the game that the Batman and I have played for so many years, winning is nothing!"

THE JOKER

MAIN CHARACTERS: Batman, The Joker
SUPPORTING CHARACTERS: Commissioner Gordon, Packy White, Alby, Bigger Melvin, Bing Hooley
LOCATIONS: Boxing gym, Alby's hotel, Gotham City Aquarium, Gotham City Harbor

PUBLICATION DATE
September 1973

EDITOR
Julius Schwartz

COVER ARTIST
Neal Adams

WRITER
Denny O'Neil

PENCILER
Neal Adams

INKER
Neal Adams

LETTERER
Unknown

BACKGROUND

The Silver Age of Comics may have been imaginative and fun, but it was seldom serious. After years of embarking on sci-fi quests and adventuring with a costumed Bat-hound, Batman reached the pinnacle of parody with 1966–1968's tongue-in-cheek *Batman* TV show. It was time for someone to put the darkness back into the Dark Knight.

This change came about most notably from the pairing of writer Denny O'Neil and artist Neal Adams. The duo returned Batman to his noir roots, beginning in the pages of *Detective Comics* #395's momentous "The Secret of the Waiting Graves." The Joker would rediscover his own dark side soon after in *Batman* #251's "The Joker's Five-Way Revenge," becoming truly murderous again instead of a harmless prankster. Batman's Rogues Gallery continued to undergo a darker rebirth, setting the tone as DC entered the period of creativity known as the Bronze Age of Comics.

The Story...

When The Joker decides to settle some old scores, Batman is drawn into a race against time to save the hardened criminals on his archenemy's hit list.

While The Joker gleefully speeds away from his latest felony **(1)**, the Bat-Signal summons the Dark Knight to the crime scene on the city outskirts. Commissioner Gordon's officers have cordoned off a body sporting a telltale death rictus **(2)**. Any hope that the murder may be the work of someone other than the Clown Prince of Crime is dashed when Batman reveals a joker playing card left at the scene.

Learning that the dead man was one of the five members of The Joker's former gang, Batman concludes that the remaining four are in mortal danger from a clown out for revenge. Boxing trainer Packy White seems the next on The Joker's hit list. Batman engages in an impromptu sparring session with the tough pugilist. Packy takes a sip from a ringside bucket of water **(3)**, his face contorts into a gruesome grin, and he falls dead.

The Joker takes a more direct approach with his third target. Reassuring the terrified crook, Alby, that he has nothing to fear, The Joker offers him a cigar **(4)**. It is packed with nitroglycerin. The Joker exits Alby's hotel room just before it erupts in flames **(5)**.

Batman next tracks down Bigger Melvin near the docks, but the former Joker henchman knocks him unconscious when his back is turned. When Batman comes to, he discovers Bigger Melvin swinging from a noose **(6)**.

After a brief clash with Batman **(7)**, The Joker departs. Just as The Joker hopes, Batman tracks him to the abandoned Gotham City Aquarium **(8)**. Bing Hooley, the fifth and final target of The Joker's vengeance, sits in a wheelchair high above a glass tank **(9)**. Within it swims a great white shark. The deal is simple: If Batman takes Hooley's place, The Joker will set his captive free. Batman agrees, but The Joker dumps both his hostages into the shark-infested water **(10)**. Riding the shark like a broncobuster, Batman defeats it and frees himself from his manacles. He then uses Hooley's sunken wheelchair as a battering ram, smashing the glass and taking off in pursuit of their grinning tormentor.

On the beach of Gotham City Harbor, Batman catches up with the fleeing Joker, flooring him with an uppercut after the villain slips on an oil slick **(11)**. Taking The Joker into custody, Batman laughs at the notion that the Clown Prince of Crime actually makes him grateful for pollution.

ARKHAM

WELCOME TO THE MADHOUSE

The Arkham Asylum for the Criminally Insane sits on the outskirts of Gotham City, home to the worst villains the city has to offer. Criminals judged insane by Gotham City's courts aren't sent to prison, they're sent to Arkham Asylum—ostensibly to receive treatment for their mental disorders and become productive citizens. But the asylum has been a poorly run hellhole and a breeding ground for psychosis ever since it was built generations ago by Amadeus Arkham. The Joker, Poison Ivy, Mr. Freeze, Two-Face, and Killer Croc are just a few examples of those often caged in Arkham Asylum's squalid cells. The asylum has been razed several times over the years, and most recently burned to the ground in the aftermath of the so-called "Joker War." However, the cursed institution seems ever fated to rise from the ashes, as corrupt as ever.

DR. JEREMIAH ARKHAM

A direct descendant of asylum founder Amadeus Arkham, Dr. Jeremiah Arkham has succumbed to the madness of the place he oversees a few times during his tenure. However, while Batman distrusts him, Jeremiah remains in charge of his family's institution, his true motives known only to himself.

REHABILITATION OR LOCKDOWN?

Much like maximum-security Blackgate Penitentiary, which houses notorious villains not deemed insane, Arkham Asylum has many safeguards to prevent escape. However, that hasn't stopped many inmates at both institutions from finding their way to freedom, sometimes repeatedly. Arkham Asylum inmates sometimes convince the doctors observing them that they have been cured, but almost all return to crime following their release. Other patients simply break out by digging tunnels, bribing guards, discovering hidden passageways, or enlisting the help of gangs on the outside.

ARKHAM ASYLUM ORIGINS

When it first appeared by name in the comic books of the 1970s, Arkham Asylum was depicted as a shadowy New England institution housing the likes of Two-Face and The Joker. As more about the asylum was revealed over the years, the building began to take on a personality as interesting as that of Gotham City itself.

AMADEUS THE ADVENTURER

Before he was driven insane by the facility he established, Amadeus Arkham met bounty hunter Jonah Hex and found himself on a series of unlikely adventures through Gotham City's underbelly. He even wrote a book about Hex entitled *Face Full of Violence*.

ASYLUM

Perimeter catwalk to central tower connecting bridge
Equipment room
Security-risk cases
Minimum confinement rooms
Main security-controlled elevator
Violent ward
Line of rear wall
Air-conditioning plant
Orderly catwalk
Engineer offices
Stores
Heating plant
Stores
Offices
Offices
Main security
Internal high-security doors

INFERNAL ARCHITECTURE

Amadeus Arkham built his namesake asylum following the brutal murders of his wife and daughter. With his sanity in tatters, Dr. Arkham designed a floorplan that evoked occult runes. He believed that the pattern would drive away the mysterious bat that haunted his dreams. To this day, inmates and administrators report that the asylum seems to breed madness. Patients are often made worse, and some staff members—such as Dr. Harleen Quinzel—have become villains themselves.

ARKHAM KNIGHT

Dr. Jeremiah Arkham isn't the last of the Arkham family. His daughter, Astrid, became a villain in her own right, deluded into thinking she holds the key to Gotham City's future through her cult-like Knights of the Sun.

UP FROM THE ASHES

Arkham Asylum has been destroyed more than once. It has been reconstructed each time, occasionally incorporating elements of the bizarre architecture laid out by Amadeus Arkham. This cycle of death and rebirth ensures that insanity is always renewed and that Arkham Asylum remains a place of bleak hopelessness. Despite the facility's terrible track record, the courts continue to send Gotham City's most dangerous maniacs to Arkham Asylum—in part because no one else will take them.

DAUGHTER OF THE DEMON

Batman agreed to help to find Rā's al Ghūl's daughter who, like Robin, seemed to have been kidnapped. Their quest ended at a Himalayan mountain fortress. There, Batman found Robin —a prisoner of Rā's al Ghūl's. The rescue had been merely a test to establish Batman's worthiness to marry Talia al Ghūl.

With his muscular manservant, Ubu, at his side, Rā's al Ghūl led Batman on a trail of carefully laid clues, all of which Batman solved.

As he freed Robin, Batman explained that he had worked out the ruse long ago. Impressed, Rā's al Ghūl praised the detective's insight.

Talia al Ghūl was no damsel in distress, but a willing participant in her father's plan.

LESLIE THOMPKINS

Every year on the anniversary of his parents' deaths, Batman visited Crime Alley to honor their memory. Leslie Thompkins, who had comforted young Bruce after the tragedy, had remained in the Crime Alley neighborhood as a charitable force for good. When Batman saw thugs harassing her, he swung into action.

Enraged by the callousness of the would-be muggers, Batman lost his usual restraint. He was about to beat them senseless, but Leslie stayed his hand.

Despite the dangers, Leslie Thompkins remained in Crime Alley to care for the needy. She is still motivated by the memory of the orphaned boy she helped long ago.

NIGHT OF THE REAPER

Even after Dick Grayson abandoned the Batcave to pursue higher education, danger followed him. As Rutland, Vermont celebrated a Super Hero masquerade party, the deadly Reaper burst onto the scene and began a string of vicious killings. Dick donned his Robin costume and teamed up with Batman to halt the Reaper's rampage.

After saying goodbye to the woman he loved, Batman hung up his costume.

In the woods, Robin found a lifeless Batman, impaled through the heart. A second look told him that the body was that of a costumed partygoer.

WHO IS THE HUNTRESS?

On the parallel world of Earth-2, Batman and Catwoman married and raised a daughter, Helena. The family was struck by tragedy when a criminal from Catwoman's past blackmailed her into committing one last crime. She died after falling from a great height—partly because of Batman's efforts to stop the heist. With her father too heartbroken to carry on his work, Helena vowed to do so in his absence, and picked up a crossbow to fight crime as The Huntress.

At her mother's graveside, Helena swore to continue the Wayne family's war on crime.

MARRIAGE IMPOSSIBLE

It was too late for Batman to save Dr. Kirk Langstrom, who had become the mutated Man-Bat after taking an experimental serum, but he hoped to save Kirk's fiancée Francine from a similar fate. However, Francine spurned Batman's help and seemed strangely determined to follow through on her marriage to the Man-Bat. Batman's worst suspicions were confirmed when he realized that Francine's pretty features were just a latex mask. She had swallowed her own dose of the serum to become a She-Bat!

CIRCUS LIFE

Having grown up in the rough-and-tumble world of Haly's Circus, Dick Grayson is accustomed to a nomadic lifestyle and has an easygoing nature that is the complete opposite to that of his brooding mentor, Bruce Wayne.

Nightwing's Escrima sticks can fire a grappling line, allowing him to swing over the rooftops like he's still on the trapeze. The sticks can also combine and lengthen to become a staff.

Nightwing's costume is insulated against extreme temperatures and electrical shocks, and protects against projectile weapons.

KEY DATA

REAL NAME Richard John Grayson

OCCUPATION Crime fighter, acrobat, detective

WEAPONS/ POWERS/ ABILITIES Escrima sticks, unparalleled acrobatic skills, master martial artist, natural leader

AFFILIATIONS Haly's Circus, Teen Titans, Outsiders, Batman, Inc., JLA

RELATIVES Jonathan and Mary Grayson (parents, deceased), Bruce Wayne (adoptive father)

FIRST APPEARANCE *Detective Comics* #38 (April 1940)

CIRCUS LIFE

Nightwing is grateful for the upbringing he received in Batman's care, but never wanted to succeed his mentor as the next Batman. He changed his mind briefly during a period when Batman was believed dead.

Nightwing's costume is streamlined for maximum mobility. Unlike many other costumed heroes, Nightwing doesn't wear a cape.

"I haven't been the 'circus kid' in years, but that doesn't mean I don't still love it." NIGHTWING

NIGHTWING

The Boy Wonder grew up! After wowing Gotham City as the original Robin, Dick Grayson used what he'd learned to launch a solo career away from home as Nightwing. Now he fights a renewed battle for justice in the neighboring harbor city of Blüdhaven.

Dick needed all his skills, intelligence, and courage while a Spyral agent .

MAKING HIS MARK

From the big top to the rooftops, Dick Grayson has never backed down from a challenge. Having learned acrobat skills as part of a traveling circus when he was child, Dick first put his talent to work as Robin, absorbing Batman's teachings but often investigating crimes on his own. Eventually, Robin flew the nest and Dick assumed a new costumed identity as Nightwing, leading the Teen Titans and briefly finding love with his teammate, Starfire.

Nightwing operated out of the corrupt city of Blüdhaven for a time, and even joined the Blüdhaven police force. He later relocated to New York City and then Chicago, with stints in Gotham City. His adventuring as Nightwing frequently brought him into contact with Barbara Gordon, the two often continuing the romance they've flirted with since both were new to wearing masks.

After a brief stint as Batman when Bruce Wayne was lost in the timestream, Nightwing himself had a turn at playing dead following a violent conflict with the other-dimensional villains of the Crime Syndicate. Grayson took the opportunity of the world at large believing him deceased to work covertly for the clandestine agency Spyral. This plot to spy on the spies eventually ended when Grayson reclaimed his Nightwing identity and returned to Blüdhaven, reestablishing himself in the world of Super Heroes.

Nightwing is an astonishing athlete whose dexterity and grace outshines the gifts of his teacher. He has proved he is a natural leader and helped found Titans Academy, a school where teenage Super Heroes can hone their powers. He now splits his time between teaching and finding a good use for the incredible fortune Alfred Pennyworth left behind for him in his will.

As the youngest member of the Flying Graysons, Dick learned to perform the quadruple somersault.

Dick wore the first version of the Nightwing costume when he was part of the New Teen Titans.

Nightwing had strong romantic feelings for Barbara Gordon. When Barbara reciprocated them, he hoped to find true love.

As a cop on the Blüdhaven police force, Dick got a street-level view of the city.

Nightwing carries a light arsenal of weapons, but his enemies should never underestimate him—they are often surprised when he outsmarts them.

BATMAN AND THE OUTSIDERS

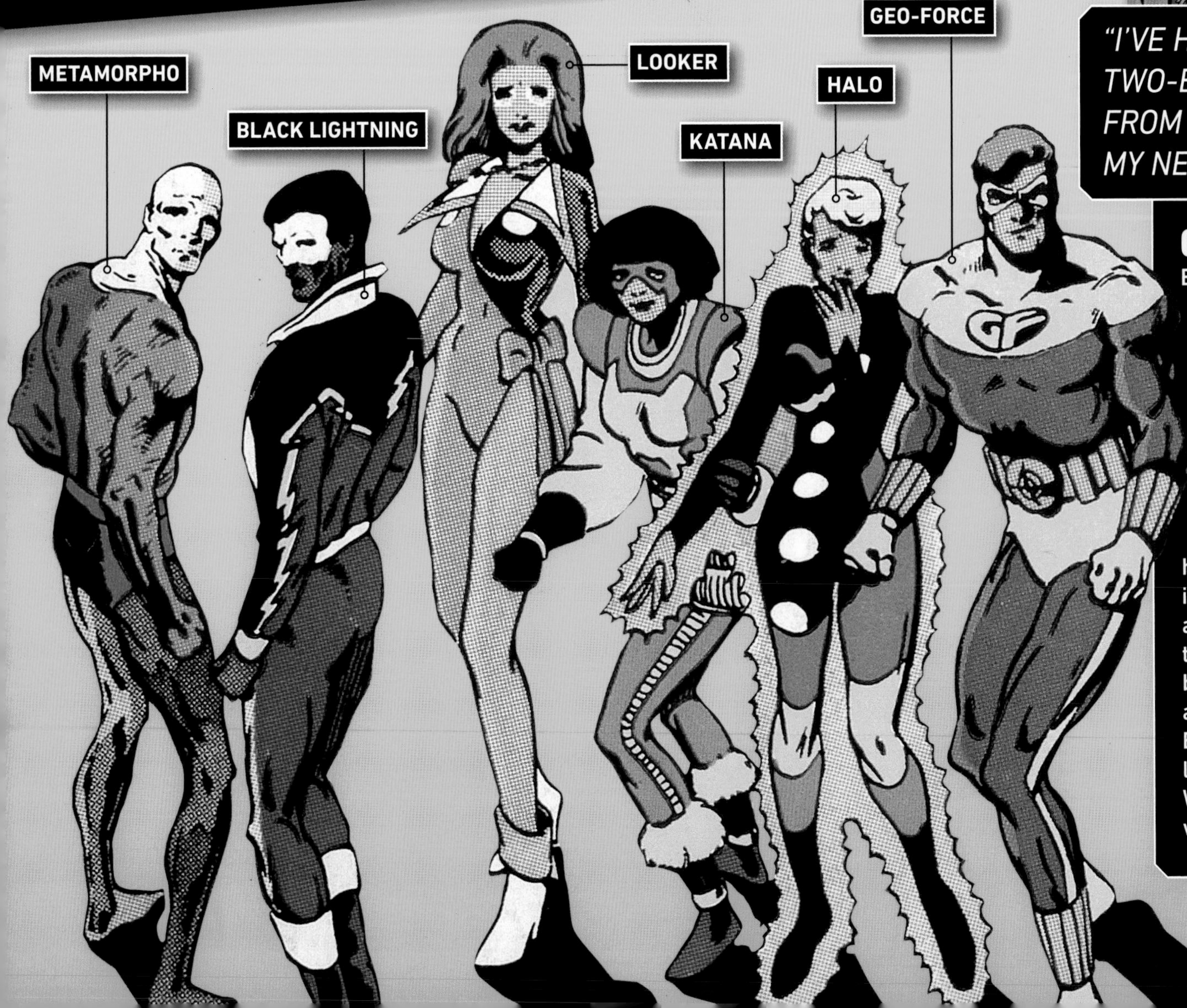
METAMORPHO
BLACK LIGHTNING
LOOKER
KATANA
HALO
GEO-FORCE

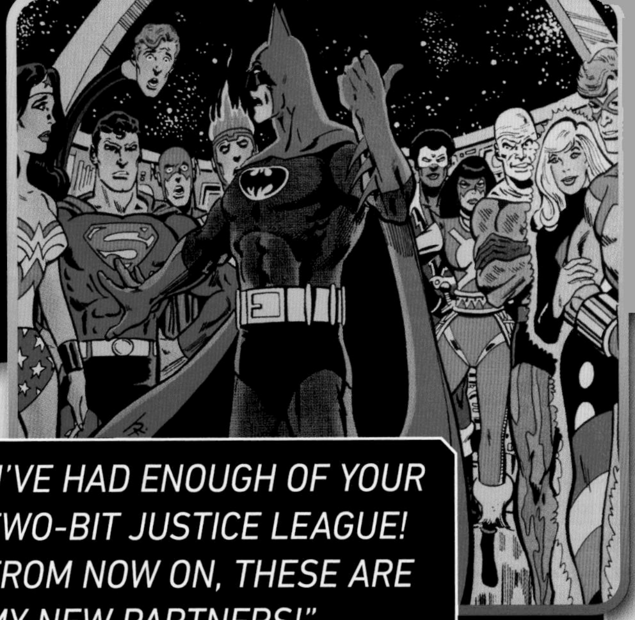

"I'VE HAD ENOUGH OF YOUR TWO-BIT JUSTICE LEAGUE! FROM NOW ON, THESE ARE MY NEW PARTNERS!"

ORIGIN

Batman doesn't take orders, he gives them! This was never clearer than in the aftermath of the Justice League of America's refusal to stop a violent revolution in the eastern European nation of Markovia. Superman had already promised the United Nations that the JLA would not interfere, so Batman had no choice but to resign his membership and build a strike team of his own. Batman and Black Lightning infiltrated Markovia, where they met the amnesiac Halo, the vengeful Katana, and the malleable hero Metamorpho. Joined by Geo-Force, heir to the Markovian aristocracy, the fledgling team defeated Baron Bedlam and restored peace to the land. The telepathic Looker, youthful Windfall, and armored Atomic Knight would later join the team's roster.

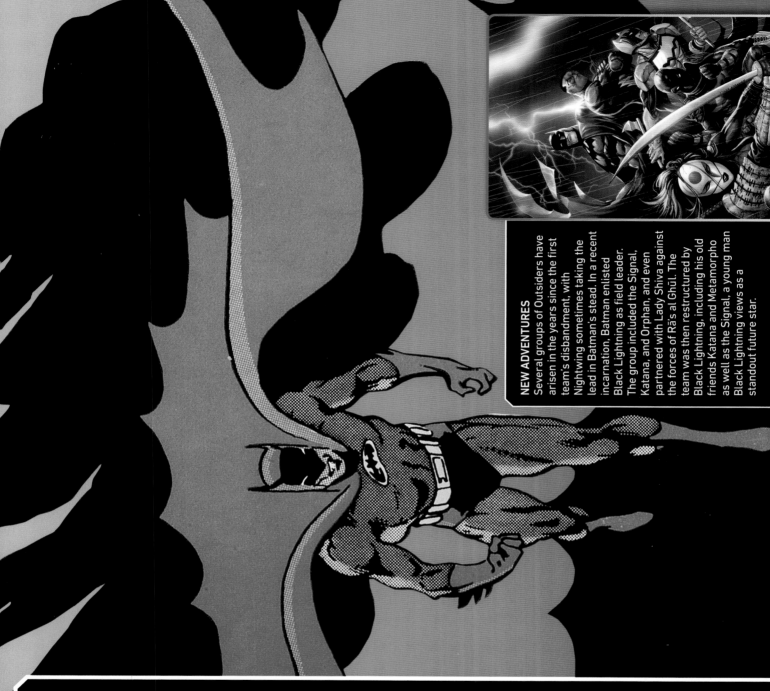

NEW ADVENTURES

Several groups of Outsiders have arisen in the years since the first team's disbandment, with Nightwing sometimes taking the lead in Batman's stead. In a recent incarnation, Batman enlisted Black Lightning as field leader. The group included the Signal, Katana, and Orphan, and even partnered with Lady Shiva against the forces of Rä's al Ghül. The team was then restructured by Black Lightning, including his old friends Katana and Metamorpho as well as the Signal, a young man Black Lightning views as a standout future star.

FEARSOME FOES

The Outsiders lived up to their name by tackling the missions that the big groups either couldn't or wouldn't take on. They didn't hesitate to break international laws if they needed to, and they made plenty of enemies along the way. The Masters of Disaster became regular foes, with members Shakedown, Coldsnap, Heatstroke, New Wave, and Windfall each possessing control over a specific element of nature. Shakedown could create powerful vibrations with his mighty strength, Coldsnap and Heatstroke could generate extreme cold and heat respectively, while New Wave could transform into living water, and her younger sister Windfall possessed the ability to manipulate the air itself. The group once nearly killed Black Lightning, but were left fraught with tensions after Windfall had a change of heart and left to join the Outsiders.

However, new threats to Batman and the Outsiders soon emerged, including the ultra-patriotic metahumans of the Force of July. Baron Bedlam even returned to the land of the living—information which Batman withheld from the Outsiders for a while, angering them and allowing Batman to quit as team leader. The gang soldiered on until their ranks were depleted during the *Millennium* invasion event.

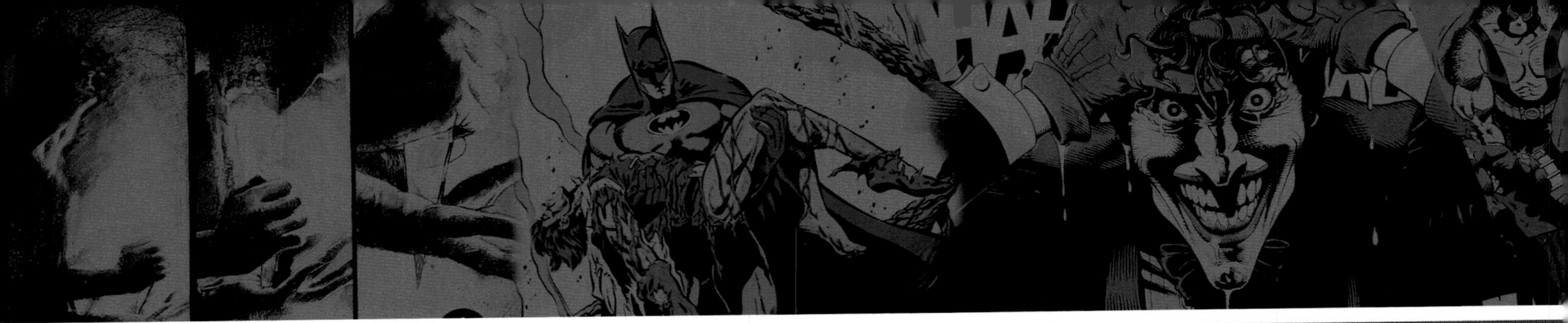

DARK AGE

MID '80s–2010

Super Hero comics earned new respect by appealing to adults, and Batman reclaimed his dangerous edge.

The year-long miniseries *Crisis on Infinite Earths* gave DC the chance to clear away generations of tangled backstory. Following this continuity-altering catastrophe, several of DC's Super Heroes received updated origins more accessible to new readers.

For Batman, it meant a gritty reboot from writer Frank Miller, *Batman: The Dark Knight Returns,* as well as a realistic, revised origin in the pages of "Year One." Later events—often of a darker, more mature nature—put Batman and his supporting cast through the proverbial ringer.

Jason Todd, the second Robin, was killed, only to be brought back to life more than a decade later. Batgirl was paralyzed and became an arguably stronger force for good in the form of the computer expert Oracle. Even Batman himself was not immune to the chaos. His back was broken by the villain Bane, and he was replaced for a time by the more violent Azrael. The Dark Knight also saw his city face plagues, earthquakes, isolation, and a gauntlet of Super-Villains.

Yet through it all, Batman made new allies, from the innovative Robin, Tim Drake, to the persistent heroine Stephanie Brown, to the fledgling Batwoman, Kate Kane. His literal family would grow as well, when the most unexpected Robin joined his team: Damian Wayne, the son Batman never knew he had.

OVERLEAF
Batman: The Dark Knight Returns #2
*(April 1986): A grim and gritty façade
masks the sophisticated storytelling and
societal commentary of writer/penciler
Frank Miller's historic work.*

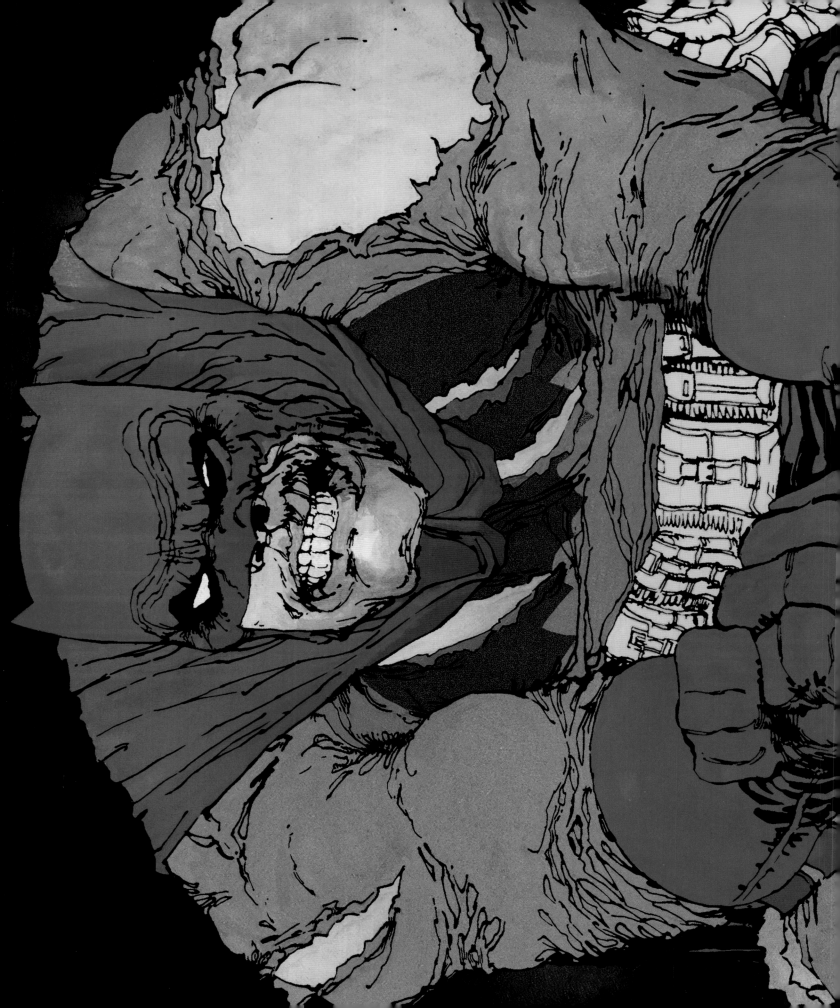

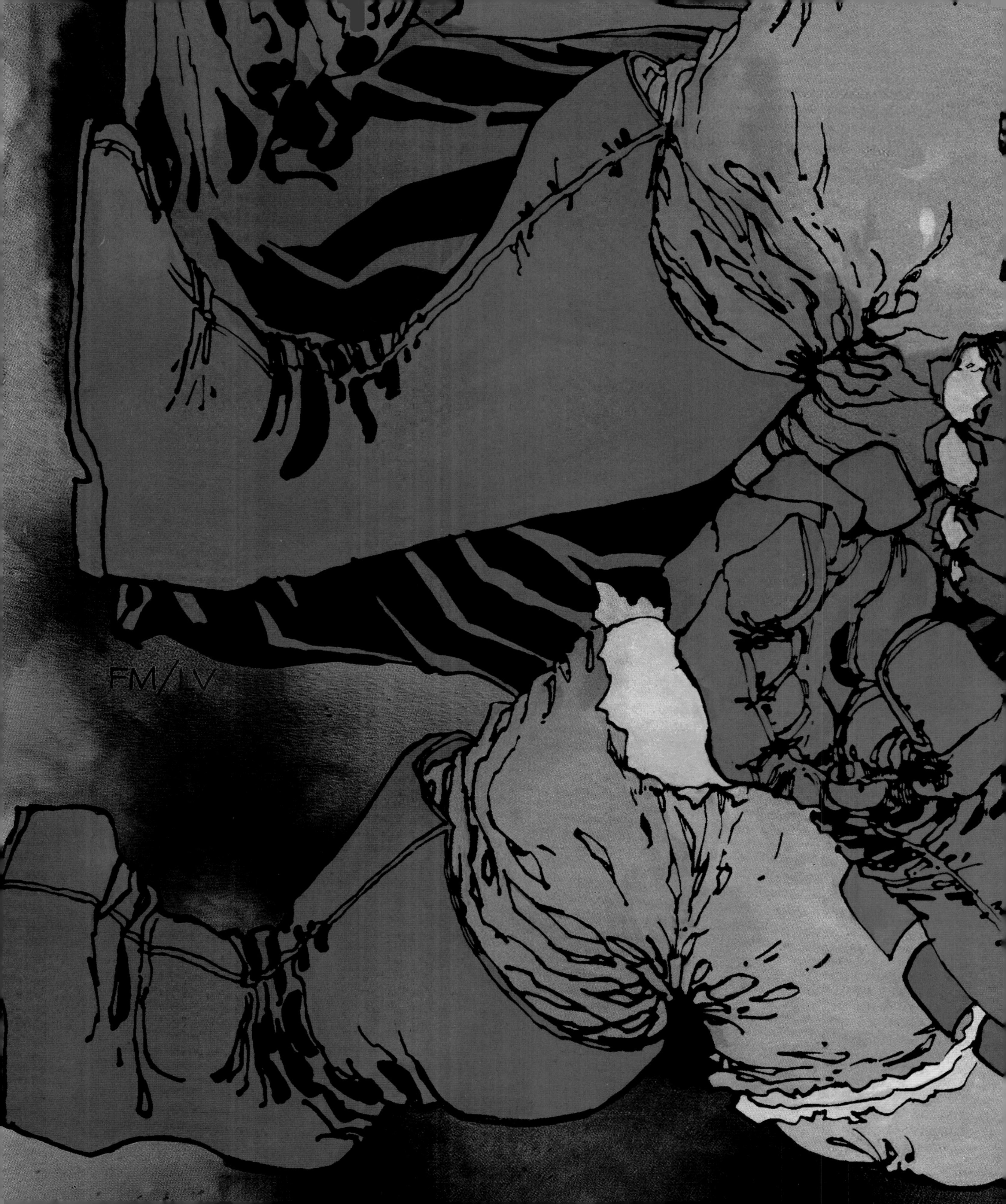
FM/LV

BATMAN: THE DARK KNIGHT RETURNS

When Harvey Dent relapsed into Two-Face to terrorize Gotham City, Batman knew he had to stop him.

A DARK FUTURE

In a shifted timeline, all Super Heroes had been hounded out of existence. Only Superman, a lackey of the U.S. government, remained. Batman had been gone for a decade, but the reemergence of old foes prompted Bruce Wayne—now in his fifties—to don the costume one last time. Opposed by a hostile mass media and a new Gotham City police commissioner, the Dark Knight recruited an army and set an example of self-determination among a populace that had grown complacent.

James Gordon left the G.C.P.D. after a lifetime of service. His successor, Commissioner Ellen Yindel, took a harsh view of Batman's vigilantism and only made things worse for the people of the city.

A NEW ROBIN

Carrie Kelley was only 13 years old, but she saw in Batman's reappearance an opportunity to reverse her directionless upbringing. Dressed in a homemade Robin costume, she shadowed Batman as he faced off with the leader of a Gotham City gang called the Mutants and saved him from certain death. Under Batman's guidance, Carrie gained discipline and direction, becoming his first soldier in a war against corruption.

Since Batman's retirement, Gotham City had fallen to the Mutants. The leader of this youth gang was a mountain of muscle who had no conscience and felt no pain. He ripped out the throat of Gotham City's mayor with his teeth to show the weakness of those who held empty titles in the city. Batman knew he had to defeat the mutant leader using his own language. Batman humiliated him in a brutal takedown, proving that he was Gotham City's alpha leader.

CELEBRITY JOKER

The Joker emerged from a catatonic state the instant he heard the name "Batman" on the evening news. He charmed his psychiatrist into believing he was sane and captured the attention of a superficial public. On live TV, The Joker killed hundreds and then lured Batman into a violent showdown. When his nemesis refused to deliver a killing blow, The Joker snapped his own neck—ensuring that Batman would face a murder charge.

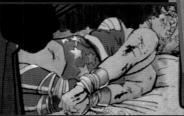

Flanked by his duped psychiatrist and a popular sex therapist, the supposedly cured Joker enjoyed a chat with the host of the David Endochrine talk show. Moments later, poison gas filled the TV studio giving every person inside a fatal, Jokerized grimace.

The Joker beat up Selina Kyle, the former Catwoman, then dressed her in a Wonder Woman costume. He left Selina bound and gagged for Batman to find.

"No, Joker. You're playing the wrong game. The old game." **BATMAN**

DARK KNIGHT VS. MAN OF STEEL

Batman's high profile had become an embarrassment to the U.S. president, who ordered Superman to eliminate his old friend. Superman anticipated a quick fight, but Batman was well prepared for their confrontation. With synthetic Kryptonite giving him the edge, Batman closed his fingers around Superman's throat—and then fell dead, the apparent victim of a heart attack.

The distant detonation of a nuclear warhead triggered an electromagnetic pulse, which plunged Gotham City into darkness. Amid the chaos, Batman led the former Mutants gang members—now calling themselves the Sons of Batman—to end the looting.

After Bruce Wayne's funeral, Bruce walked away from his grave. His death was a ruse! In a new headquarters, Batman formed an army, with Robin and the Sons of Batman as his first draftees.

KEY ISSUES

#404–407

BATMAN Year One

> "You've eaten Gotham's wealth. Its spirit. Your feast is nearly over. From this moment on—none of you are safe."
>
> BATMAN

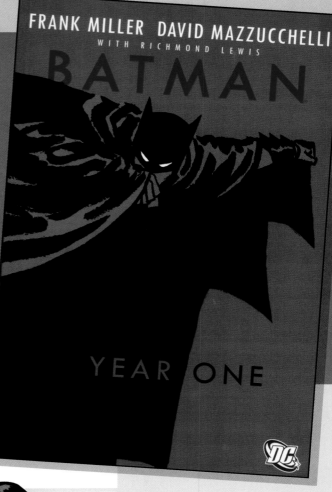

FRANK MILLER · DAVID MAZZUCCHELLI
WITH RICHMOND LEWIS

BATMAN

YEAR ONE

MAIN CHARACTERS: Batman, James Gordon
SUPPORTING CHARACTERS: Barbara Gordon, Detective Flass, Commissioner Loeb, Sarah Essen, "The Roman," Catwoman
LOCATIONS: Police headquarters, Wayne Manor, Gotham City slums, Falcone's mansion, Gotham River

BACKGROUND

Frank Miller's *Batman: The Dark Knight Returns* set a new standard for ambitious graphical storytelling, but it was a future story with little impact on DC's overall continuity. Inspired by Miller's success, DC commissioned the writer to update the mainstream Batman's origins in the wake of the companywide revisions brought about by the *Crisis on Infinite Earths* crossover. Miller's gritty Gotham City—as yet untouched by super-villainy—is plagued by common street crime, an epidemic desperately in need of eradication.

The four-part "Batman: Year One" didn't appear as a standalone miniseries, but rather as issues #404–407 of the main *Batman* title. Miller and artist David Mazzucchelli told parallel tales, contrasting Jim Gordon's first months at the Gotham City Police Department with Bruce Wayne's experimental efforts to become a crime-fighting vigilante. The two men demonstrate why they are the heroic champions needed by a corrupt city, even though their methods differ.

PUBLICATION DATE
February–May 1987

EDITOR
Denny O'Neil

COVER ARTIST
David Mazzucchelli

WRITER
Frank Miller

PENCILER/INKER
David Mazzucchelli

COLORIST
Richmond Lewis

LETTERER
Todd Klein

The Story...

James Gordon and Batman show their mettle as the future champions of Gotham City, fighting crime and corruption in their own ways in this updated origin story.

Lieutenant Gordon, recently transferred from the Chicago police force, arrives in Gotham City just as Bruce Wayne returns home after years spent abroad following his parents' murders **(1)**. Setting up home in Gotham City with his pregnant wife Barbara, Gordon is shown the ropes of the Gotham City Police Department by his new partner, Detective Flass **(2)**. Men like Flass ignore the weak, protect the powerful, and take bribes at every turn.

Flass encourages Gordon to embrace the perks offered by a broken system. Gordon refuses to bend, even when pressured by the corrupt Commissioner Loeb. As Bruce Wayne hones his skills at Wayne Manor **(3)**, a cocky Flass and a gang of officers decide to beat up Gordon to teach him a lesson **(4)**.

Dressed in street clothes, Bruce Wayne ventures into the most dangerous Gotham City backstreets to protect the innocent. He soon finds himself involved in a fight with a street hustler and his employee, Selina Kyle. **(5)**. After being stabbed in the melee and then shot by a police officer, Bruce returns home to Wayne Manor, barely clinging to life.

While Jim Gordon refuses to back down and confronts Flass **(6)**, back at Wayne Manor, Bruce is mournfully contemplating his future, when a bat smashes through the window of his study **(7)**. Inspired, he decides to don a bat-like costume that will strike fear into the hearts of criminals. Dressed as the mysterious Batman, Bruce begins to turn the tide against the muggers, murderers, and Mafiosos dominating Gotham City.

At a private banquet for the city's biggest criminal power brokers, Batman threatens the rich and powerful, making him Commissioner Loeb's number one enemy **(8)**. This leads to the G.C.P.D. nearly trapping Batman in an old tenement, a fate Batman escapes, inspiring witness Selina Kyle to eventually adopt her own costume as Catwoman.

Meanwhile, due to his ongoing affair with fellow cop, Sarah Essen **(9)**, Gordon is tormented by the reality of his crumbling marriage **(10)**. After Commissioner Loeb tries to force his loyalty through blackmail **(11)**, Gordon comes clean with his wife. With this bargaining chip removed, Loeb—operating on orders from crime boss "The Roman"—arranges the kidnap of Gordon's newborn son. An out-of-costume Batman saves Gordon's child, earning Gordon's lifelong friendship, even if Gordon claims to be unable to see Bruce's face **(12)**.

Later, as G.C.P.D. headquarters buzzes with news about a villain called The Joker, Gordon heads for the building's roof. Turning on the newly installed Bat-Signal, he awaits the arrival of his new, costumed ally in the fight against crime **(13)**.

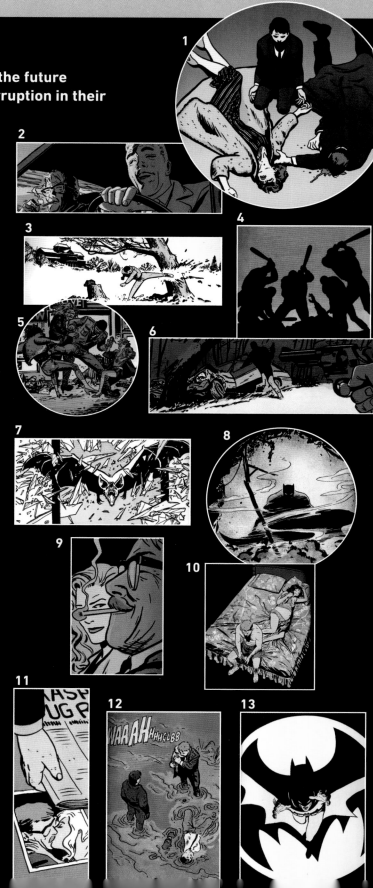

BATMAN: THE KILLING JOKE

The Joker kidnapped Commissioner Gordon and paralyzed Barbara Gordon in a tale that shed light on one possibility of The Joker's mysterious origin.

A MAD PLAN

The Joker was convinced of one simple truth: all it takes is one bad day for a normal person to slip into insanity. But it wasn't enough to just believe this theory; he had to test it. He chose Police Commissioner James Gordon as his subject. After breaking into Gordon's home, taking him captive, and leaving his daughter Barbara bleeding from a gunshot wound, The Joker forced Gordon into a nightmarish ride through an abandoned amusement park. Batman rushed to stop it, but The Joker had planned for that, too. Through it all, a flashback sequence revealed the possible origin of The Joker before his own "bad day."

DOUBLE TROUBLE
Escaping from Arkham Asylum was easy for The Joker. The hard part was tricking people into thinking he had never left! The Joker left a duplicate in his place, but when Batman questioned him and noticed his pale skin was just white makeup, the game was up.

It was a quiet evening at the Gordon household when Barbara Gordon answered a knock at the door to find The Joker pointing a gun at her. She had no time to react before he fired.

By leading Batman into a Hall of Mirrors, The Joker tried to show him that the two of them had more in common than he realized. Batman didn't agree.

ORDER VS CHAOS

The Joker invaded the Gordon home with ruthless force. Barbara Gordon fell to the floor after taking a bullet, her legs paralyzed from the injury, while The Joker's henchmen beat and kidnapped Commissioner Gordon. The Joker took photos of Barbara lying among the carnage, later projecting them on giant screens for Commissioner Gordon to watch at his horror-show funhouse.

The Joker's macabre circus assistants used cattle prods to keep Gordon in line.

ORDER VS. CHAOS

Batman tracked down The Joker, freed Commissioner Gordon, then went deeper into the theme park to find the villain behind the crimes. As Batman worked his way past The Joker's death traps, he was taunted by The Joker's proclamations that both hero and villain shared the same degree of insanity. But Batman would not crack, and he swiftly ended The Joker's rampage.

When The Joker told Batman a joke, Batman was so caught up in the absurdity of their situation he could not help but laugh.

BIRTH OF THE JOKER

In this theory of The Joker's origin, an unnamed man had a wife who loved him, a baby on the way, and ambitions to earn a living as a stand-up comedian—but he couldn't scare up any laughs. To help pay the bills, he agreed to assist in a one-time criminal caper, hoping that for once the cards would come up in his favor.

Troubled and insecure about his failure to provide for his wife and unborn child, the man who would become The Joker agreed to lead the notorious Red Hood mob through a chemical plant on their way to a robbery.

The crooks ordered the mourning man to wear the costume of the Red Hood, explaining that it would boost their gang's hoodlum reputation.

Just before the robbery, the tragic comedian was devastated by the news that his wife and their unborn baby had died in an accident at their home.

Despite his terrible news, the gang insisted the robbery move forward as scheduled. Chased by Batman and unable to see anything in his Red Hood getup, the man who would become The Joker fell into a chemical stew that bleached his skin white and dyed his hair bright green.

After the day's events, the sight of his changed appearance pushed The Joker to breaking point. His only refuge was madness—and a new villain was born.

Bruce was worried that Jason Todd had become too brutal in his approach to fighting crime. When Bruce decided to temporarily relieve the second Robin of his duties, Jason stormed off. Disillusioned, he began a solo mission to locate his biological mother.

Jason found his mother, Sheila Haywood, aiding famine victims in a refugee camp in Ethiopia.

His oldest enemy crossed the ultimate line, forcing Batman to live with Robin's death on his conscience.

DEATH IN THE FAMILY

THE FINAL HOUR

The Joker's scheme to steal medical supplies in Ethiopia brought The Joker—with Batman on his trail—into a collision with Robin's family reunion. Seizing an opportunity when Batman wasn't around, The Joker beat Robin with a crowbar, then left him and his mother inside a locked warehouse containing a ticking time bomb.

Jason Todd's biological mother looked on as her son was beaten unconscious by The Joker.

Robin had escaped from death traps countless times, but on this day his number was up.

FALLEN SOLDIER

Batman arrived at the scene too late to stop The Joker's time bomb from exploding and taking his partner's life. Batman recovered Jason Todd's body from the wreckage and mourned the first Robin to die in the line of duty. The Joker had to be punished, but first Batman returned to Gotham City to bury Jason.

Batman carried overwhelming guilt over Jason Todd's death and resolved to work alone. But Batman wasn't the same without his partner, and soon Tim Drake became the third Robin.

ARKHAM ASYLUM

A SERIOUS HOUSE ON SERIOUS EARTH

> "You're in the real world now, and the lunatics have taken over the asylum."
>
> THE JOKER

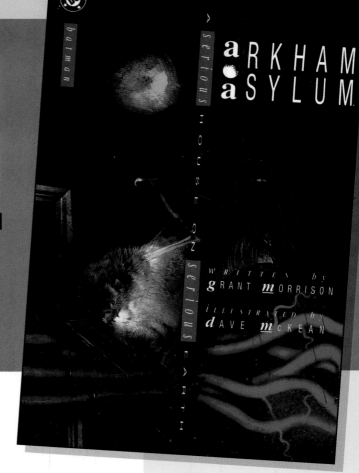

MAIN CHARACTERS: Batman, The Joker
SUPPORTING CHARACTERS: Amadeus Arkham, Commissioner Gordon, Dr. Ruth Adams, Two-Face, "Mad Dog" Hawkins, Clayface, Doctor Destiny, Mad Hatter, Killer Croc, Dr. Charles Cavendish
LOCATIONS: Arkham Asylum

BACKGROUND

When a man dresses up like a bat to avenge his dead parents, where does one draw the line between sanity and madness? Writer Grant Morrison explored this theme in the dreamlike graphic novel *Arkham Asylum: A Serious House on Serious Earth*. During a wave of late '80s stories that brought mature themes and psychological complexity to Batman's world, Arkham Asylum took its action inside—within the walls of the asylum and the recesses of Batman's brain.

The impressionistic art of Dave McKean illuminated a journey through the asylum that doubled as an exhumation of long-buried secrets. Morrison's narrative weaved between the creation of the asylum in the 1920s and the present day, and referenced everything from the occult to the I-Ching. The story also cemented Arkham Asylum as a place of primal nightmares.

PUBLICATION DATE
October 1989

EDITOR
Karen Berger

COVER ARTIST
Dave McKean

WRITER
Grant Morrison

ARTIST
Dave McKean

LETTERER
Gaspar Saladino

The Story...

The inmates are running free at Arkham Asylum, and Batman goes in alone despite worries for his own mental state.

In a prologue set in 1901, the young Amadeus Arkham is left alone to care for his mentally ill mother **(1)**. Horrified by her suffering, Arkham pledges to study psychiatry in order to help those with similar afflictions.

In modern-day Gotham City, The Joker and his accomplices take the staff of Arkham Asylum hostage. Batman enters the facility alone to prevent further violence **(2)**.

Batman's arrival is met with great amusement by The Joker **(3)**. The Dark Knight soon meets the Arkham staffers, among them Dr. Ruth Adams, who theorizes that The Joker is gifted with "super sanity." She has also weaned Two-Face off his coin and onto a tarot deck, to provide him with more choice options than a simple yes or no **(4)**.

Having lured his prey into the asylum, The Joker announces the rules of a new game to the inmates—to hunt Batman! After shooting a hostage in the head, he forces Batman to start running, pursued by the residents of the asylum.

In a flashback to the 1920s, Amadeus Arkham has now become a noted psychologist. Agreeing to treat the mass murderer "Mad Dog" Hawkins, he returns from a trip to find the bodies of his wife and daughter—Mad Dog's newest victims. Despite this, Arkham opens his asylum, accepting Hawkins as his first patient. After enough time has passed to allay suspicion, Arkham takes his revenge by frying the unrepentant killer on an electroshock couch.

Back in the present day, Batman is beset by the self-loathing sickness of Clayface **(5)**, the impotent rage of Doctor Destiny **(6)**, and the Mad Hatter's reality-bending riddles **(7)**. In the past, Amadeus Arkham **(8)** gradually becomes obsessed with the vision of a giant bat **(9)**, becoming an inmate in his own asylum, surrounded by occult runes scratched into the walls and floor with his fingernails **(10)**.

Meanwhile, Batman withstands the fury of Killer Croc **(11)** and soon encounters the asylum's current administrator, Dr. Cavendish. Gripped by the same madness that consumed Amadeus, Cavendish reveals that he triggered the breakout himself. He is prepared to do even worse, but Dr. Adams slashes the administrator's throat with a knife.

The Joker remains king of Arkham Asylum, leaving it to Two-Face to determine Batman's fate. Two-Face flips his coin, stating that if the scarred side comes up, Batman will die **(12)**. If the unblemished side shows, he will go free. The result is freedom for Batman. Unseen by the other inmates, Two-Face studies the coin as Batman leaves the asylum. It sits in his palm, scarred side face up.

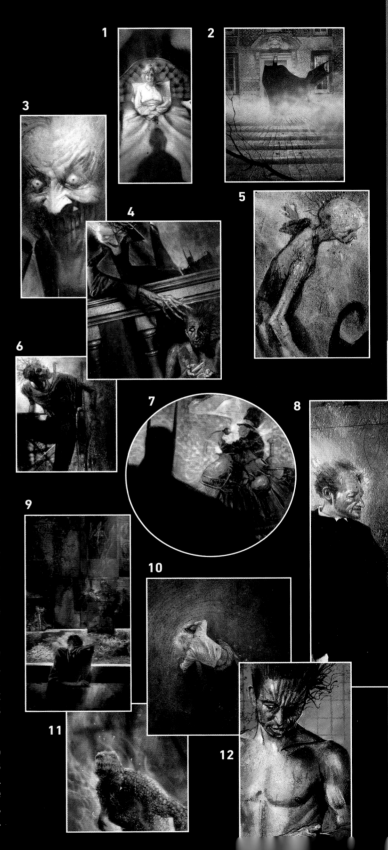

Though he had faced a thousand foes, the Dark Knight finally met his match when Bane broke the Bat.

Packing hi-tech weaponry, Bane freed the inmates of Arkham Asylum.

KNIGHTFALL

A HERO MEETS HIS END

Juiced up with the superpowered steroid Venom, Bane is a towering grappler who seems to be made of solid muscle. But he also possesses a keen strategic mind, and his plan for wearing down Batman succeeded where other schemes had failed. After freeing Gotham City's villains from Arkham Asylum, he steered Batman into dozens of fights, studying his enemy's techniques at a distance. Then, when Batman's stamina was spent, Bane delivered the final blow.

With Venom chemicals invigorating his hulking physique and boosting his rage, Bane hoisted the defeated Batman in triumph.

After battling his Rogues Gallery for days on end, Batman returned to the peace of Wayne Manor to rest. But it was no safe harbor. Alfred lay unconscious on the floor, and Bane was spoiling for a fight.

Batman and Bane's battle took them down into the Batcave. Among the trophies of Batman's triumphs, Bane beat down his exhausted opponent.

The Mad Hatter sent his mind-controlled monkey henchmen to battle Batman.

Amygdala unleashed shocking violence on anyone who was a threat—even Batman.

Poison Ivy infected innocents with plant pollen, turning them into an army of zombie slaves.

The tally marks on Mister Zsasz's skin number his kills—and he wanted to add one more victim.

Saving the people of Gotham City was always Batman's first priority when his enemies triggered city-wide disasters.

Batman tackled the flames of pyromaniac Firefly and gave The Joker a kicking.

RUN RAGGED

Freeing Arkham Asylum's patients to run riot across the city was Bane's masterstroke. He knew Batman could not ignore citizens in danger, and that he would not sleep until every killer was caught. Robin and The Huntress tried to help, but Batman fought alone against enemies, including the hypnotic Poison Ivy, the bloodthirsty Mister Zsasz, and the combined team of The Joker and Scarecrow, before he could take a break.

Batman knew he could only go on fighting for so long.

BREAKING A BAT

After cornering Batman in Wayne Manor, Bane had his enemy at his mercy. Batman fought back, but his blows were weak and his moves countered. Though he could have easily killed his enemy, Bane chose to let Batman live on, a broken man. "Death would only end your agony—and silence your shame," he said.

With a brutal slam across his knee, Bane crushed Batman's vertebrae.

AZRAEL

Azrael took up the mantle of the bat while Bruce Wayne rehabilitated from his injuries, with Wayne acting as his mentor. Wayne was later forced to fight his protégé to reclaim his identity.

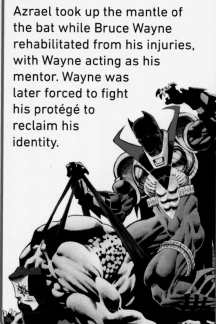

#1

BATMAN: THE LONG HALLOWEEN

"We can all talk around it, but— we know what needs to be done."

BATMAN

MAIN CHARACTERS: Batman, Captain James Gordon, Harvey Dent, Carmine "the Roman" Falcone, Catwoman
SUPPORTING CHARACTERS: Alberto Falcone, Richard Daniel, Johnny Viti, Barbara Gordon, Gilda Dent
LOCATIONS: Carmine Falcone's mansion, Gotham City Bank boardroom, Gotham City police headquarters, Gotham City warehouse, Harvey Dent's home

BACKGROUND

This issue marked the start of writer Jeph Loeb and artist Tim Sale's stylish, 13-part *Batman: The Long Halloween*. Its storyline took Batman back to the early years of his crime-fighting career, serving as a sequel of sorts to Frank Miller and David Mazzucchelli's "Year One" (February–May 1987) and inspiring further collaborations between the award-winning team of Loeb and Sale.

A murder mystery formed *The Long Halloween*'s backbone, as Batman, Police Captain James Gordon, and District Attorney Harvey Dent raced to apprehend the mysterious Holiday Killer, who struck once a month on days of public celebration. However, the story's real heart was its exploration of the professional partnership between the three men, and the heartbreaking manner in which it splintered after Dent was scarred by acid and transformed into the horrifying Super-Villain Two-Face.

PUBLICATION DATE
December 1996

EDITOR
Archie Goodwin

COVER ARTIST
Tim Sale

WRITER
Jeph Loeb

PENCILER
Tim Sale

INKER
Tim Sale

COLORIST
Gregory Wright

LETTERER
Richard Starkings

The Story...

Batman teams up with Police Captain James Gordon and District Attorney Harvey Dent to take on Gotham City's godfather, Carmine "The Roman" Falcone.

Batman is beginning to make his mark in Gotham City, but it remains under the thumb of Carmine "The Roman" Falcone, head of the notorious Falcone crime family. When Bruce Wayne receives an invitation to the wedding of Falcone's nephew, Johnny Viti, he knows it comes with strings attached **(1)**. As a member of the board at the Gotham Bank and one of the most powerful men in the city, Bruce knows that Falcone hopes to persuade him to help convince the bank to launder money for the mob. Bruce isn't afraid to reject Falcone to his face **(2)**. He walks out of Falcone's office and rejoins the wedding festivities, where he is cheered by the presence of his friend, the alluring Selina Kyle.

District Attorney Harvey Dent hasn't been invited to the gala, but in the parking lot of Falcone's mansion apartment, he jots down license plate numbers in his ongoing effort to collect evidence against the mob boss **(3)**. Later, Batman breaks into Falcone's safe and takes his private ledger, but has to fight off Catwoman, who has her own designs on Falcone's secrets **(4)**.

Soon after, Batman meets with Dent and police captain James Gordon **(5)** to discuss dismantling organized crime in Gotham City **(6)**. Batman then produces the Falcone ledger **(7)** to prove his dedication to the cause.

Later, despite Falcone's continued scheming, Batman convinces bank president Richard Daniel to vote against Falcone's interests. However, Daniel's act of defiance earns him a death sentence, carried out with cold precision.

The Falcones are soon beset by trouble of a different sort when the Holiday Killer strikes for the first time. On Halloween night, Carmine Falcone's newly wed nephew, Johnny Viti, is shot dead in his bathtub, with a Jack-o'-lantern left as a calling card **(8)**. To make matters worse for Carmine Falcone, Dent and Batman locate his stockpiled profits in a warehouse. **(9)**. With a single match **(10)**, Dent ignites a blaze that consumes the warehouse and the ill-gotten gains within **(11)**.

Harvey Dent returns home to his wife Gilda **(12)**. However, moments later, his home explodes, further igniting a war that will last for a year and become known as the "Long Halloween" **(13)**.

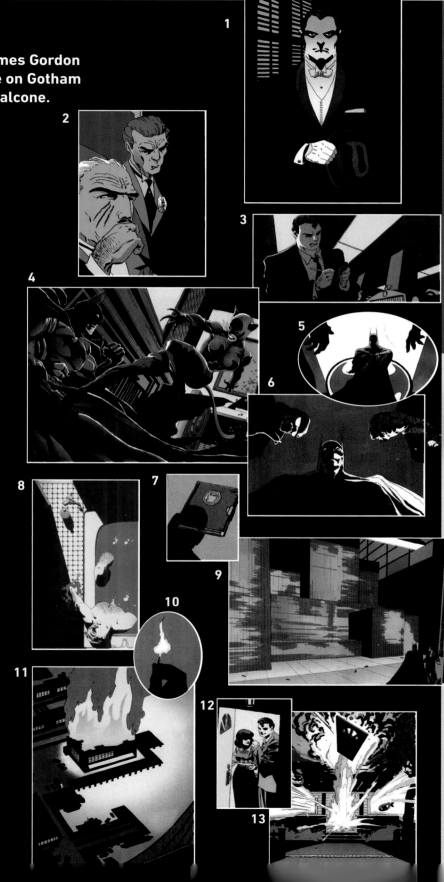

FALCONE
CRIME FAMILY

Vincent Falcone (father)

Carla Viti (sister)

Lucia Viti (niece)

Johnny Viti (nephew)

Sofia Gigante (daughter)

Mario Falcone (son)

Alberto Falcone (son)

CARMINE FALCONE
The kingpin of the Falcone family, Carmine "The Roman" Falcone had both Gotham City's mayor and its police commissioner on his payroll and ran the entire city from behind the scenes. His headaches began with the raids conducted by Batman and district attorney Harvey Dent, but his son Alberto turned against his own family by becoming the Holiday Killer. Carmine enlisted help from Gotham City's costumed freaks, but he lost his life after Harvey Dent became the crazed Two-Face.

GOTHAM CITY'S ORIGINAL GANGSTERS

When Batman arrived on the scene, old-world crime families like the Falcones had Gotham City in their pocket. The vigilante smashed their operations and inspired a new breed of costumed Super-Villains who had no respect for tradition. The Falcone family was the first to feel the effects of the new order.

The Falcones enjoyed an exuberant lifestyle in Gotham City, and the wedding of Carmine Falcone's nephew, Johnny Viti, was a typically lavish affair, with all members of the criminal empire in attendance.

Catwoman was no friend to the Falcones. Carmine Falcone got his facial scars after a swipe from her claws, while Carmine's daughter, Sofia Gigante, targeted the Cat for elimination.

SELINA KYLE

The mysterious Selina Kyle had the charm to win an invitation to the wedding of Carmine Falcone's nephew, and the guts to return after dark as Catwoman so she could break into Falcone's safe. Her connection to the Falcone family remained a mystery to Batman, though rumors swirled that Selina might be Carmine Falcone's daughter.

Though she fought the Falcones, Catwoman wasn't on Batman's side either.

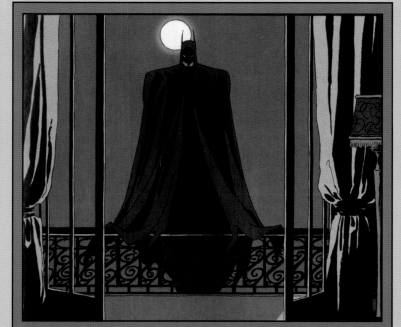

BATMAN AND THE FALCONES

Years ago, Bruce Wayne's father Thomas saved Carmine Falcone from a gunshot wound, and the Mafia don felt that he owed a debt to the Wayne family. He never knew that Bruce had taken up the identity of Batman, thwarting and humiliating Carmine at every turn. When Batman torched the Falcones' warehouse containing millions of dollars in cash, Carmine called for his head.

"THE ROMAN" EMPIRE [FAMILY TREE]

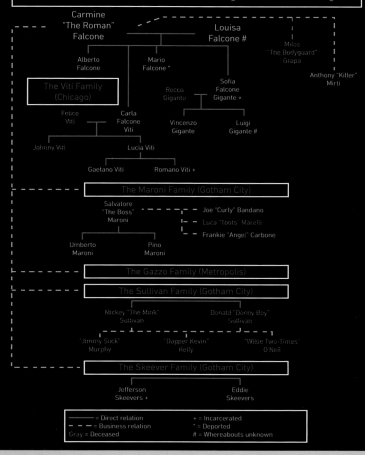

Carmine "The Roman" Falcone — Louisa Falcone #

- Alberto Falcone
- Mario Falcone *
- Milos "The Bodyguard" Grapa
- Anthony "Killer" Mirti

The Viti Family (Chicago)

- Rocco Gigante
- Sofia Falcone Gigante +

- Felice Viti — Carla Falcone Viti
- Vincenzo Gigante
- Luigi Gigante #

- Johnny Viti
- Lucia Viti

- Gaetano Viti
- Romano Viti +

The Maroni Family (Gotham City)

- Salvatore "The Boss" Maroni
  - Joe "Curly" Bandano
  - Luca "Toots" Marelli
  - Frankie "Angel" Carbone

- Umberto Maroni
- Pino Maroni

The Gazzo Family (Metropolis)

The Sullivan Family (Gotham City)

- Mickey "The Mink" Sullivan
- Donald "Donny Boy" Sullivan

- "Jimmy Suck" Murphy
- "Dapper Kevin" Kelly
- "Willie Two-Times" O'Neil

The Skeever Family (Gotham City)

- Jefferson Skeevers +
- Eddie Skeevers

——— = Direct relation	+ = Incarcerated
– – – = Business relation	* = Deported
Gray = Deceased	# = Whereabouts unknown

THE MARONI FAMILY

The Maroni family was the chief rival to the Falcone family in Gotham City's underworld. Sal Maroni infamously threw acid into D.A. Harvey Dent's face during a courtroom trial, inadvertently creating Two-Face. The Maronis and the Falcones both found themselves under fire from the Holiday Killer, and accused each other of orchestrating the mysterious assassinations.

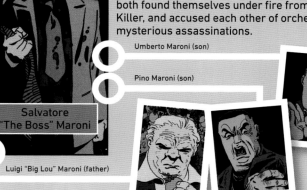

Salvatore "The Boss" Maroni

Umberto Maroni (son)

Pino Maroni (son)

Luigi "Big Lou" Maroni (father)

BIRDS OF PREY

BLACK CANARY
One of the founding members of the Birds of Prey, Black Canary proved the perfect partner for Oracle. She is an expert martial artist who possesses the metahuman ability to shatter eardrums with her ultrasonic Canary Cry. With Justice League experience and a tendency to challenge Oracle when the two disagree, she is the heart and soul of the BOP team.

THE HUNTRESS
Putting her time in the covert group Spyral behind her, Helena Bertinelli found that being The Huntress helped her deal with her anger issues. While her moral compass sometimes pointed in a different direction than the rest of the Birds, they were always able to find a common target in the distance. And no one is as good at hitting targets as The Huntress and her crossbow.

HARLEY QUINN
After clearing her criminal record by serving in the Suicide Squad, Harley Quinn teamed with the Birds of Prey a few times in her continued effort to turn over a new leaf. Her zany sense of dark humor didn't always mesh with the other Birds, but they could recognize her dedication to bettering Gotham City—even if her methods included using a comically large mallet.

THE FEARLESS FLOCK

This covert strike force populated by a diverse range of crime fighters came into existence under the direction of Barbara Gordon during her time as the information broker Oracle. While Barbara monitored trouble spots from the Birds of Prey's headquarters, Black Canary, Huntress, and other operatives executed global field missions.

ORACLE

After an injury left her paralyzed from the waist down, Police Commissioner James Gordon's daughter, Barbara, was forced to abandon her role as Batgirl. Instead, she became the computer virtuoso known only as Oracle. By tapping surveillance cameras and hacking into computer feeds, she acted as the eyes and ears of the Birds of Prey, calling the shots from thousands of miles away.

LADY BLACKHAWK

Before the *Flashpoint* event altered continuity, the Birds of Prey found a pilot in the form of Lady Blackhawk. Trained by the international team of aviators known as the Blackhawks, Zinda Blake was an expert pilot qualified to fly everything from helicopters and jet fighters to massive cargo carriers. Transported decades into the future, she became a long-serving member of the Birds of Prey, and was loved for her big heart and her ability to drink anyone under the table.

THE QUAKE
An earthquake killed thousands and left Gotham City's infrastructure in ruins. With no money in the city's budget and no outside parties willing to finance the necessary repairs, the outlook looked grim.

E GANGS MOVE IN
magnitude 7.6 earthquake had freed inmates from ham Asylum and Blackgate Penitentiary. With the r-empty city at their mercy, criminals carved out ir own fiefdoms. Between them, Two-Face and e Penguin controlled the most territory.

Bruce Wayne left Gotham City to plead its case in Washington, D.C. His plans fell on deaf ears, so he found himself traveling for the first few months of No Man's Land, punishing himself for losing his city.

Helena Bertinelli, otherwise known as The Huntress, remained in Gotham City to protect the helpless and assumed the identity of Batgirl. Batman approved of Helena's new identity, recognizing that Gotham City's survivors needed a Bat-like symbol of hope in his absence. But soon things turned sour. Two-Face's gang went on the offensive, reclaiming territory that Batgirl had thought secure.

THE STREET DEMONZ

KILLER CROC

TWO-FACE

THE PENGUIN

NO MAN'S LAND

| SCARFACE | POISON IVY | BLACK MASK |

POWER SHIFT

Not every criminal had evil intentions. Batman ceded Robinson Park to Poison Ivy provided she harmed no Gotham City citizens who had retreated there—mostly children who had been orphaned in the quake. But reestablishing law and order meant winning Gotham City back from the gangs headed up by the likes of Two-Face, The Penguin, and The Joker. James Gordon and his law-enforcing Blue Boys formed an alliance with Two-Face and his gang to put an end to the worst of the fighting, but Gordon's former friend betrayed him. First, Two-Face tried to kill Gordon, then he subjected him to a mock trial for breaking their alliance. G.C.P.D. detective Renee Montoya appealed to Harvey Dent's sense of justice, deeply buried within Two-Face's psyche, and convinced him to acquit Gordon.

Two-Face hired top assassin David Cain to eliminate Gordon. Cain's daughter Cassandra stopped her father and joined Batman's team, taking over from The Huntress as the newest Batgirl.

As the No Man's Land period reached its end, The Joker shot and killed Sarah Essen, James Gordon's wife. Gordon took revenge by putting a bullet in The Joker's knee.

REBUILDING

Metropolis mogul Lex Luthor created the turning point in the No Man's Land saga. He convinced the U.S. government to rescind its No Man's Land order by presenting his plans to restore Gotham City. A joint effort by LexCorp, Wayne Enterprises, and the U.S. Army Corps of Engineers got the city back on its feet. Lex, of course, had ulterior motives, but he failed in his scheme to seize control of entire blocks of Gotham City real estate.

GOTHAM CITY STANDS ALONE

The earthquake left devastation in its wake. Gotham City's citizens waited for disaster relief, but soon learned that the U.S. government had written off Gotham City as a lost cause. Not only would the quake damage go unrepaired, but city services—including the police—would be discontinued. All residents were ordered to leave, with bridges dynamited to prevent anyone from returning. But some Gothamites remained. The stubbornly loyal and the desperately poor became prey for the gangs—the new leaders of No Man's Land Gotham City. Criminals battled for control of each block. Opposing them stood the "Blue Boys," Commissioner Gordon's volunteer police officers. At first Batman seemed to have abandoned the city, but once Bruce Wayne returned from a failed mission to Washington, D.C., Gotham City once again fell under the protection of the Bat.

BRUCE WAYNE: MURDERER?

The real killer framed Bruce by dumping Vesper's bullet-riddled body in a Wayne Manor hallway. Moments after Bruce discovered it, the G.C.P.D. burst in with weapons drawn, and found him holding Vesper in his arms.

A WANTED MAN

Batman's crime-fighting crusade was brought to a halt when Bruce Wayne became a suspect in the murder of his ex-girlfriend, radio host Vesper Fairchild. Unable to account for his whereabouts without revealing his double life, Bruce was held in Blackgate Penitentiary. With his bodyguard Sasha Bordeaux also under arrest for the crime, it was left to Bruce's inner circle to prove his innocence.

"Given Mr. Wayne's wealth and resources, I feel it is in the best interest of the city that he be held without bail."

FUGITIVE

Bruce escaped from custody during a prison transfer. It made him look even guiltier, but it meant he could now launch his own investigation as Batman. Although he insisted on going it alone, it was the efforts of Batman's team that identified assassin David Cain as the murderer and Lex Luthor as the author of the smear campaign.

The hardened criminals of Blackgate thought a frightened billionaire would be an easy target, but Bruce Wayne easily took down the gang of inmates who rushed his cell.

Every member of Batman's inner circle pitched in to exonerate him. Robin, Nightwing, Batgirl, Spoiler, Oracle, and Alfred uncovered new details on Vesper's death and determined how the killer had got past the manor's security systems.

Doubts as to whether her boss fully trusted her led Sasha Bordeaux to resign her bodyguard position at the end of her ordeal.

SPOILER BECOMES ROBIN

Having proven her crime-fighting skills as Spoiler, Stephanie Brown was thrilled when Batman agreed to train her as Robin. But he fired her for disobeying orders, and in a bid to regain his trust she implemented one of his plans for subduing the Gotham City underworld. Unfortunately, Stephanie had only half understood the plan, and when it all went wrong the city fell into chaos.

In Batman's plan, his agent, Matches Malone, would bring all Gotham City's rival gangs under his own control. Stephanie didn't know that Batman was Malone, and when he failed to show at the meeting she set up, the gangsters opened fire on each other. A city-wide bloodbath was to follow.

WAR GAMES

A full-scale gang war proved disastrous for Gotham City—and for Stephanie Brown's position within Batman's organization.

ALL-OUT WAR

As gang war raged in Gotham City, Batman planned to draw every gang member to a pre-arranged location where his ally Orpheus would leave them open to mass arrest by the G.C.P.D. But the criminal Black Mask killed Orpheus and spurred the mob to even greater acts of violence.

After torturing Stephanie Brown for information about Batman, Black Mask shot her and left her for dead. She would be secretly nursed back to health by Dr. Leslie Thompkins. Continuing his rampage, Black Mask destroyed the clocktower headquarters of Oracle and the Birds of Prey.

BLACK MASK RULES

The massacre wiped out a substantial portion of Gotham City's underworld hierarchy, including costumed gangs and old-world crime families. By the time the last shots had been fired, Black Mask stood unopposed at the top of Gotham City's criminal order. He wasted no time in flaunting his power.

A SHARED PAST

A prestigious Gotham City surgeon, Dr. Thomas Elliot is also one of Bruce Wayne's oldest friends. When the two were children, Bruce's father saved the life of Tommy's mother. But Tommy knew the act had robbed him of the chance to inherit his family's large fortune, and he vowed to take revenge. Many years later—and now somehow armed with the secret of Bruce's double identity—Tommy Elliot became the mysterious bandaged villain named Hush.

A new foe sets a grand plan in motion. But his mask of bandages conceals a face that Bruce Wayne knows well.

HUSH

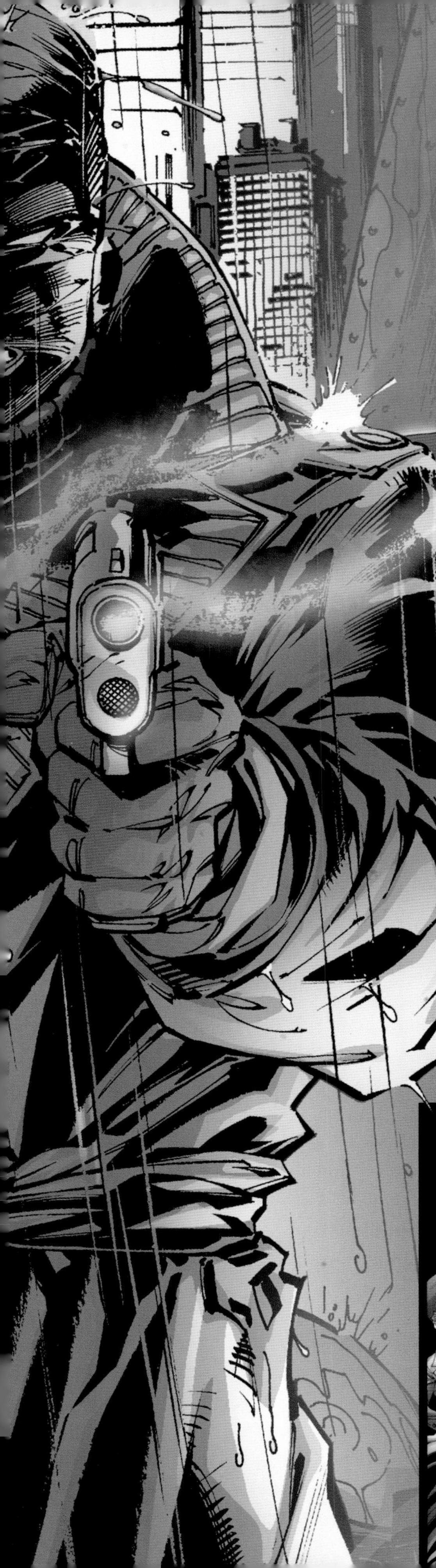

THE FIRST CONTENDER

Investigating a kidnapping, Batman entered the lair of Killer Croc, one of his most bestial opponents. Batman couldn't imagine the drumbeat of clashes with his enemies that would follow, all of them orchestrated by a strange new villain known only as Hush.

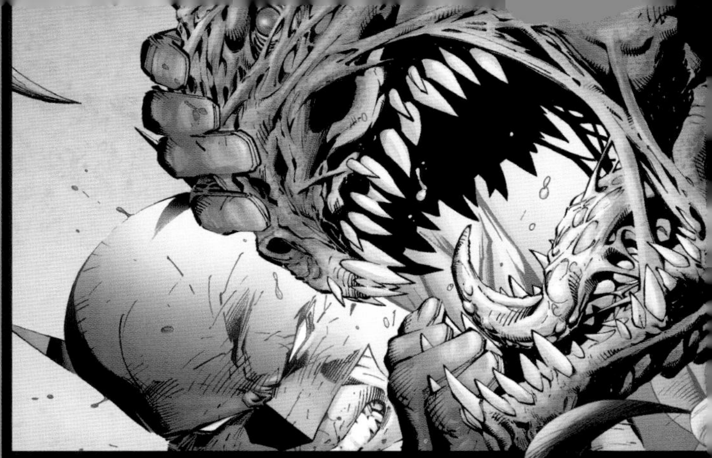

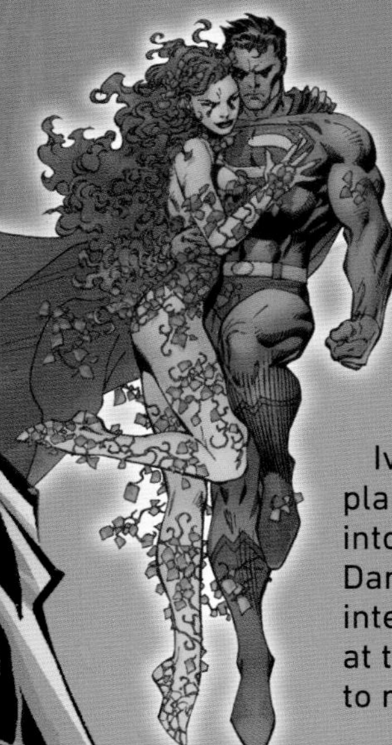

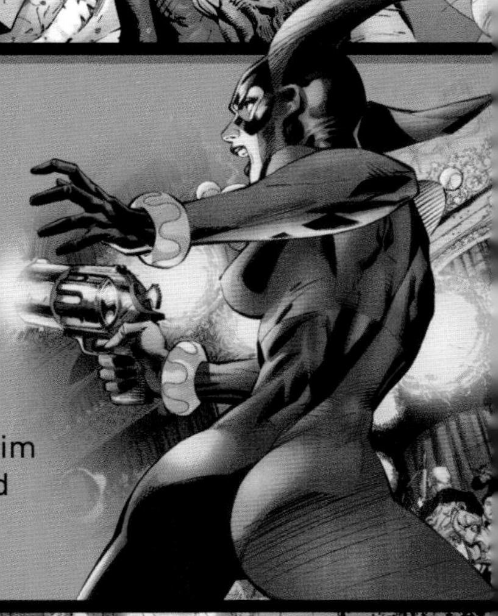

ROGUES GALLERY

Poison Ivy and Harley Quinn took their own shots at Batman as Hush's vengeful scheme unfolded. Ivy enslaved Superman using plant pheromones and ordered him into battle against an outmatched Dark Knight, while Harley Quinn interrupted Bruce Wayne's night at the theater when she tried to rob the packed house.

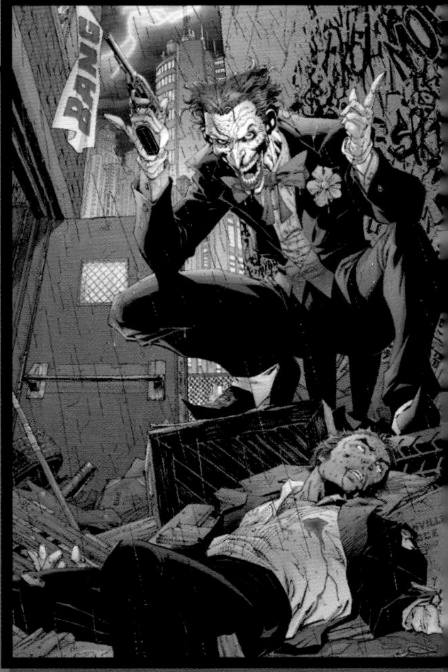
BANG

FLIPPING THE SCRIPT

Just as Tommy Elliot began to surface as a potential suspect for Hush's crimes, he took a fatal bullet. The Joker appeared to have fired the shot and Batman nearly beat him to death with his fists—not realizing he had been fooled by Hush. The shapeshifting Clayface had played the role of Elliot's corpse as Hush looked on approvingly from the shadows.

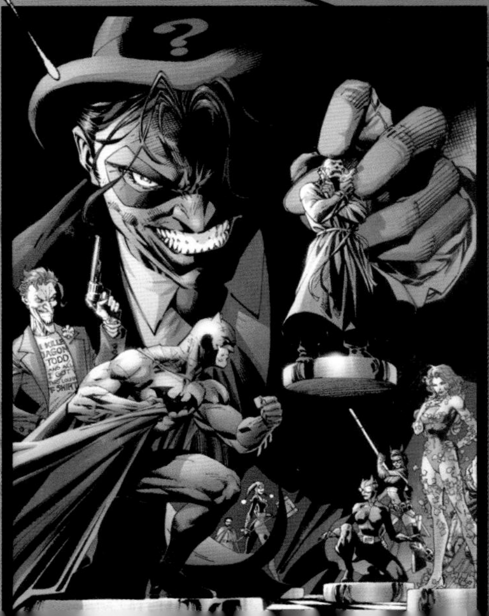

THE "HUSH" PLOT

Hush might have gotten things moving, but it was The Riddler who ultimately profited from them. The Riddler had joined forces with Elliot, and was running what he called the "Hush" plot behind the scenes. The Riddler had also deduced Batman's secret Bruce Wayne identity.

#6 IDENTITY CRISIS

DC
IDENTITY
CRISIS
#6
OF 7
DEAD END!
BRAD
MELTZER
RAGS
MORALES
M.R.
BAIR

"This is Batman we're talking about! You can't do that to Batman!"
THE FLASH

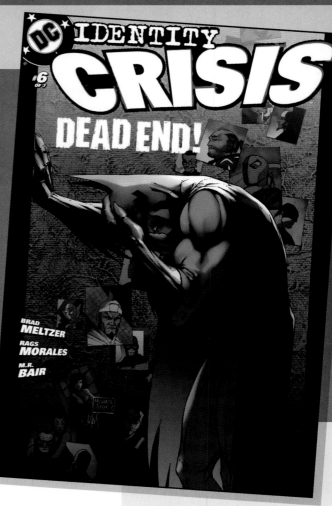

MAIN CHARACTERS: **Batman, Robin, Green Arrow, The Flash, Captain Boomerang**
SUPPORTING CHARACTERS: **Doctor Light, Calculator, Deadshot, Merlyn, Monocle, Zatanna, Dr. Mid-Nite, Mister Terrific, The Atom**
LOCATIONS: **Gotham City, JLA satellite, New York City, Ivy Town**

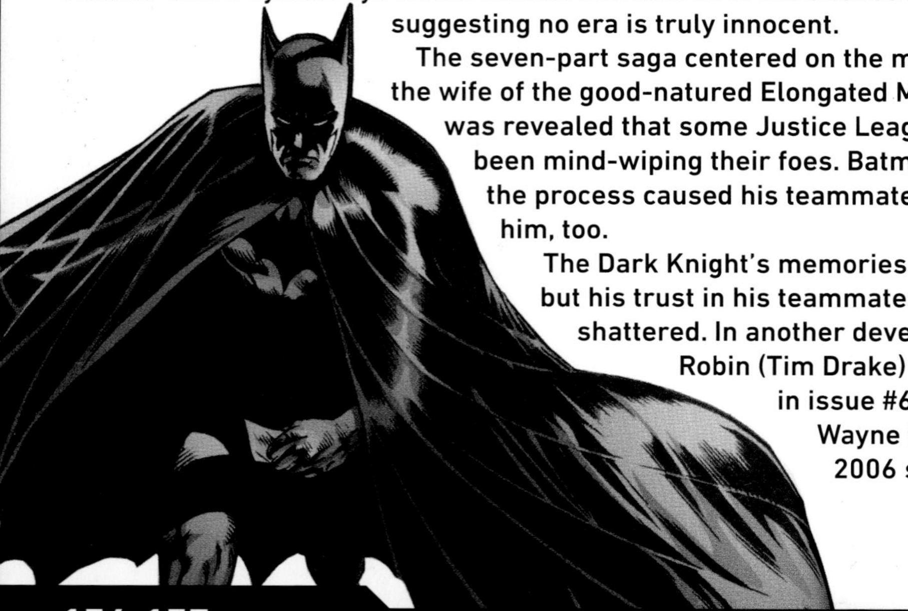

PUBLICATION DATE
January 2005

EDITOR
Mike Carlin

COVER ARTIST
Michael Turner

WRITER
Brad Meltzer

PENCILER
Rags Morales

INKER
Michael Bair

COLORIST
Alex Sinclair

LETTERER
Kenny Lopez

BACKGROUND

Though it bore the same "crisis" keyword as *Crisis on Infinite Earths*, 2004's *Identity Crisis* spent more time on personal revelations than cosmic crusades. Writer Brad Meltzer cast a cynical eye on the classic adventures of the Justice League of America, suggesting no era is truly innocent.

The seven-part saga centered on the murder of Sue Dibny, the wife of the good-natured Elongated Man. By issue #6, it was revealed that some Justice League members had been mind-wiping their foes. Batman's objection to the process caused his teammates to brainwash him, too.

The Dark Knight's memories later returned, but his trust in his teammates was forever shattered. In another development, the third Robin (Tim Drake) became an orphan in issue #6, prompting Bruce Wayne to adopt him in a 2006 storyline.

The Story...

Batman is too late to prevent the death of Robin's father, but he is about to witness a shocking act that breaks his trust in his teammates.

Tim Drake—the third Boy Wonder—rushes to his father's home only to discover two bodies lying on the floor. Jack Drake and the assassin Captain Boomerang have killed one another in a showdown. Even though Tim Drake knows his father's condition is fatal, he makes frantic efforts at resuscitation. With the words, "I've got you," Batman gently pulls him away. Tim, like Bruce, is now an orphan **(1)**.

Jack Drake isn't the only man who has left behind a son. Owen Mercer, the new Captain Boomerang, arrives at the scene and demands to see his father's body. The authorities refuse to give him access **(2)**. The younger Captain Boomerang stalks off, determined to live up to his father's legacy.

His setback is offset by victories for costumed criminals throughout the legal system. Deadshot, Merlyn, and the Monocle all escape prosecution for their crimes due to their participation in dangerous missions for the U.S. government's Suicide Squad program **(3)**. Doctor Light—responsible for an earlier brutal assault on Sue Dibny aboard the Justice League of America's satellite—is also unpunished **(4)**.

Meanwhile, The Flash confronts Green Arrow about an incident from the history of the Justice League **(5)** and Green Arrow then confesses what the League has tried to keep under wraps for years. In the aftermath of Doctor Light's attack on Sue, he and several other League members voted to use Zatanna's magical powers to erase the villain's memories. They were interrupted in the middle of the act by a shocked Batman **(6)**. The Dark Knight could not believe that his teammates would eliminate anyone's ability to make their own decisions **(7)**. The other Leaguers were left to decide what to do next, and the majority agreed to work Zatanna's magic on Batman, too.

Batman hasn't yet discovered the full truth about his teammates' actions, however. Continuing his investigation into Sue Dibny's murder, he returns to the Batcave to analyze the forensic data from Sue's autopsy. At the same time, at the Justice Society of America's headquarters, Dr. Mid-Nite and Mister Terrific are pursuing the same line of investigation **(8)**. Both parties come to the same conclusion: Only a person capable of size-changing could have killed Sue **(9)**. Batman rushes into action **(10)** seeking out Ray Palmer, the hero known as The Atom. By the end of the case, Batman has deduced the murderer's identity (Palmer is innocent), and that trust shared with his teammates can easily be broken.

UNDER THE RED HOOD

The Red Hood was someone Batman never thought to see again. Jason Todd was back from the dead!

REGENERATION
Jason Todd required the restorative waters of a Lazarus Pit to bring him back to full health.

Ignoring Batman's strict rule against the use of firearms, Jason Todd took every advantage, no matter the price. Armed with a rapid-fire cannon, he cut down a gang of street dealers without thinking twice about the body count.

AAK AAK

IN THE CROSSHAIRS

Black Mask had risen to dominate Gotham City's underworld, but the Red Hood spoiled his triumph by killing his aides. Black Mask hired mercenaries like Mr. Freeze to tackle the Red Hood, hoping to eliminate the newcomer before he threatened Black Mask himself.

BACK WITH A VENGEANCE

Though he died at the hands of The Joker, Jason Todd—who had fought alongside Batman as the second Robin—returned to life. Jason remembered everything that had been done to him by The Joker, and he blamed Batman for not stopping his murderer when he had the chance. With a dangerous edge and a complete disregard for Batman's "no killing" rule, Jason returned to Gotham City and assumed the identity of the Red Hood. His target for extermination was the gangster Black Mask, whose criminal gang controlled most of Gotham City's underworld.

In Batman's eyes, anyone who recklessly uses deadly force to fight their cause is no hero. Batman moved to shut down the Red Hood's crime-fighting operation long before he discovered the vigilante's identity.

Jason delivered brutal payback to the man who had killed him. He beat The Joker with a crowbar—just as The Joker had done to him when he was Robin—leaving him close to death.

PRODIGAL SON

From the subtlety in the Red Hood's fighting style, Batman immediately suspected that the fallen Robin had returned. After he unmasked Jason, Batman hoped he could rehabilitate his former pupil. But in his failure, he knew he had made a new enemy. Eventually, Jason's anger would abate, and he would regain some of Batman's trust. While they remain allies, Jason's willingness to use lethal force continues to drive a wedge between himself and his mentor.

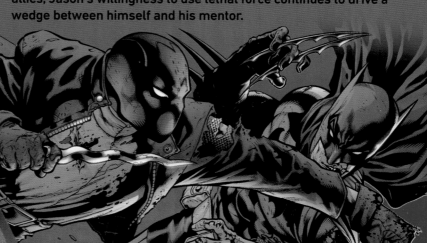

INFINITE CRISIS

During the *Crisis on Infinite Earths*, a hero named Alexander Luthor helped to save the universe by combining many realities into one. When he next appeared, he was a corrupted madman intent on remaking the universe to his own design.

ON THE DEFENSIVE

Following Alexander Luthor's preliminary assault, Batman met with Superman and Wonder Woman aboard the Justice League's orbital HQ. The three didn't yet know their enemy's true goals, and tensions between them stood in the way of cooperation on a counterattack. When the alien warlord Mongul arrived to mop up any survivors of Alexander's attack, the heroes were barely able to fight him off. An angry Batman concluded that this was one crisis he would face alone.

Batman felt his colleagues had betrayed his trust. He pushed aside offers of help, even from Alfred.

"You know, there was one thing your father never wanted to be. Alone." ALFRED

A SECOND SUPERMAN

Somebody else remembered the way things were before the *Crisis on Infinite Earths*. A pre-*Crisis* version of Superman urged Batman to join Alexander's cause, showing him visions of friends and family members who had existed on alternate Earths erased during the first *Crisis*. They could all live again, if multiple realities were restored.

BROTHER EYE

The Brother Eye surveillance satellite, built by Batman, became self-aware and turned living beings into OMAC cyborgs. Alexander used it to spread chaos.

A NEW PLAN

The stakes had now become far too great for Batman to handle everything on his own. Booster Gold and a new, teenaged Blue Beetle became his first recruits in a mission to strike at Brother Eye. As Batman's squad rocketed into space, Superman and Wonder Woman took aim at Alexander Luthor's other agents.

TAKING DOWN THE EYE

Batman and his team penetrated Brother Eye's defenses and stormed the corridors leading to the AI core. Brother Eye fought back against its creator, but Batman had a secret weapon in Mister Terrific, whose hi-tech innovations made him invisible to machines. An adjustment to the satellite's engines sent Brother Eye into an orbital death spiral from which Batman himself narrowly escaped.

FATAL DECISION

Alexander Luthor's scheme lay in ruins and Batman had the villain at his mercy. For an instant he considered using a gun to end the threat forever, but remembered his vow to never take a life. However Alexander soon found himself cornered by The Joker, who sprayed his face with acid before putting a bullet in his head.

"You didn't let The Joker play."

LEX LUTHOR

Batman and Superman
are outstanding partners.
Superman's ability to fly,
invulnerability, and heat
vision make him nearly
unstoppable—and he's even
more effective when guided
by Batman's tactical genius.

MORTAL ENEMIES?
Batman is aware that a mind-controlling villain could turn Superman
against him, and that he can't match the Man of Steel in a contest of
strength. He has wisely prepared countermeasures for emergency
use, including compact explosives to distract Superman and
inner-ear-scrambling sonic screechers to disorient him. Batman's
final line of defense is a ring containing a shard of Kryptonite.

BATMAN & SUPERMAN

WORKING TOGETHER

Batman and Superman were suspicious of each other at first, but over time they became trusted allies who could act as a tightly synced fighting squad when needed. Because Gotham City and Metropolis are close neighbors, the two heroes often collaborate when tracking down members of their respective Rogues Galleries. Batman and Superman are also founding members of the Justice League, which gives them international—and sometimes intergalactic—jurisdiction. Pitted against their many foes, the two heroes must use their individual skills as a combined force.

ALWAYS OUTNUMBERED

It is always a bad idea to challenge Batman and Superman, but this fact does not stop their enemies from trying to get the best of the formidable pairing. After Lex Luthor placed a billion-dollar bounty on their heads, the two heroes found themselves cornered in Washington, D.C. by a dangerous group of villains that included Giganta, Black Manta, The Cheetah, King Shark, and a host of other hopefuls with greed in their hearts.

WORLD'S FINEST

While they often have to be talked into spending time together socially, Bruce Wayne and Clark Kent enjoy each other's company, despite rarely agreeing on any given topic. Even though Batman rarely admits it, he and Clark are indeed more than allies, they're truly friends.

"I've always felt that people should take responsibility for their actions, not excuse them."

BATWOMAN

BATWOMAN

Gotham City's criminals have learned to fear Kate Kane! With resources to rival those of Bruce Wayne, Batwoman combats threats ranging from simple muggings to the elaborate and twisted Religion of Crime.

A traumatic kidnapping during their childhood forever changed the destinies of Kate and her twin sister.

HONOR AND DUTY

Batman may originally have been her inspiration, but Batwoman has become a hero in her own right.

Kate Kane grew up within the wealthiest Gotham City family not named Wayne. As a child, she saw her mother and twin sister Beth gunned down during a botched kidnapping, and grew up under the heavy-handed influence of her father, U.S. Army Colonel Jacob Kane. Kate studied at the United States Military Academy at West Point before she was asked to leave for refusing to hide her personal relationship with another woman from her superiors. She has since been romantically involved with Renee Montoya and Maggie Sawyer, both women sharing her passion for justice, law, and order.

Kate found inspiration in Batman's example after the hero helped her during an encounter with a mugger. With assistance from her father, she underwent intense physical training. The Kane family fortune paid for her high-tech Batsuit and an arsenal of gadgets, and an interior section of the R. H. Kane Building became her secret headquarters.

During a period when Batman left Gotham City to pursue a spiritual journey overseas, Kate made her first patrol as the mysterious, flame-haired Batwoman. She faced Bruno Mannheim, the leader of the Religion of Crime, and later the eerie woman known only as "Alice." Batwoman's world shattered when Alice revealed herself as Beth Kane, Kate's own twin who had survived the childhood hostage raid but suffered deep psychological damage in the years since.

Finding teamwork more to her liking than she originally let on, Kate teamed with her cousin, Bette Kane (aka Hawkfire), as her protégée in her war against crime, and later worked with Red Robin and a group of Gotham City heroes including Batman. The group eventually disbanded, but Batwoman continues her fight against injustice on her own, sometimes operating out of an underwater hideout in Gotham Ciy Harbor called the Batcove.

With a knife throw, Batwoman took out Bruno Mannheim, leader of the Religion of Crime. It was one of the first challenges she faced as a crime fighter in Gotham City.

Batwoman's father urged her to ignore rumors of her sister's survival, but she was determined to discover the truth.

Kate's first serious romantic relationship was with G.C.P.D. police detective Renee Montoya.

The enigmatic Alice vanished in the waters of Gotham City Harbor, but returned, calling herself Red Alice.

Batwoman has the same red hair color as her Kate Kane persona, but employs a long wig when in the cape and cowl to better hide her identity.

KEY DATA

REAL NAME Katherine "Kate" Kane

OCCUPATION Adventurer, international operative, socialite

WEAPONS/POWERS/ABILITIES Batarangs, extendable staff, Utility Belt gadgets, military training in armed and unarmed combat

AFFILIATIONS Batman, Inc.

RELATIVES Jacob Kane (father), Gabrielle Kane (mother, deceased), Beth Kane (sister), Bette Kane (cousin), Bruce Wayne (cousin)

FIRST APPEARANCE *52* #7 (June 2006)

Batwoman's crime-fighting suit contains a layer of impact-dispersing Kevlar weave, much like the Batsuit worn by Batman.

TEACHER AND STUDENT
Though Bette Kane had previous crime-fighting experience as the costumed Flamebird, she didn't share Kate's disciplined military upbringing and found it hard to win her approval. However, through hard work she graduated to a new Super Hero identity as Hawkfire.

Every inch of Batwoman's costume is functional. Her no-slip, steel-toed boots provide both traction and kicking power.

GOTHAM KNIGHTS
Under the leadership of both Batman and Batwoman, this rather informal team of Gotham City operatives included founder Red Robin, Orphan, Spoiler, and even a temporarily reformed Clayface. They later incorporated both Azrael and Batwing into their ranks.

THE WEEPING WOMAN
Batwoman faced a deadly challenge in the form of a supernatural spirit that targeted Gotham City's children and dragged them to watery graves. While stopping the spirit, known as the Weeping Woman, Kate began a relationship with Maggie Sawyer of the G.C.P.D.

Can Harvey Dent ever be free of Two-Face? Harvey's slide back into villainy shattered Batman's trust.

FACE THE FACE

Plastic surgery had repaired Harvey's scars, but it could not heal his spirit.

Harvey was tormented by the voice of Two-Face inside his head.

FROM HERO TO VILLAIN

When Batman traveled abroad for a year, he left Gotham City in good hands. Back when he was the city's district attorney, Harvey Dent had been Batman's ally in the fight against mob corruption. And now, with his looks and sanity restored thanks to the plastic surgery of Dr. Thomas Elliot (also known as Hush), Harvey was Batman's first choice to carry out nighttime patrols in his absence. But Harvey Dent hadn't erased his split personality—he had only pushed it aside.

Batman had reason to suspect that Harvey was involved in the murders of several low-level villains, but he trusted his friend. Despite that, Harvey fell into a whirlpool of paranoia when named as a suspect.

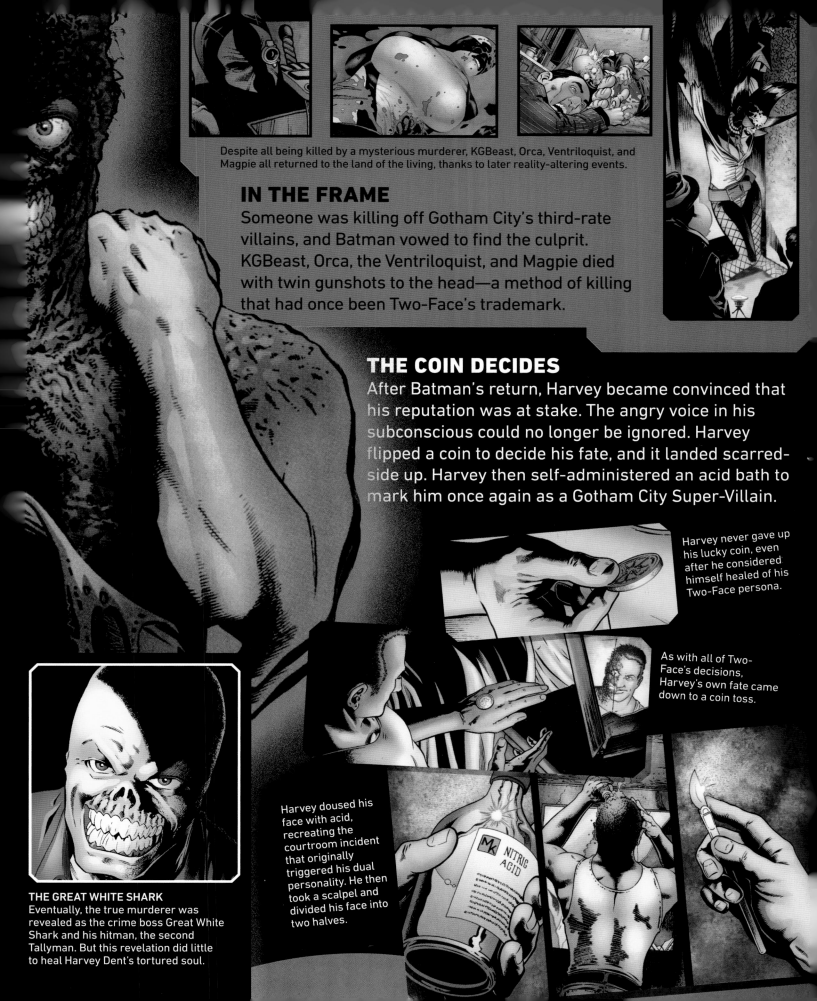

Despite all being killed by a mysterious murderer, KGBeast, Orca, Ventriloquist, and Magpie all returned to the land of the living, thanks to later reality-altering events.

IN THE FRAME

Someone was killing off Gotham City's third-rate villains, and Batman vowed to find the culprit. KGBeast, Orca, the Ventriloquist, and Magpie died with twin gunshots to the head—a method of killing that had once been Two-Face's trademark.

THE COIN DECIDES

After Batman's return, Harvey became convinced that his reputation was at stake. The angry voice in his subconscious could no longer be ignored. Harvey flipped a coin to decide his fate, and it landed scarred-side up. Harvey then self-administered an acid bath to mark him once again as a Gotham City Super-Villain.

Harvey never gave up his lucky coin, even after he considered himself healed of his Two-Face persona.

As with all of Two-Face's decisions, Harvey's own fate came down to a coin toss.

Harvey doused his face with acid, recreating the courtroom incident that originally triggered his dual personality. He then took a scalpel and divided his face into two halves.

THE GREAT WHITE SHARK
Eventually, the true murderer was revealed as the crime boss Great White Shark and his hitman, the second Tallyman. But this revelation did little to heal Harvey Dent's tortured soul.

ENTERING THE BATCAVE

Batman's ten-year-old son Damian grew up in the cruel care of the League of Assassins. A lethal killer, he was heralded since birth as heir to the world-conquering legacy of his mother, Talia, and his grandfather, Rāʾs al Ghūl. Batman didn't know if he could fully overcome Damian's indoctrination, but he brought his son to the Batcave to begin his training.

Talia al Ghūl was one of Batman's deadliest foes. To Batman's surprise, she also turned out to be the mother of his son, Damian!

BATMAN AND SON

Surrounded by colorful sculptures and pop art prints, Batman foiled a horde of sword-wielding Ninja Man-Bat warriors. But he wasn't prepared for the surprise that Talia al Ghūl had in store.

MAN-BAT ARMY

Talia re-entered Batman's life when she attacked an art museum with a commando squad of ninjas, who had been mutated into flying freaks by Dr. Kirk Langstrom's Man-Bat serum. It was one step in Talia's plan for global domination. When Batman stopped her, Talia seized the chance to introduce her unruly son to his unwitting father. Damian was in need of discipline, and Talia knew Bruce Wayne was the man to teach it to him.

Tim Drake only wanted to be friends, but Damian was conditioned to see him as a rival—and a threat.

TRIAL BY COMBAT

Following the traditions of the League of Assassins, Damian believed he had to earn his father's respect by defeating the current Robin, Tim Drake. Damian donned his own version of the Robin costume and headed into Gotham City to join Batman's war on crime. He killed a low-level crook known as the Spook to demonstrate his commitment, but only proved how much he still had to learn: His father's mission is one of redemption, not capital punishment.

ANGER ISSUES

As Robin, Damian has struggled to curb his violent impulses and youthful arrogance. He made lethal mistakes while working directly with Batman, as well as during his tenure as leader of various incarnations of the Teen Titans. His journey is far from over and he continues to hunt for his place in the world.

The Spook may have been a professional crook, but he didn't deserve the punishment Damian dished out. His career was ended with a horrific beheading.

BATMAN R.I.P.

BREAKING DOWN BATMAN

Some years ago, Batman spent ten days in a sensory-deprivation tank to sharpen his mind. The researcher in charge of the treatment was Dr. Simon Hurt—in actuality a mystically long-lived ancestor of Batman's named Thomas Wayne. Following apparent orders from the demon god Barbatos, Hurt had subliminally planted the phrase "Zur-En-Arrh" in Batman's mind. When triggered, the phrase rendered Batman delirious and vulnerable. Together with the Club of Villains—which included Le Bossu, Charlie Caligula, King Kraken, Scorpiana, and El Sombrero—Hurt planned to push Batman to breaking point.

Incapacitated by Dr. Hurt's hypnotic "trigger phrase," Batman lay helpless as Hurt and the Club of Villains infiltrated the Batcave. They beat Alfred senseless, then drugged Bruce Wayne before dumping him, dazed and confused, onto the streets of Gotham City to fend for himself.

THE BATMAN OF ZUR-EN-ARRH

Bruce Wayne could not remember who he was or how he wound up in a Gotham City alleyway, but he soon found strength by seizing upon the belief that he was a hero called the Batman of Zur-En-Arrh. He fashioned a Batman costume from rags and sought guidance from a figment of his imagination in the shape of the interdimensional imp Bat-Mite. These subconscious rituals helped Batman hold onto his sanity and prepare a counterattack against Dr. Hurt.

"THE BATMAN OF ZUR-EN-ARRH!"

THE JOKER'S GAME

Dr. Hurt invited The Joker to play a key role in his plot against Batman, but The Joker had his own plans for the Dark Knight and wasn't accustomed to taking orders. He wreaked havoc, even killing members of the Club of Villains, then revealed that he thought Dr. Hurt's plot was a farce all along— after years of trying to kill Batman, The Joker knew the Dark Knight would not be defeated.

BORN AGAIN

The Batman of Zur-En-Arrh traced the Club of Villains to Arkham Asylum. They captured him again and buried him alive in a shallow grave, planning to dig him up after he suffered brain damage from the lack of oxygen. The Dark Knight regained his strength and his mental sharpness, and fought his way free of the coffin and the layers of dirt imprisoning him. The real Batman was back!

#6
FINAL CRISIS

"I made a very solemn vow about firearms. But for you, I'm making a once-in-a-lifetime exception."

BATMAN

MAIN CHARACTERS: Batman, Darkseid, Superman
SUPPORTING CHARACTERS: Wonder Woman, Green Arrow, Supergirl, Mary Marvel, The Flash, Black Racer
LOCATIONS: Legion of Super-Heroes arsenal, Blüdhaven, Darkseid's singularity

BACKGROUND

From the 1980s onward, DC drummed up sales for its interconnected comics with special crossovers. These events often had "crisis" in the title, a traditional DC buzzword that had originated in Silver Age tales of the original *Justice League of America* title. The 2008–2009 crossover *Final Crisis* shocked readers by offering up what appeared to be Batman's dying act in his crusade against crime.

The Dark Knight uncharacteristically packed a futuristic firearm to defeat the godlike Darkseid. Batman wounded the villain before appearing to perish under Darkseid's counterattack: the lethal beams of the Omega Sanction.

After *Final Crisis*, Batman's presumed death kicked off a race to find his successor. It also gave his allies an occasion to memorialize the man who had given his life to alter events on a cosmic scale.

PUBLICATION DATE
January 2009

EDITOR
Eddie Berganza

COVER ARTIST
J. G. Jones

WRITER
Grant Morrison

PENCILERS
J. G. Jones, Carlos Pacheco, Doug Mahnke, Marco Rudy

INKERS
J. G. Jones, Jesus Merino, Christian Alamy, Marco Rudy

COLORISTS
Alex Sinclair and Pete Pantazis

LETTERER
Rob Clark Jr.

The Story...

The fate of the universe hangs in the balance as the Dark Knight of Gotham City takes on the might of the terrifying Fourth World god, Darkseid.

The entirety of time and space has been thrown into turmoil in the cataclysmic struggle known as the *Final Crisis*. It is left to Earth's protectors to stand against the conquering forces of Darkseid, but their ranks are broken. Darkseid has dragged the planet's population under his spell by eliminating free will. Wonder Woman has already become Darkseid's slave, with Green Arrow and others also joining the cause of evil.

While Superman seeks the Legion of Super-Heroes' "miracle machine" in the 31st century **(1)** and Supergirl spars with Mary Marvel **(2)**, The Flash tries to battle Darkseid by harnessing the power of the deity of death, Black Racer **(3)**. Batman, however, penetrates the walls of the singularity that shields Darkseid's inner sanctum, relying on stealth to approach the god's throne. Calling on Batman to reveal himself **(4)**, Darkseid gloats that the Dark Knight will soon be forced to embrace the brainwashed "peace" of anti-life.

However, Batman has applied his knowledge of forensics to solve the case of the Fourth World god Orion, who has fallen victim to an assassin's bullet. Batman has reached two conclusions: Darkseid orchestrated Orion's death to usher in the current crisis; and the bullet fired from the murder weapon was cast from pure radion—the only known substance in the universe with the power to kill a god.

Armed with a Fourth World firearm loaded with the radion bullet recovered from the Orion crime scene **(5)**, Batman breaks his own personal code and fires the gun, just as Darkseid fires his infamous Omega Beams **(6)**. Batman's radion bullet strikes Darkseid in the shoulder **(7)**. Batman murmurs "gotcha"—just before Darkseid's Omega Beams seemingly tear him to atoms **(8)**.

An enraged Superman **(9)** later recovers what is believed to be Batman's corpse **(10)**. The fallen hero is laid to rest near the graves of Thomas and Martha Wayne. However, Darkseid's act has not killed Batman: It has caused him to become unstuck in time.

BLACKEST NIGHT

The Green Lantern Corps is one of seven interstellar forces, including the Red Lanterns of rage and the Blue Lanterns of hope, that represent different colors and emotions. The absence of color once had a champion, too, in the death-obsessed Black Hand. He sought to raise fallen heroes as Black Lanterns, and the key to his scheme was the freshly buried body of Batman!

Black Lantern symbol

Though living, Wonder Woman, Superman, and Green Arrow were all overpowered by Black Lantern rings. They were made vulnerable by their past experiences of death and resurrection.

WHITE LANTERN

The colors of the seven Lantern Corps combined to make white light, ending the Blackest Night and activating a White Lantern ring that Batman would briefly control.

GRAVE ROBBER

Black Hand lacked the power to create an entire Black Lantern Corps by himself, so he enlisted the help of Nekron, the Lord of Death. From an unmarked grave near the tombstones of Thomas and Martha Wayne he dug up the remains of Bruce Wayne, who had been laid to rest after his apparent death at the hands of Darkseid. The body would later be revealed as a cloned fake, but this did not spoil Black Hand's plan. He only needed to stir the emotions of those who remembered Batman.

THE DEAD RISE

Thousands of Black Lantern rings activated by Nekron resurrected dead heroes and villains as hateful shells of their former selves. Batman's living allies, including Commissioner Gordon, Barbara Gordon, Nightwing, and Robin fought off their advance, while the seven Lantern Corps joined forces against Nekron.

Using Batman's skull as a talisman, Black Hand forged an empathic link with those who had known Batman best. Ragged strips of flesh suddenly reanimated Batman's body, turning the hero into an undead horror. Confronted with their friend's transformation, Superman and other defenders dropped their guard and became mindless agents of Nekron.

Batman was dead—or so the world believed. Who would carry on the Dark Knight's crime-fighting legacy?

BATTLE FOR THE COWL

GOTHAM CITY NEEDS BATMAN

With Bruce Wayne supposedly laid to rest beside the graves of his parents, the members of Batman's inner circle were torn over what to do next. Having served as the original Robin, Dick Grayson was the obvious choice to don the cape and cowl of his fallen mentor—but being Batman was an honor he didn't feel worthy of accepting. Others had their own designs on the cowl, including two more Robins. Jason Todd believed Gotham City needed a ruthless Batman that acted as judge, jury, and executioner, and Tim Drake was forced to grow up before he was ready in order to stop him. As Black Mask plunged the city into chaos, Gotham City cried out for a savior. Where was Batman?

BLACK MASK

A Gotham City with no Batman was an easy target for a criminal with no conscience. When Black Mask arrived, he freed the city's worst villains from Arkham Asylum and Blackgate Penitentiary, reveling in the madness that ensued.

JASON TODD

Back from the grave and angrier than ever, Jason Todd had convinced himself that Batman's "no killing" rule was what prevented the original hero from achieving true greatness. Jason geared up in a modified Batsuit and set out to scare Gotham City's crooks into submission— even if he had to leave behind a few bodies as examples to others.

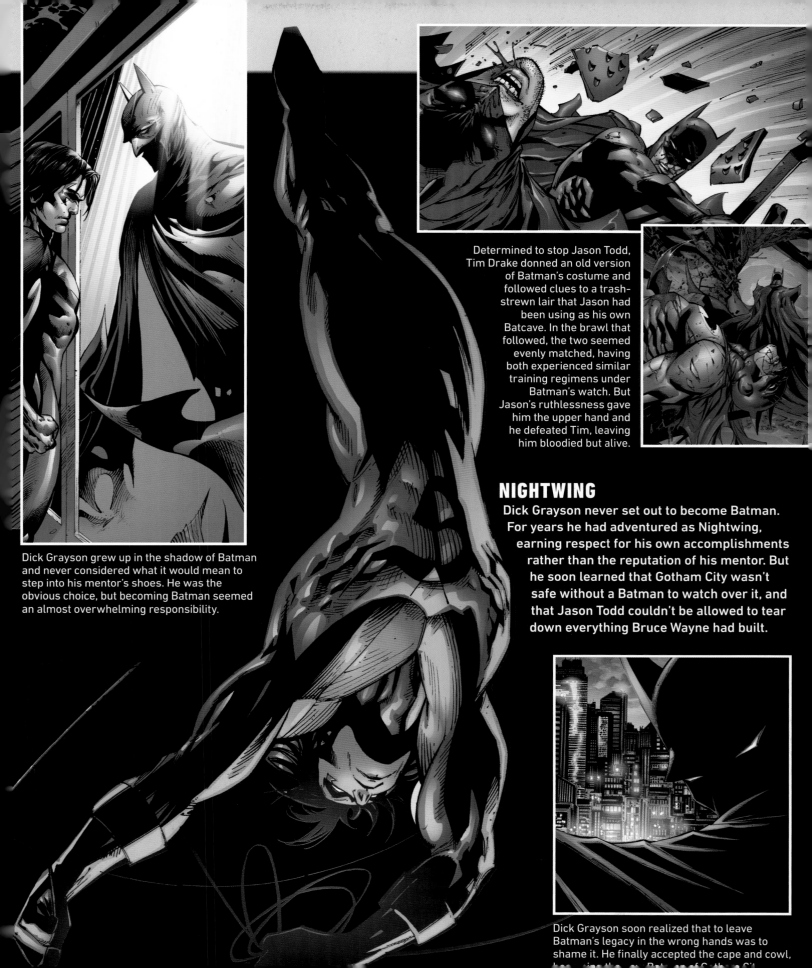

Dick Grayson grew up in the shadow of Batman and never considered what it would mean to step into his mentor's shoes. He was the obvious choice, but becoming Batman seemed an almost overwhelming responsibility.

Determined to stop Jason Todd, Tim Drake donned an old version of Batman's costume and followed clues to a trash-strewn lair that Jason had been using as his own Batcave. In the brawl that followed, the two seemed evenly matched, having both experienced similar training regimens under Batman's watch. But Jason's ruthlessness gave him the upper hand and he defeated Tim, leaving him bloodied but alive.

NIGHTWING

Dick Grayson never set out to become Batman. For years he had adventured as Nightwing, earning respect for his own accomplishments rather than the reputation of his mentor. But he soon learned that Gotham City wasn't safe without a Batman to watch over it, and that Jason Todd couldn't be allowed to tear down everything Bruce Wayne had built.

Dick Grayson soon realized that to leave Batman's legacy in the wrong hands was to shame it. He finally accepted the cape and cowl,

Superman, Booster Gold, Green Lantern, and the time-traveling Rip Hunter searched for Batman through time.

Bruce Wayne was thought dead but he was actually lost in time. His journey home took him through the past, present, and future.

THE RETURN OF BRUCE WAYNE

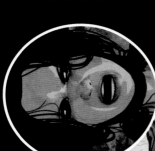

A young warrior of the Miagani became Bruce Wayne's prehistoric, Robin-like squire.

CAVEMAN

After arriving in prehistory, in the territory that would one day become Gotham City, Bruce Wayne led a persecuted tribe to victory over his immortal enemy Vandal Savage and a band of Neanderthals. He left the people of the Miagani tribe with a story that would echo throughout the ages.

Bruce's ancestor, Nathaniel Wayne, gave orders for the accused witch Annie to be hanged.

WITCH HUNTER

A time-skip sent Bruce to Puritan-ruled Gotham City in 1640, where he took the name "Mordecai" and investigated accusations of local witchcraft. He was unable to save a woman from death by hanging before another time-skip moved him forward once again.

CHASING TIME

When Darkseid blasted Batman with his Omega beams, he sent him through time—an act meant to kill the Dark Knight slowly. Each time-skip would infuse Batman with Omega energy until it had built up to such a degree that it threatened the universe itself.

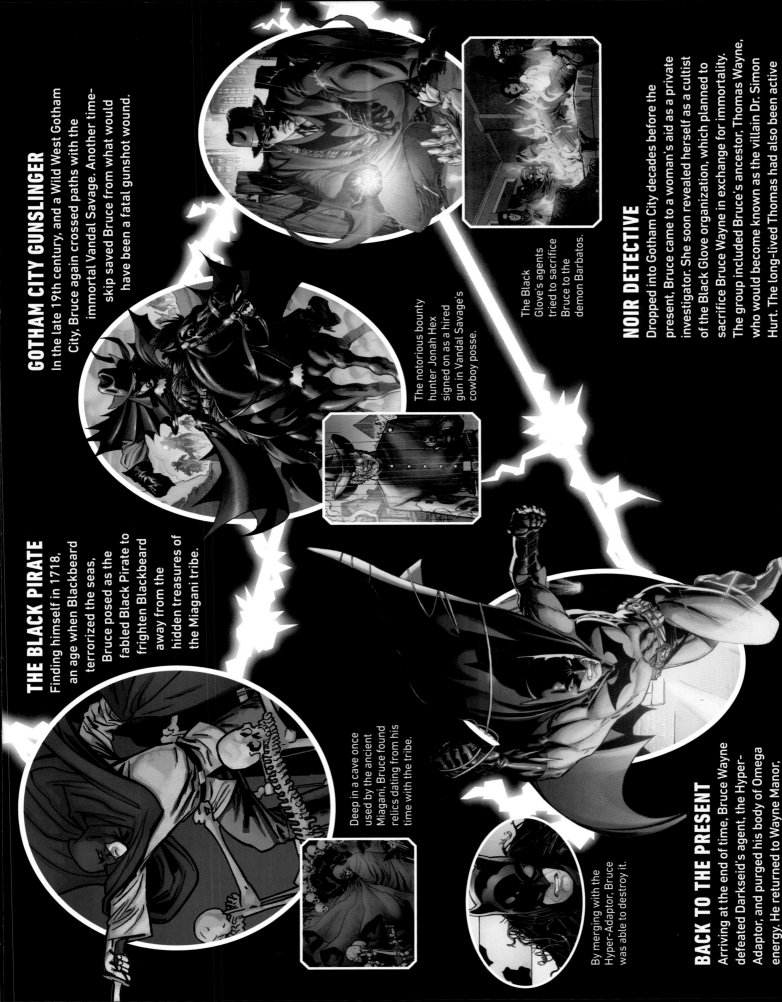

GOTHAM CITY GUNSLINGER

In the late 19th century, and a Wild West Gotham City, Bruce again crossed paths with the immortal Vandal Savage. Another time-skip saved Bruce from what would have been a fatal gunshot wound.

The notorious bounty hunter Jonah Hex signed on as a hired gun in Vandal Savage's cowboy posse.

The Black Glove's agents tried to sacrifice Bruce to the demon Barbatos.

NOIR DETECTIVE

Dropped into Gotham City decades before the present, Bruce came to a woman's aid as a private investigator. She soon revealed herself as a cultist of the Black Glove organization, which planned to sacrifice Bruce Wayne in exchange for immortality. The group included Bruce's ancestor, Thomas Wayne, who would become known as the villain Dr. Simon Hurt. The long-lived Thomas had also been active when Bruce had appeared earlier in the 19th century.

THE BLACK PIRATE

Finding himself in 1718, an age when Blackbeard terrorized the seas, Bruce posed as the fabled Black Pirate to frighten Blackbeard away from the hidden treasures of the Miagani tribe.

Deep in a cave once used by the ancient Miagani, Bruce found relics dating from his time with the tribe.

By merging with the Hyper-Adaptor, Bruce was able to destroy it.

BACK TO THE PRESENT

Arriving at the end of time, Bruce Wayne defeated Darkseid's agent, the Hyper-Adaptor, and purged his body of Omega energy. He returned to Wayne Manor, ready to reclaim the title of Batman.

BATMAN INCORPORATED

"Batman is everywhere." BRUCE WAYNE

BATMAN GOES GLOBAL

When traveling through time, Batman had glimpsed a dire threat in his future. To combat this new evil, Bruce Wayne shocked the public when he announced Wayne Industries' plans for Batman, Inc.—an international initiative to install licensed Batman agents across the planet. What the original Batman had done for Gotham City, Wayne argued, the legend of Batman could do for the entire world. As the program took hold, the mysterious new enemy Batman had foreseen emerged with a similar goal of worldwide expansion. Batman needed every member of Batman, Inc. to fight back against the mysterious cabal known only as Leviathan.

Bruce Wayne's public role as Batman, Inc.'s financial backer helped to dispel rumors that he was secretly the Batman of Gotham City.

Flanked by a squad of Batman-like robots, Bruce Wayne demonstrated that automated agents could play a valuable role in stopping street-level crime.

BATMAN

Origin: U.S.
Bio: Bruce Wayne adopted a new costume after his return from the timestream. This Batsuit included his familiar yellow oval symbol; however this one lit up to intimidate criminals.

RED ROBIN

Origin: WORLDWIDE
Bio: As Red Robin, Tim Drake broadened his crime-fighting jurisdiction on an international scale. Within Batman, Inc., Red Robin led a team of Outsiders consisting of Metamorpho, Looker, Katana, Halo, and Freight Train.

BATGIRL

Origin: U.S.
Bio: Stephanie Brown filled the role of Batgirl during the early missions of Batman, Inc., while Barbara Gordon assisted as the computer expert Oracle. After the history-changing *Flashpoint* event, Stephanie departed the team.

BATMAN (DICK GRAYSON)

Origin: U.S.
Bio: After the formation of Batman, Inc., Dick Grayson continued wearing the Batman costume he had first put on during Bruce Wayne's absence. The presence of two Batmen helped underscore the ever-vigilant mission of Batman, Inc.

ROBIN

Origin: U.S.
Bio: Damian Wayne, the current Robin, signed on to his father's newest project as a loyal operative. He chased down leads concerning the evil Leviathan organization, but the revelation of Leviathan's true mastermind came as a shock.

THE HOOD

Origin: U.K.
Bio: George Cross works for the British intelligence service MI5 and models himself after Robin Hood, taking from the rich and giving to the poor. The Hood played a key role in helping Batman, Inc. neutralize the villainous Doctor Dedalus.

EL GAUCHO

Origin: ARGENTINA
Bio: A founding member of the now-defunct Batmen of All Nations, El Gaucho is a prominent Argentinean hero whose signature weapon is the bola. In his other identity of Santiago Vargas he is a wealthy and respected landowner.

BATWOMAN

Origin: U.S.
Bio: The military-trained Batwoman fitted in well within Batman, Inc.'s hierarchy. She assisted the team on a mission to the Falkland Islands, where she investigated the sinister Doctor Dedalus and his ties to the Leviathan syndicate.

KNIGHT AND SQUIRE

Origin: U.K.
Bio: Knight and Squire were high-profile heroes in the UK, with a long history of working with Batman. The Knight was Cyril Sheldrake, who succeeded his father in the role, and was later succeeded by his former Squire, the scrappy Beryl Hutchinson.

NIGHTRUNNER

Origin: FRANCE
Bio: A newer recruit into Batman, Inc., Bilal Asselah is a French Muslim who lives in suburban Paris. His advanced parkour free-running skills make him a nimble guardian of the city's people.

MAN-OF-BATS AND RAVEN RED

Origin: U.S.
Bio: This father/son duo operates from a Sioux reservation in South Dakota, U.S.A. Man-of-Bats was once a proud member of the Batmen of All Nations. His son, Raven Red, has expressed a desire to emerge from his father's shadow.

BATWING

Origin: DEMOCRATIC REPUBLIC OF CONGO
Bio: David Zavimbe is a police officer in the city of Tinasha in the Democratic Republic of Congo. He also coordinated Batman, Inc.'s operations throughout Africa in his role as Batwing. Luke Fox later adopted the Batwing moniker.

BLACK BAT

Origin: Hong Kong, China
Bio: With combat skills and extensive field experience as a former Batgirl, Cassandra Cain was Batman, Inc.'s agent in Hong Kong, China, under her shortlived identity of Black Bat.

DARK RANGER

Origin: AUSTRALIA
Bio: Johnny Riley was Batman, Inc.'s Australian representative and the second-generation successor to the country's original Ranger. Dark Ranger's jetpack allows him to fly and he carries a pulse weapon to fight off attackers.

BATMAN OF MOSCOW

Origin: RUSSIA
Bio: The Russian representative of Batman, Inc. died after facing rival crime fighter Morgan Ducard, who is otherwise known as Nobody. Ducard "erased" the Batman of Moscow by submerging him in a vat of acid.

BATMAN OF JAPAN

Origin: JAPAN
Bio: As the former sidekick of Mr. Unknown, Jiro Osamu helped Batman avenge Mr. Unknown's death and agreed to join Batman, Inc. as Batman of Japan, often teaming with fellow hero Shy Crazy Lolita Canary.

WINGMAN

Origin: U.S.
Bio: Jason Todd secretly took up the mantle of a new Wingman in order to operate in Batman's covert interests inside Batman, Inc. Surprisingly, this mantle was later adopted by Jason's dad, Willis Todd.

MODERN AGE
2010 AND ON...

Batman was now a bigger star than ever and led the relaunch of a new DC universe.

In late 2011, the *Flashpoint* event altered the DC universe to such an extent that even after it ended and the universe was restored, Batman's reality was left forever changed. This new continuity was the result of DC's decision to reboot its entire universe in the initiative known as the *New 52*. Every title was restarted with a first issue, including the long-lived series *Batman* and *Detective Comics*. The Dark Knight had a new costume and a compressed timeline, while other heroes were updated to an even greater degree.

By 2016, it was clear a few key elements were missing from some corners of the DCU. To restore these beloved continuity fragments, DC introduced the *Rebirth* event. This restarted the *Batman* title once more, while restoring *Detective Comics* to its classic numbering. *Detective Comics* soon arrived at its historic 1000th issue, followed by the equally momentous issue #1027, which celebrated Batman's debut from a thousand issues prior.

To further embrace all that came before, the company-wide *Infinite Frontier* rebranding of 2021 amended the DC universe once more. The heroes suddenly remembered nearly all of the adventures that had been lost to them from various crises. The future was now full of possibilities, and Batman was more integral to this bold new direction than any other Super Hero.

OVERLEAF
Detective Comics #1027 (November 2020): Batman has stayed on mission for more than a thousand Detective Comics' *issues, as wells as numerous other comic book series.*

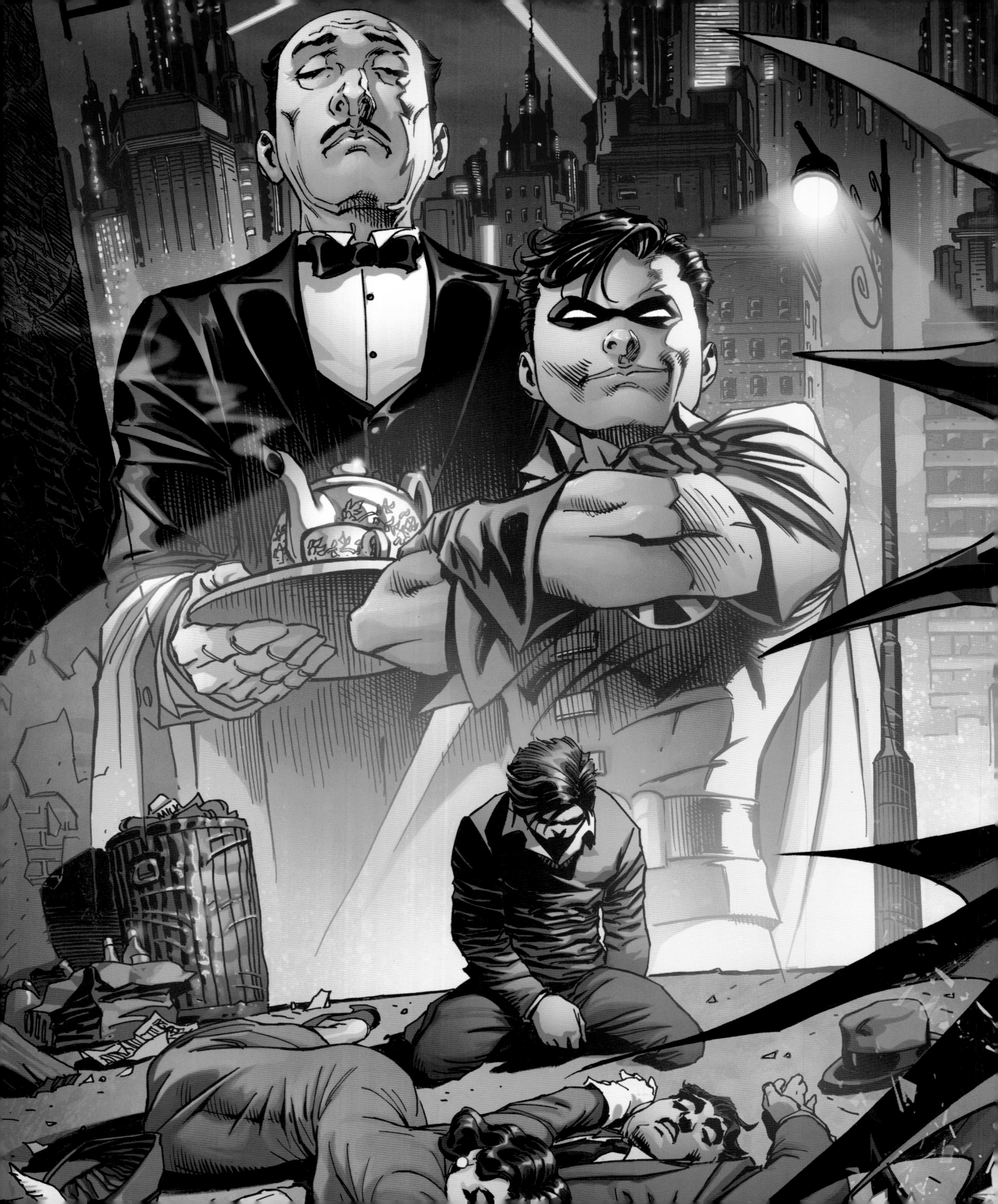

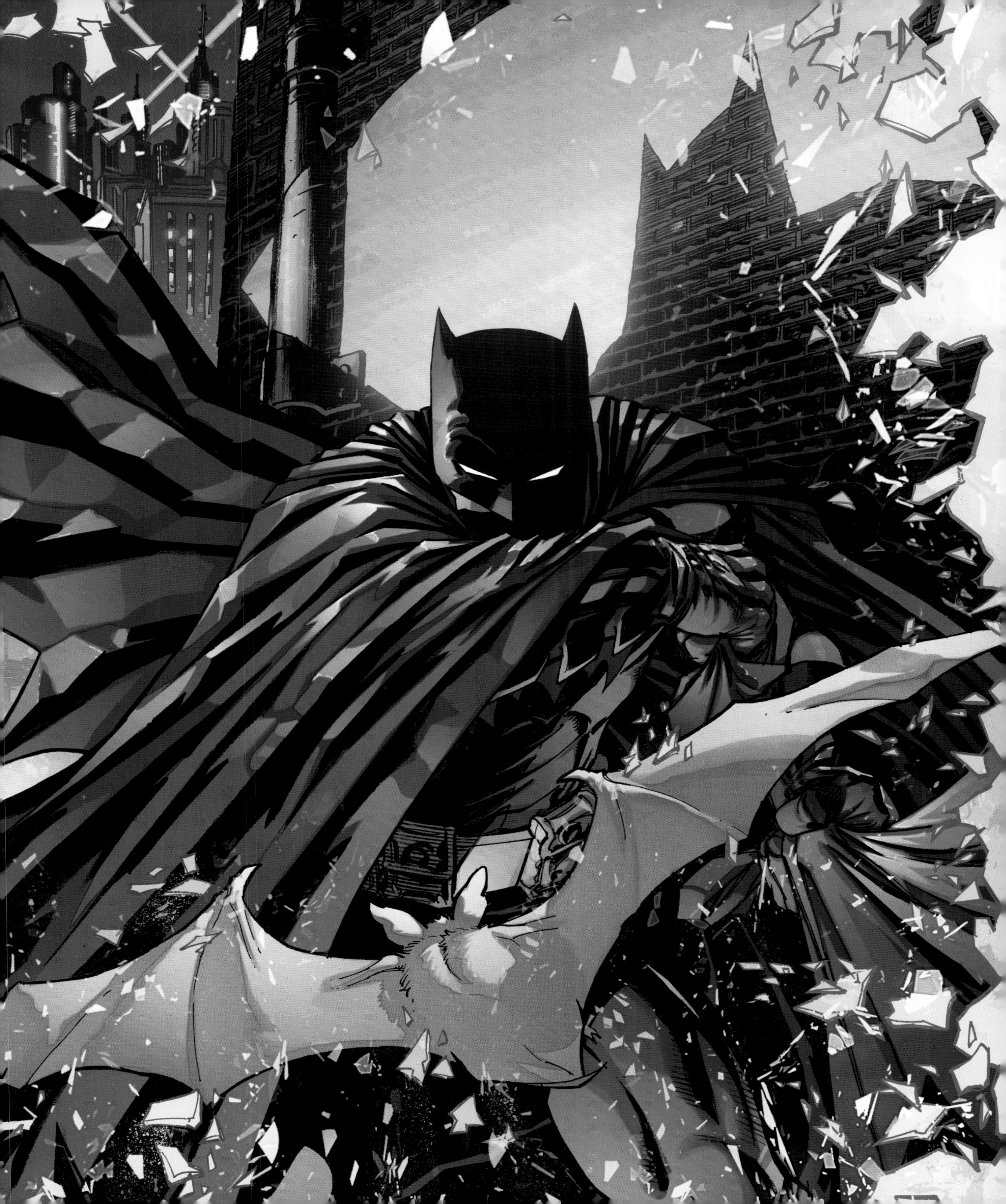

FLASHPOINT

The Flash awoke to a world in which his late mother lived, a global Super Hero war raged, and Dr. Thomas Wayne was Batman!

BROKEN TIMELINE

Waking up in a strange new timeline, The Flash struggled to make sense of things. Some Super Heroes did not exist, others were at war, and he had lost his powers. Inside his ring, The Flash found not his own costume but that of his enemy, the Reverse-Flash. He was sure the Reverse-Flash had altered history. Enlisting the aid of Batman—Bruce Wayne's father—The Flash rallied other heroes for a showdown with the Reverse-Flash.

Wayne Manor had fallen to ruin, but it still held Batman's secrets.

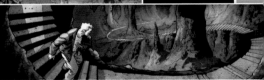

ENTERING THE BATCAVE

The world might have been turned upside down, but The Flash believed that there was one person he could trust in any reality—Batman. Inside the Batcave, however, he encountered a Dark Knight he did not recognize. The shifting *Flashpoint* timeline had caused Dr. Thomas Wayne to become Batman, and he scoffed at The Flash's description of a world where his son Bruce had lived and become a hero to all. After a while, Dr. Wayne put aside his doubts and began to listen. Somehow The Flash's tale rang true. Finally convinced, Batman generated an artificial lightning strike to restore The Flash's speed powers.

One look in Batman's eyes, told The Flash how deep the changes to history had gone

Hooked to an electrical rig, The Flash received a jolt that mimicked the accident that had originally blessed him with super-speed.

new Gotham City ill a refuge of d order thanks to orts of its Batman, homas Wayne. This night had a brutal ept sharp by the y of the mugger who d killed his only son, The incident had so atized Thomas' wife, , that she had ed a breakdown came Gotham nfamous villain ker.

SUBJECT 1

Batman hoped that a secret prisoner held by the U.S. government's Project Superman might be able to help them. Joined by the Super Hero Cyborg, he and The Flash penetrated the Project Superman vault to find Subject 1, a young Kryptonian named Kal-El who had never felt the energizing rays of Earth's yellow sun.

Despite a lifetime in solitary confinement, Subject 1 had a kind heart and helped his rescuers escape the facility. However, once outside the vault he panicked and flew away.

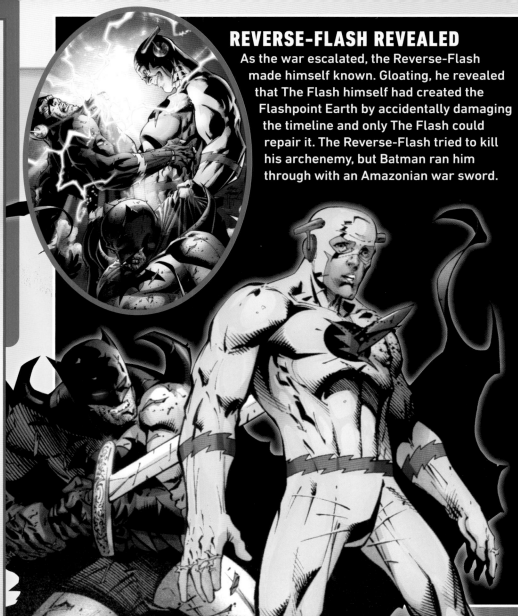

REVERSE-FLASH REVEALED

As the war escalated, the Reverse-Flash made himself known. Gloating, he revealed that The Flash himself had created the Flashpoint Earth by accidentally damaging the timeline and only The Flash could repair it. The Reverse-Flash tried to kill his archenemy, but Batman ran him through with an Amazonian war sword.

THE RETURN

To mend the timeline, The Flash would have to undo everything that had led to this moment, erasing the only world Dr. Thomas Wayne knew. The Flash raced back through the timestream, carrying a letter for Bruce from the father he would never know. Both The Flash and Batman's costumes were different when The Flash reached his destination. Something was new about this familiar world...

"Love always, your father—Thomas."

#1
BATMAN

"Gotham is 'Batman.' Gotham is 'Batman's city.' Gotham is 'The Bat...'"

BATMAN

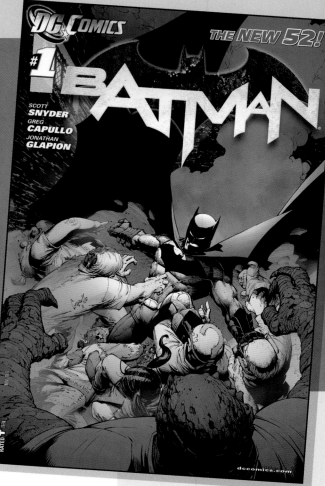

MAIN CHARACTERS: Batman, Nightwing (Dick Grayson), Commissioner Gordon
SUPPORTING CHARACTERS: Mr. Freeze, Scarecrow, Clayface, Robin (Damian Wayne), Red Robin (Tim Drake), Vicki Vale, Lincoln March, Harvey Bullock
LOCATIONS: Arkham Asylum, G.C.P.D. headquarters, the Batcave, Wayne Manor, Gotham City slums

BACKGROUND

The *Flashpoint* crossover event in 2011 gave DC the opportunity to make some changes. By restarting each of their titles with a first issue and introducing a slew of new series, they introduced *The New 52*, 52 monthly books in a reimagined DC universe. While Batman's corner of the DC universe wasn't affected as drastically as other comics—as in the completely retconned *Teen Titans* or *Justice League*—there were still major differences from the pre-*Flashpoint* world, including the costumes of his cast of characters.

Two of *The New 52* marquee titles were *Detective Comics* and *Batman*. For the first time in over seven decades, both comics restarted with new #1 issues, jumping right into the action with a de-emphasis on past continuity. In *Batman #1*, writer Scott Snyder drew parallels between Batman and Gotham City as the epic introduction of the Court of Owls unfolded.

PUBLICATION DATE
November 2011

EDITOR
Mike Marts

COVER ARTIST
Greg Capullo

WRITER
Scott Snyder

PENCILER
Greg Capullo

INKER
Jonathan Glapion

COLORIST
FCO Plascencia

LETTERERS
Richard Starkings, Jimmy Betancourt

The Story...

A new era dawns for Batman in an adventure through the key locations of the Dark Knight's legend, including Arkham Asylum, the Batcave, and the mean streets of Gotham City.

While Batman is putting down a riot at Arkham Asylum **(1)** that involves Mr. Freeze, Scarecrow, Clayface, and others, the sudden appearance of The Joker threatens to turn the tide in the villains' favor **(2)**. However, The Joker fights on Batman's side **(3)**!

Later, Batman regroups with Commissioner Gordon on the rooftop of G.C.P.D. headquarters and reveals that an Arkham guard may have unlocked the cells to trigger the evening's bedlam. Returning to the Batcave **(4)**, Batman finds The Joker waiting for him. All becomes clear when Dick Grayson drops his impressive holographic disguise **(5)**.

At Wayne Manor, Bruce reconvenes with Damian Wayne and Tim Drake **(6)** at his latest fundraiser. Bruce Wayne proudly announces Wayne Industries' plans to revitalize Gotham City's downtown infrastructure **(7)**, omitting to mention that the reconstruction will hide the installation of secret "bat bunkers" throughout the city.

Among those present is Vicki Vale of the *Gotham Gazette*, who introduces Bruce to mayoral candidate Lincoln March **(8)**. March hints that he has equally big plans for the city, but Bruce excuses himself from further mingling. His covert contact lens eyewear surveillance has pieced together the content of a murder investigation call between Commissioner Gordon and G.C.P.D. detective Harvey Bullock. It is time for Bruce to help Gotham City as Batman **(9)**.

Detective Bullock is unfazed by the Dark Knight's sudden appearance at the crime scene in the city's slums, and brings his visitor up to speed. The victim, skewered by razor-tipped throwing knives which avoided major arteries, died after a drawn-out ordeal. The handle of each knife bears the mark of an owl, a traditional symbol of Gotham City. Batman detects the smell of linseed oil **(10)**, and borrows Bullock's lit cigar to ignite a spill on the wall. There, written in flame, are the words: "BRUCE WAYNE WILL DIE TOMORROW."

One more clue remains. Batman analyzes a tissue sample found beneath the victim's fingernails, and Alfred calculates a DNA match at the Batcave that points to Dick Grayson **(11)**. But the real killer is still out there, and Batman's investigation will soon throw a light on the ultra-secretive Court of Owls.

BATMAN THE NEW 52!

The events of *Flashpoint* brought about a new status quo, and reaffirmed Batman's role as a central figure of the heroic age. Batman's past history had been altered as a fallout of the event, as had that of the Justice League and the Teen Titans—indeed the entire DC Multiverse. Batman and his allies' costumes were significantly different, leaning more toward a segmented armor aesthetic, and the Dark Knight's timeline was compressed to help reduce his age and years in service in his cape and cowl. With son Damian serving as Robin, Batman faced opposition from unfamiliar enemies and the emergence of a centuries-old secret society known as the Court of Owls. The Dark Knight's influence could also be seen close to home in the vigilance of Batgirl, Batwoman, and Nightwing, and on a global scale through the actions of Batwing and Red Hood and the Outlaws.

BATMAN

Bruce Wayne might be one of Gotham City's most prominent citizens, but even he dismissed the mysterious Court of Owls as nothing more than a nursery-rhyme fantasy. But the secret society was all too real. Batman discovered that its members had murdered Bruce's ancestor, Alan Wayne, nearly a century before. Now, in the modern era, they sent their assassin Talon to kill Bruce. After restarting his investigation into the clandestine organization, Batman learned that Lincoln March, a man who claimed to be his long lost brother, was the Court's lead operative.

DETECTIVE COMICS

A new villain joined Batman's Rogues Gallery when the Dollmaker sliced his way into the Gotham City headlines. This twisted new foe was employed to remove The Joker's face, ushering in a new era for the Clown Prince of Crime, one that led into a later crossover event throughout the bat-books called *Death of the Family*. Wearing his skinned face like a macabre mask, The Joker looked as outwardly horrific as he was internally.

BATMAN: THE DARK KNIGHT

Most of Gotham City's problems begin at Arkham Asylum. In the pages of the new title *Batman: The Dark Knight*, Batman faced the threat of the villain White Rabbit haunting that institution's corridors. That led to a meeting with the Venom-injected Two-Face and the larger looming threat of Bane. Further stories in this fledgling title pitted the Dark Knight against dark foes like the Mad Hatter and Scarecrow, revealing secrets from the pasts of some of Batman's most deadly foes.

BATMAN AND ROBIN

Batman had already trained four Robins, but his experience counted for little when his son Damian became the fifth to carry the name. Damian's upbringing among the League of Assassins—a group of killers headed by his mother, Talia al Ghūl—gave the latest Robin a ruthless streak and a cocky arrogance. At first, he sought to control these qualities under the guidance of his father. But when Morgan Ducard, also known as Nobody, tried to lure Damian away from his father and teach him to mete out "true" justice as both judge and executioner, Ducard's approach appealed to Damian's ingrained killer instincts. Ducard's actions nearly succeeded in driving a wedge between father and son—and Batman and Robin.

BATWING David Zavimbe was Africa's protector within Batman, Inc.

CATWOMAN Selina Kyle sharpened her claws battling the Russian mob.

BATWOMAN Kate Kane became Gotham City's newest hero.

TEEN TITANS Red Robin (Tim Drake) joined Superboy and Kid Flash.

RED HOOD AND THE OUTLAWS These outcasts accepted each other when no one else would.

BIRDS OF PREY Black Canary, Katana, Poison Ivy, and Starling formed the new team.

NIGHTWING Dick Grayson protected Gotham City and later moved to Chicago.

BATGIRL Barbara Gordon was back in the Batgirl costume and better than ever.

JUSTICE LEAGUE Batman was a core member of this mighty super-group.

JUSTICE LEAGUE INTERNATIONAL A second team followed Batman's example.

COMRADES IN ARMS
From the alleys of Gotham City to the peaks of the Himalayas, Batman's colleagues and protégés continued to carry out their own crime-fighting campaigns.

ZERO YEAR

The *New 52* Batman gets a matching new origin story in an epic that introduces the Dark Knight to a new generation.

STARTING FROM ZERO

Following the *Flashpoint* event, it was clear that some of Batman's past had been altered. His costume was different and his timeline had been significantly condensed. However, it wasn't until the 12-part "Zero Year" flashback story debuted in the main *Batman* title that readers finally learned the extent of the alterations made to the Dark Knight's personal history.

SUIT UP

Batman's "Zero Year" costume harkened back to his Batsuit from his first appearance: purple gloves, a more simplistic bat-symbol, and a wing-like cape.

THE FIRST BATCAVE

Six years prior to his recent adventures, a young Bruce Wayne returned to Gotham City. He had been traveling around the globe, training from a variety of masters, and was finally ready to embark on his campaign against crime. With help from Alfred Pennyworth, Bruce set up a hi-tech headquarters secreted inside a nondescript brownstone.

RED HOODLUMS

As Bruce got the lay of his old hometown, he learned of the Red Hood Gang. Led by the brilliant schemer Red Hood One, the gang eventually destroyed Bruce's brownstone, nearly killing the inexperienced Wayne in the process. Injured and forced to retreat to his family estate of Wayne Manor, Bruce found the inspiration he needed when a bat perched on the bust of his father.

PHILIP KANE

The brother of Bruce's mother Martha, Philip welcomed his nephew back to Gotham City. Bruce would later discover that Kane was secretly in league with the Red Hood Gang, an allegiance that would eventually result in Kane's murder.

THE JOKER

Clad in his first Batsuit and now operating out of the caverns below Wayne Manor, Batman embarked on his mission in Gotham City. He faced down the Red Hood Gang at ACE Chemical, a battle that culminated with Red Hood One falling into a vat of chemicals. Even in the continuity of *The New 52*, The Joker's birth was unavoidable.

THE BATMOBILE

Batman introduced his first Batmobile during "Zero Year," a stylish model capable of flight.

DOCTOR DEATH

Batman fought new villain Doctor Death, realizing only too late that the malformed criminal was working for The Riddler. While Batman was occupied, The Riddler blew the city's retaining walls and a superstorm flooded Gotham City.

THE RIDDLER

Edward Nygma worked as Philip Kane's top strategist, but maintained his own secret agenda. As his plan progressed, Nygma would reemerge as The Riddler.

NEW WHEELS

Batman adopted a practical Batcycle and survival suit when navigating Gotham City's savagely rough terrain.

AN URBAN JUNGLE

After being incapacitated from his fight with Doctor Death, Bruce awoke to a changed Gotham City. With the tunnels flooded, the bridges rigged with explosives, and the streets overgrown with vegetation from research stolen from Dr. Pamela Isley, Nygma now controlled everything within city limits. Nevertheless, Batman had been nursed back to health by the young Duke Thomas and his kind family, and the Dark Knight soon teamed with Lucius Fox and Lieutenant James Gordon to challenge The Riddler's rule. Batman eventually outsmarted the overconfident Riddler, stopped Gotham City from suffering further destruction, and even returned power to the grid. With the Batman back, Gotham City could start on the road to recovery.

SUPERHEAVY

ENDGAME

Seemingly aware of Bruce Wayne's alter ego, The Joker had unleashed a series of violent attacks on Batman and Gotham City. These brazen actions reached their crescendo when the Clown Prince of Crime released his virus on the city. After Batman discovered a cure, he and The Joker duked it out in a cavern near a pool of a mysterious healing metal called Dionesium. Their fight was bloody and brutal, and both died in the struggle.

BUILDING A BETTER BATMAN

Batman was dead, but Gotham City still needed him. So the G.C.P.D. decided to take matters into their own hands. Under the guidance of new Commissioner Maggie Sawyer and industrialist Geri Powers, a special task force was launched, with former commissioner James Gordon filling the role of a city-sponsored Dark Knight. With his mustache gone and a Mohawk shaved into his trim hair, the 46-year-old Gordon piloted a sophisticated armor dubbed the Rookie and set out to protect the streets from a variety of threats.

COMMISSIONER BATMAN

Gordon wore a more traditional Batsuit underneath his Rookie armor. This Batsuit was black and yellow, and could turn nearly invisible via digital camouflaging. Still a cop at heart, Gordon also relied on a gun, but one that fired non-lethal, mini Batarangs.

NEW EQUIPMENT

Batman is always well equipped, even when it's not Bruce Wayne wearing the cowl. Gordon's Batman employed a giant Bat-Truck—his so-called "rolling cave"—that cost more than $15 million. His team operated out of a Bat-Blimp that could launch Gordon in his Rookie armor from the Gotham City sky.

BATMAN'S REBIRTH

While the real Batman had indeed "died" fighting The Joker, Bruce Wayne had survived. Working with his old flame Julie Madison at the Lucius Fox Center For Gotham Youth, Bruce had recovered from his death thanks to the effects of the Dionesium metal. However, his memories of life as Batman were gone. Once he realized that he was needed to fight Mister Bloom and protect his city, Bruce used a hi-tech invention—his "final machine"—to upload his memories and skills as Batman into his mind. He donned a new Batman costume, one with a purple inner cape and yellow outlined bat-symbol, and arrived to help Gordon stop Mister Bloom. With the rightful Batman now protecting Gotham City once more, Jim Gordon returned to his post as police commissioner, putting his Dark Knight duty behind him.

MISTER BLOOM

Dealing in a potent and deadly advanced drug, the grotesquely elongated Mister Bloom became Gordon's first true Super-Villain foe. When Bloom eventually grew to the size of a skyscraper, it took a mech-sized suit of Batman armor to finally take him down.

DARK NIGHTS: METAL

The Dark Multiverse invades the DC Multiverse, with a league of evil Batmen leading the charge.

THE MANTLING

Ever since he had unwillingly tampered with time, Batman was a marked man. When Darkseid sent him through the timestream during the events of *Final Crisis*, Batman had angered a powerful entity known as Barbatos. Barbatos targeted Batman, and began preparing him in a process called mantling, through which the Dark Knight would be exposed to five powerful metals.

ELEMENT X

In order to stop Barbatos, the Justice League wore armor made of 10th Metal built for them at the Forge of Worlds. Using this metal to reach out to the cosmos, they overcame the darkness and in doing so, created a unity that resulted in a bold new era for the Justice League. However, in doing so, they pierced the mysterious Source Wall at the universe's edge and soon faced new threats from the beyond.

Shortly after Batman's return to the present, he encountered Electrum, a regenerative metal used by the Talon soldiers of the Court of Owls. Next, after Batman and The Joker fought to the death, they were brought back to life by Dionesium, a pool of green liquid metal. Batman's memories returned to him thanks in part to the Promethium components of his hi-tech "final machine," but he then unknowingly exposed himself to the substance most closely associated with the Super Hero Hawkman, Nth Metal. During these experiments, Batman's new partner in training, Duke Thomas, had his own metahuman powers activated. As Duke gained the light-manipulating powers he would use as the Signal, a ripple traveled across the dimensions. It reached the Dark Multiverse, a realm of impossibly dark temporary realities existing on the flipside of the true Multiverse.

Batman desperately tried to save his allies from the threat he knew was fast approaching, but a conflict with the Court of Owls exposed him to yet another metal, named Batmanium. Once Batman came into contact with it, the mantling was complete, and a twisted group of Barbatos' top agents from the Dark Multiverse were unleashed upon the Earth.

THE BATMEN OF THE DARK MULTIVERSE

The agents of Barbatos (1) included: 2 The Drowned (an evil Batman/Aquaman hybrid); 3 The Devastator (Batman/Doomsday); 4 The Murder Machine (Batman/Cyborg); 5 Groblins (evil Robins); 6 The Batman Who Laughs (Batman/The Joker); 7 The Merciless (Batman/Ares); 8 The Red Death (Batman/The Flash); 9 The Dawnbreaker (Batman/Green Lantern).

THE BATMAN WHO LAUGHS

After Barbatos' defeat, The Batman Who Laughs continued his nefarious plotting. He set up his own perverse Batcave beneath Gotham City's Monarch Theater, and began infecting the Dark Knight's allies with Dark Metal. James Gordon was his first victim, as the heroic top cop unwittingly became The Batman Who Laughs' pawn, named the Commissioner. Other heroes who served in the Batman Who Laughs' corrupted army included Shazam, Blue Beetle, Donna Troy, Supergirl, and Hawkman.

MEETING NEW HEROES

Batman had faced a literal rebirth when he reclaimed his mantle from James Gordon, but soon, the DC universe faced another shift in continuity, one created due to the meddling of a cosmic-level being. A few heroes and villains returned to life, histories were partially restored, and some new faces emerged.

Among those new heroes were Gotham and Gotham Girl, Hank and Claire Clover. They had powers similar to those of Superman, and they saved Batman's life, rescuing him from a crashing plane. However, the more Gotham and Gotham Girl used their powers, the more they drained their life energy; each superhuman feat shortened their lifespans. Due to manipulation by Hugo Strange and the Psycho-Pirate, Gotham was driven insane and died in a mad rampage. Gotham Girl was also psychologically harmed, causing Batman to hunt down the Pirate to cure her.

THE SQUAD

Bane was holding Psycho-Pirate at his Santa Prisca stronghold in. To help Gotham Girl, Batman had to seize the Pirate. To that end, he assembled his own Suicide Squad team, including Catwoman. They broke into Bane's base and Catwoman bested Bane. The team then returned to Gotham City, unaware that this had been part of Bane's plan all along.

BATMAN VS. BANE

While Bane was seemingly broken in the aftermath of Batman's suicide mission, the relationship between Batman and Catwoman was anything but. The two grew closer, even as Bane returned to Gotham City. Bane attacked the Bat-Family, but was soon forced to fight through a gauntlet of villains inside Arkham Asylum in order to get at the Dark Knight. Batman then triumphed over the rage-fueled Bane—or so he thought.

Bruce Wayne and Selina Kyle had flirted with a relationship ever since the birth of their Batman and Catwoman personas. But can a Dark Knight and a Feline Fatale ever truly settle down?

THE WEDDING

AT FIRST SIGHT

While they often argued whether they had first met on a boat or on the street, Batman and Catwoman couldn't deny that their mutual attraction was growing stronger. Using the diamond Catwoman first stole on that original boat caper, Batman got down on one knee and proposed.

COLD FEET

Before the big night, a clash with The Joker and a chat with her old friend Holly Robinson planted doubts in Selina's mind. Did she have the right to marry someone as driven as Batman? Could a Batman every truly be both happy and effective? On the night they were to be married, Selina left Bruce at the proverbial altar, the rooftop of Finger Tower.

TO THE NINES

Both Bruce Wayne and Selina Kyle chose their wedding attire carefully. Even though Selina had access to the Wayne Family fortune, she decided to steal her elegant wedding dress in the dead of night. Old habits die hard for Gotham City's most notorious cat burglar.

VENGEANCE OF BANE

Catwoman left Gotham City, leaving Batman distraught and riddled with doubt. The Dark Knight hadn't yet realized that Bane had engineered the breakup; both The Joker and Holly Robinson had been working for him. Bane's plan had been slowly proceeding, ever since he'd engineered the plane crash that introduced Batman to Gotham and Gotham Girl. And it had worked perfectly. Bane had broken Batman like never before, but his ultimate motive was still unclear...

A GRIM RETURN

Emotionally numb, Batman renewed his war on crime. As if to remind himself of past feats, he wore a black and gray Batsuit that he had not worn for years.

Bane had played the long game, and his plans were about to come to fruition, with all of Gotham City as his prize.

CITY OF BANE

CRAKK

FLASHPOINT OF NO RETURN

Bane had played possum inside his cell in Arkham Asylum. While the rest of Gotham City believed him a defeated, raving lunatic, Bane continued to enact his plans for Gotham City and Batman. With only the Dark Knight realizing the truth, the police began to view Batman's fixation with Bane as an obsession. This only worsened when Batman woke up in Arkham Asylum, after having been subjected to fear-gas-induced nightmares. He fought his way out, but began to question his own grasp on reality even as Bane physically bested him and left him nearly dead in the care of none other than Bruce's "father," Thomas Wayne from the *Flashpoint* reality. Batman escaped Thomas, and disappeared from Gotham City altogether.

Thanks to help from nefarious super-speedster the Reverse-Flash, Thomas Wayne had made his way to Batman's Earth. This gun-toting Batman had teamed with Bane, pretending to take orders from him. When Bruce Wayne left, Thomas was handed Gotham City. He served as its Batman under Commissioner Hugo Strange, backed by a police force made up of Arkham Asylum villains. The Ventriloquist served as Thomas' "Alfred" and Gotham Girl his "Robin." Bane held the real Alfred captive, and had issued a firm decree: If any member of Batman's Family set foot in Gotham City, Alfred would be put to death.

THE DEATH OF ALFRED

Brash and impulsive as ever, Robin ignored Bane's rule and entered Gotham City. Thomas Wayne took Robin captive, and Bane snapped Alfred's neck in front of the boy's eyes.

BAT AND CAT

While Bane took Gotham City, Batman began to retrain his body and mind for the task at hand. Traveling with Catwoman, the two rekindled their romance, and achieved their goal of cutting off Bane's supply of Super-Venom, the drug with which Bane powered his brainwashed enforcer, Gotham Girl.

REMATCH

Returning to Gotham City, Batman defeated Bane with help from Catwoman. However, this moment of triumph was interrupted when Batman was shot by Thomas Wayne. Revealing his true colors, Wayne then shot Bane as well.

BANE'S GOTHAM CITY POLICE

Brainwashed by Hugo Strange and the Psycho-Pirate, Super-Villains Professor Pyg, Two-Face, and even The Riddler served Bane as members of his G.C.P.D. Batman and Catwoman had to take out these "officers" one by one in order to get to Bane.

BATMAN VS. BATMAN

With Batman injured, Thomas revealed that Alfred had been murdered. Stricken with grief, Batman brutally fought this alternate version of his father. In Thomas's mind, he was doing everything he could to protect his son from the curse of being Batman. It was why he teamed with Bane to try to force Bruce out of the role. But when their fight was over, only one Batman was left standing. The true Dark Knight: Bruce Wayne.

#1
BATMAN: THREE JOKERS

> "We do what we always do.
> We try to make a better Joker."
>
> THE JOKER

MAIN CHARACTERS: Batman, the Three Jokers, Batgirl, Red Hood
SUPPORTING CHARACTERS: Alfred Pennyworth, Joe Chill, Thomas and Martha Wayne, The Joker's goons, Commissioner Gordon, Harvey Bullock, G.C.P.D. officers, The Joker's victims, Gaggy LOCATIONS:
Wayne Manor, the Batcave, Park Row, a Gotham City gym, a Gotham City cemetery, Ace Chemical, The Joker's cabin, Gotham Aquarium, 17th and Broadway

BACKGROUND

Often at the forefront of large-scale DC continuity-altering events, writer Geoff Johns had written the *DC Universe: Rebirth* one-shot special as well as "The Darkseid War" in the pages of *Justice League*, the latter with star artist Jason Fabok. Both series dealt in part with Batman discovering that he had battled not one, but three different Jokers throughout the years.

With these teasers firmly in place, Johns and Fabok reteamed to deliver the three-issue prestige format *Batman: Three Jokers*. This miniseries fully embraced the aesthetic of the landmark *Batman: The Killing Joke*, from the embossed lettering and close-up imagery of the covers, to the nine-panel grid format inside each densely packed issue. And while it's unclear exactly on which Earth the events of this story fall in the DC Multiverse, there is no doubt of its direct continuation of the plot of *The Killing Joke*, revealing new insights into The Joker's past.

PUBLICATION DATE
October 2020

EDITOR
Mark Doyle and
Amedeo Turturro

COVER ARTIST
Jason Fabok

WRITER
Geoff Johns

PENCILER
Jason Fabok

INKER
Jason Fabok

COLORIST
Brad Anderson

LETTERER
Sam Rosen

The Story...

Batman discovers that there have been three Jokers active throughout his career, as the Clown Princes of Crime plot their latest personal attack on the Dark Knight.

Injured from his latest exploit, Batman stumbles home to Wayne Manor. While Alfred stitches him up, the Dark Knight's mind drifts to the villains who have given him his many scars **(1)**, none more than The Joker.

When three murders occur simultaneously in the city, each crime attributed to The Joker, Batman and allies Batgirl (Barbara Gordon) and Red Hood (Jason Todd) investigate. Three grinning victims dressed as the original Red Hood, are discovered at Ace Chemical **(2)**.

Soon after, The Joker, driving a stolen Ace tanker truck, arrives at an isolated cabin in the woods. Once inside, all three Jokers are accounted for: the scheming world-weary Criminal **(3)**; the Hawaiian shirt clad Comedian, driven mad after the death of his wife and unborn child; and the quirky, murderous Clown **(4)**.

Back in Gotham City, the Red Hood has discovered seawater on a wrench used by a Joker goon, a clue he follows to the Gotham Aquarium with Batman and Batgirl. The trio is greeted by a Joker-envenomed shark **(5)** and a gang of henchmen, led by The Joker's former sidekick, Gaggy. The heroes defeat the villains and apprehend the criminals' true leader, the Clown Joker **(6)**. Batman then leaves to investigate another Joker sighting. The Clown Joker taunts the Red Hood and, before Batgirl can stop him, Jason shoots and kills the Clown **(7)**.

The story continues into the following two issues, climaxing in a showdown at the Monarch Theater **(8)** where Batman is forced to save the life of his parents' murderer, Joe Chill **(9)**. This delays the three Jokers' plan to make Joe Chill the next Joker. The scheme is permanently ended when the Comedian Joker shoots and kills the Criminal Joker. After giving himself up to the police, the lone remaining Joker claims that he knows the secret identities of all the Dark Knight's allies.

But there are some secrets The Joker doesn't know. Batman has long ago deduced The Joker's true name; he also knows that The Joker's wife and child are living in Alaska **(10)**. This particular secret the Dark Knight resolves to guard from The Joker with his life.

THE JOKER

CHAOS REIGNS

The Joker was tired of games. He was no longer willing to pretend that he didn't know that Bruce Wayne and Batman were the same man. While masquerading as the Designer—a villain from Gotham City's past—he kept Batman busy with five hired assassins. Then he used the Designer's old masterplan to steal Wayne Industries' assets, including Bruce Wayne's personal fortune. Now worth over $100 billion, The Joker enlisted a clown army and plunged the city into chaos.

HOSTILE TAKEOVER

The Joker now had his own lawyer, a criminal called the Underbroker, and a new moll, by the name of Punchline. With these loyal helpers, The Joker took over Wayne Industries and turned public opinion against Bruce Wayne, claiming Wayne embezzled money to his "ally" Batman. Punchline broke into the Tricorner Yards division of Wayne Industries, took Lucius Fox hostage, and stole Batman's fleet of vehicles.

PUNCHLINE

After Harley Quinn had decided to turn her life around and try her hand at playing the hero, Alexis Kaye became The Joker's new right-hand woman, Punchline. A former college student obsessed with The Joker, she was a natural fit—violent, scheming, and lacking any remorse for her victims.

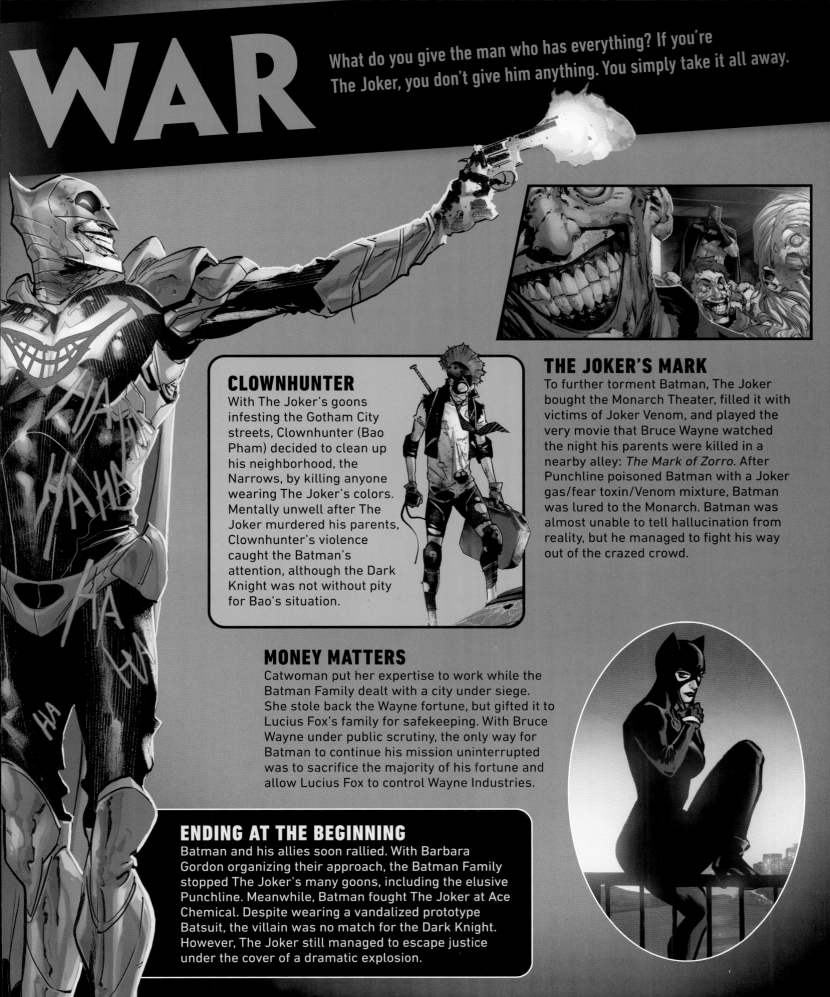

WAR

What do you give the man who has everything? If you're The Joker, you don't give him anything. You simply take it all away.

CLOWNHUNTER

With The Joker's goons infesting the Gotham City streets, Clownhunter (Bao Pham) decided to clean up his neighborhood, the Narrows, by killing anyone wearing The Joker's colors. Mentally unwell after The Joker murdered his parents, Clownhunter's violence caught the Batman's attention, although the Dark Knight was not without pity for Bao's situation.

THE JOKER'S MARK

To further torment Batman, The Joker bought the Monarch Theater, filled it with victims of Joker Venom, and played the very movie that Bruce Wayne watched the night his parents were killed in a nearby alley: *The Mark of Zorro*. After Punchline poisoned Batman with a Joker gas/fear toxin/Venom mixture, Batman was lured to the Monarch. Batman was almost unable to tell hallucination from reality, but he managed to fight his way out of the crazed crowd.

MONEY MATTERS

Catwoman put her expertise to work while the Batman Family dealt with a city under siege. She stole back the Wayne fortune, but gifted it to Lucius Fox's family for safekeeping. With Bruce Wayne under public scrutiny, the only way for Batman to continue his mission uninterrupted was to sacrifice the majority of his fortune and allow Lucius Fox to control Wayne Industries.

ENDING AT THE BEGINNING

Batman and his allies soon rallied. With Barbara Gordon organizing their approach, the Batman Family stopped The Joker's many goons, including the elusive Punchline. Meanwhile, Batman fought The Joker at Ace Chemical. Despite wearing a vandalized prototype Batsuit, the villain was no match for the Dark Knight. However, The Joker still managed to escape justice under the cover of a dramatic explosion.

DARK NIGHTS: DEATH METAL

The world is reshaped in the dark image of the all-powerful Batman Who Laughs, with only a few Super Heroes left to stand in his way.

BLACK LANTERN BATMAN

Wearing a Black Lantern ring, riding a motorcycle made out of a Joker dragon skeleton, and armed with a large scythe, the true Batman rebelled against The Batman Who Laughs. However, as his ring would indicate, Batman had been killed some time ago, and was only a reanimated corpse, a shadow of the hero he had been in life.

PERPETUA

When the Justice League defeated Barbatos using 10th Metal, their victory came at a cost. They had unwittingly broken the Source Wall at the edge of the universe, allowing for the eventual return of Perpetua, the mother of the Multiverse itself. A supreme cosmic being, Perpetua chose Superman's archfoe Lex Luthor to be her right-hand agent on Earth. Eventually, however, The Batman Who Laughs usurped that position, convincing Perpetua to let him rewrite reality in his own terrifying image.

METALVERSE

In The Batman Who Laugh's hellish reality, the very continents had taken the form of a bat. The Batman Who Laughs led an army of Dark Multiverse Batmen and ruled over the few surviving heroes, including Wonder Woman, Aquaman, and Harley Quinn.

THE DARKEST KNIGHT

Not content with his own Earth, The Batman Who Laughs wanted his own Multiverse. After he was killed in a fight with Wonder Woman and her invisible chainsaw, The Batman Who Laugh's brain was placed into the body of a Bruce Wayne who had the godlike abilities of the entity called Doctor Manhattan. Soon, The Batman Who Laughs evolved even further into the shadow-like Darkest Knight.

A BATMAN FOR ALL SEASONS

The Batman Who Laughs employed a variety of Dark Multiverse Batmen, including the living monster truck Batmobeast; the robot dinosaur from the Batcave given an evil Batman mind named Batmanasaurus Rex; the magical Bat-Mage; the mad scientist Dr. Arkham; and even an entire sentient city called Castle Bat.

ROBIN KING

Every Batman needs a Robin, and the Darkest Knight found his in the form of Robin King. This young Bruce Wayne hailed from a Dark Multiverse world in which he not only killed Joe Chill, but killed his parents as well on that fateful night outside the Monarch Theater. Transformed into a Groblin, he was then promoted by The Batman Who Laughs to serve as his demented Robin King.

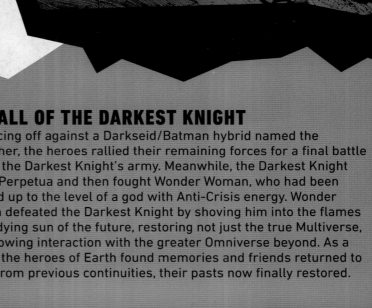

THE FALL OF THE DARKEST KNIGHT

After facing off against a Darkseid/Batman hybrid named the Darkfather, the heroes rallied their remaining forces for a final battle against the Darkest Knight's army. Meanwhile, the Darkest Knight bested Perpetua and then fought Wonder Woman, who had been charged up to the level of a god with Anti-Crisis energy. Wonder Woman defeated the Darkest Knight by shoving him into the flames of the dying sun of the future, restoring not just the true Multiverse, but allowing interaction with the greater Omniverse beyond. As a result, the heroes of Earth found memories and friends returned to them from previous continuities, their pasts now finally restored.

INFINITE FRONTIER

It's a brand new day for Batman and Gotham City. The Batman Family faces infinite possibilities as they set out to explore a restored DC universe brimming with potential.

FORT GRAYE

After "The Joker War" saw the bulk of his fortune transferred to the Fox family, Bruce Wayne decided on a simpler approach to life. He moved to the heart of Gotham City, to a brownstone in the Fort Graye neighborhood. While he was closer to the action than he'd been with his commute from Wayne Manor, his life in Fort Graye meant actually getting to know his neighbors, and keeping his nocturnal activities a secret from the nosier ones.

THE GARAGE

Underneath Bruce Wayne's Fort Graye home sat Batman's garage, a simpler Batcave than any he'd employed in recent years. Batman intended this to be just one of several mini-caves spread around the city to allow him access to his gear at a moment's notice.

THE ORACLE RETURNS

During "The Joker War," Barbara Gordon operated from behind her computer screen, her skills needed more than ever. She soon decided to adventure as Batgirl only sparingly, working instead as Oracle with both Orphan and Spoiler as her Batgirl agents in the field.

ROBIN REBELS

After resorting to extreme and lethal methods while leading an incarnation of the Teen Titans, Damian Wayne broke away from the Batman Family. He decided to test his mettle by entering an exclusive fighting competition on a remote location of regenerative properties named Lazarus Island.

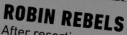

THE GHOST-MAKER

Possessing many of the same fighting skills as Batman owing to training with many of the same masters, the Ghost-Maker attempted to "fix" Gotham City, despite a long-standing truce to stay out of Batman's hometown. While Ghost-Maker viewed Bruce Wayne's commitment to non-lethal crime fighting as a weakness, he decided to follow his rules while he remained in Gotham City, partnering with perhaps the only man he has ever regarded as an equal.

DEAD OR ALIVE

After the conclusion of "The Joker War," Arkham Asylum was mostly destroyed in an attack attributed to The Joker. The most wanted man in Gotham City, The Joker fled the country, pursued by former G.C.P.D. Commissioner James Gordon, who accepted a contract on The Joker's head.

ALWAYS AN OUTLAW

No longer working with his team of Outlaws, the Red Hood was finding it difficult to change his modus operandi. He agreed to commit to Batman's no-killing rule, but soon stepped over the line when stopping a drug-dealing, negligent father. Always looking for redemption, the Red Hood remained tortured by his past.

BATMAN BEYOND
After Bruce Wayne retired from crime fighting, the mantle of Batman fell to high-schooler Terry McGinnis. Wearing a sleek black interpretation of the famous costume, Terry became the new face of heroism for the people of Neo-Gotham City. By working alongside Police Commissioner Barbara Gordon, Terry became the Batman for a new generation. He was later joined by the daughter of Nightwing—Elainna Grayson—who became the new Batwoman, and even his brother Matt, who temporarily stepped into the part of Robin.

BATMAN & DRACULA: RED RAIN
Vampires ruled Gotham City from behind the scenes, with Dracula as their unholy lord. Initially incredulous, Batman was forced to accept the truth after he suffered a wound that turned him into a member of their undead clan. Despite his transformation, Batman remained committed to law and order, and teamed up with a vampire hunter to track down Dracula and put an end to his centuries-long reign. Batman, now possessing supernatural strength, vampiric fangs, and bat-like wings, soared above Gotham City as its immortal guardian.

GOTHAM BY GASLIGHT
After witnessing the deaths of his parents at the hands of a coach robber, Bruce Wayne became the Batman of the year 1889. Though he was successful at stopping street-level smash-and-grabs, Batman faced a challenge when Jack the Ripper's arrival in Gotham City took things to a terrifying new level. The police arrested Bruce as a suspect in the Ripper murders but he managed to deduce the killer's true identity from behind bars. After breaking out of jail and apprehending the Ripper himself, Batman was able to resume his role as Gotham City's protector.

ALTERNATE REALITIES

BATMAN: YEAR 100

One hundred years after the first reported sightings of Batman in 1939, a familiar hero stood up to an oppressive governmental regime. The Gotham City of 2039 was a police state with its citizens under constant surveillance—the kind of place where an urban legend like the Batman was not supposed to exist. But the Batman of this era had friends, including a new Robin and a G.C.P.D. officer descended from James Gordon. Playing up to the myths, Batman wore ceramic teeth that made him resemble a monster and used fear to uncover a conspiracy to bioengineer a worldwide pandemic.

KINGDOM COME

After a new crop of vigilantes won praise for their bloodthirsty approach to peacekeeping, Earth's original heroes felt they were no longer needed. But after the American heartland was destroyed by a nuclear bomb, Superman was prompted to assemble an old-guard Justice League to rein in the new extremists. Batman believed that Superman's actions edged dangerously close to fascism and gathered his own team in response. Lex Luthor appeared to share Batman's concerns, but Batman betrayed the villain at the last minute, leading to a three-way battle against a backdrop of imminent nuclear annihilation.

FUTURE STATE

In a Gotham City patrolled by the private security force known as the Magistrate, Bruce Wayne was presumed dead, but continued to fight crime from the shadows in a more utilitarian Batsuit. Meanwhile, Lucius Fox's son —Tim "Jace" Fox—served as the more public Batman, embarking on his own crime-fighting career despite opposition from the relentless Magistrate. Elsewhere in this dystopia, Tim Drake remained active as Robin, Dick Grayson fought for the Super Hero community as Nightwing, and Red Hood joined the Magistrate to work against the organization from the inside.

In the past, the future, and on other versions of Earth, Batman is still a significant figure. The different incarnations of Bruce Wayne might lead unfamiliar lives, but a childhood tragedy always steers them toward dark vigilantism. Later generations of Batmen are inspired by Bruce Wayne's example and endeavor to carry on his work.

INDEX

Page numbers in **bold** refer to main entries; comic book series are in *italics*.

ACKNOWLEDGMENTS

The publishers have made every effort to identify and acknowledge the artists and writers whose work appears in this book.

Artists, Inkers, and Colorists: Neal Adams, Christian Alamy, Juan Albarran, Oclair Albert, Laura Allred, Mario Alquiza, Brad Anderson, Murphy Anderson, Jim Aparo, Aspen Studios, Terry Austin, Tony Avina, Ramon Bachs, Mark Bagley, Michael Bair, Jim Balent, Matt Banning, David Baron, Eduardo Barreto, Eddy Barrows, Chris Batista, Moose Baumann, David M. Beaty, Jordie Bellaire, Ed Benes, Ryan Benjamin, Joe Bennett, Lee Bermejo, Liz Berube, Shannon Blanchard, Fernando Blanco, Bret Blevins, Blond, Karine Boccanfuso, Brian Bolland, Tamra Bonvillain, Brett Booth, Doug Braithwaite, Elizabeth Breitweiser, Norm Breyfogle, John Broome, Bob Brown, Steve Buccellato, Mark Buckingham, Álvaro Martínez Bueno, Rick Burchett, Chris Burnham, Jack Burnley, Sal Buscema, Jim Calafiore, Robert Campanella, J. Scott Campbell, Greg Capullo, Claudio Castellini, Keith Champagne, Richard Chasemore, Chris Chuckry, June Chung, Vicente Cifuentes, Scott Clark, Andy Clarke, Gene Colan, Kevin Conrad, Will Conrad, Jorge Corona, Jeromy Cox, Andrew Dalhouse, Rodolfo Damaggio, Carlos D'Anda, Tony S. Daniel, Alan Davis, Shane Davis, Mike DeCarlo, Luciana Del Negro, Edgar Delgado, John Dell, Jesse Delperdang, Mike Deodato, Tom Derenick, D'Israeli, Rachel Dodson, Terry Dodson, Horacio Domuingues, Ming Doyle, Christian Duce, Dale Eaglesham, Steve Epting, Jason Fabok, Romulo Fajardo, Jr., Nathan Fairbairn, Mark Farmer, Wayne Faucher, Javier Fernandez, Raúl Fernández, Eber Ferreira, Juan Ferreyra, Nick Filardi, David Finch, Walt Flanagan, Sandu Florea, John Floyd, Jorge Fornés, Francesco Francavilla, Derek Fridolfs, Richard Friend, Lee Garbett, José Luis García-López, Stefano Gaudiano, Mitch Gerads, Noelle Giddings, Joe Giella, Keith Giffen, Dick Giordano, Jonathan Glapion, Patrick Gleason, Mick Gray, Sid Greene, Mike Grell, Paul Gulacy, Culley Hamner, Ian Hannin, Scott Hanna, Ed Hannigan, James Harvey, Jeremy Haun, Rob Haynes, Doug Hazlewood, Andrew Hennessey, Clayton Henry, Hi-Fi Design, John Higgins, Bryan Hitch, Matt Hollingsworth, Richard Horie, Tanya Horie, David Hornung, Sandra Hope, Adam Hughes, Rob Hunter, Carmine Infantino, Frazer Irving, Mikel Janín, Klaus Janson, Georges Jeanty, Jorge Jimenez, Phil Jimenez, Jock, Sam Johns, J. G. Jones, Joëlle Jones, Kelley Jones, Malcolm Jones III, Ruy José, John Kalisz, Bob Kane, Gil Kane, Stan Kaye, Karl Kesel, Leonard Kirk, Tyler Kirkham, Don Kramer, Andy Kubert, Michel Lacombe, Julia Lacquement, José Ladrönn, Andy Lanning, David Lapham, Serge LaPointe, Michael Lark, Stanley Lau, Ian Laughlin, Bob Layton, Jae Lee, Jim Lee, Pat Lee, John Paul Leon, Richmond Lewis, Kirk Lindo, Kinsun Loh, Aaron Lopresti, Lee Loughridge, Adriano Lucas , Doug Mahnke, Guy Major, Alex Maleev, Clay Mann, Seth Mann, Guillem March, David Marquez, Laura Martin, Marcos Martin, Shawn Martinbrough, Marcos Marz, Ron Marz, José Marzán, Jr., Francesco Mattina, J. P. Mayer, Randy Mayor, David Mazzucchelli, Ray McCarthy, Tom McCraw, Scott McDaniel, Luke McDonnell, Ed McGuinness, Dave McKean, Jamie McKelvie, Mark McKenna, Bob McLeod, Shawn McManus, Gleb Melnikov, Adriana Melo, Jaime Mendoza, Jesus Merino, Mike Mignola, Danny Miki, Al Milgrom, Brian Miller, Frank Miller, Steve Mitchell, Sheldon Moldoff, Shawn Moll, Dan Mora, Rags Morales, Tomeu Morey, Win Mortimer, Patricia Mulvihill, Dustin Nguyen, Tom Nguyen, Graham Nolan, Mike Norton, Phil Noto, Irv Novick, Kevin Nowlan, Ben Oliver, Ariel Olivetti, Glen Orbik, Jerry Ordway, Andy Owens, Carlos Pacheco, Carlo Pagulayan, Jimmy Palmiotti, Peter Pantazis, Yanick Paquette, Charles Paris, Lucio Parrillo, Sean Parsons, Allen Passalaqua, Bruce D. Patterson, Jason Pearson, Andrew Pepoy, George Pérez, Pere Pérez, Rich Perotta, Hugo Petrus, Sean Phillips, FCO Plascencia, Ivan Plascencia, Paul Pope, Howard Porter, Joe Prado, Arif Prianto, Bruno Premiani, Javier Pulido, Frank Quitely, Stefano Raffaele, Pamela Rambo, Jay David Ramos, Rodney Ramos, Norm Rapmund, Fred Ray, Brian Reber, Bruno Redondo, Sal Regla, Ivan Reis, Rod Reis, Chris Renaud, Sabine Rich, David Roach, Darick Robertson, Jerry Robinson, Roger Robinson, Kenneth Rocafort, Irvin Rodriguez, John Romita, Jr., Alex Ross, Riley Rossmo, George Roussos, Stéphane Roux, Adrienne Roy, Joe Rubinstein, Marco Rudy, Neil Ruffino, P. Craig Russell, Matt Ryan, Tim Sale, Daniel Sampere, Alejandro Sánchez, Amilton Santos, Joe Shuster, Damion Scott, Nicola Scott, Trevor Scott, Stjepan Šejić, Mike Sekowsky, Jerry Serpe, Bill Sienkiewicz, Alejandro Sicat, Walt Simonson, Alex Sinclair, James Sinclair, Paulo Siqueira, Jeremiah Skipper, Cam Smith, J. D. Smith, Pam Smith, Ryan Sook, Aaron Sowd, Dick Sprang, Chris Sprouse, John Stanisci, Joe Staton, Peter Steigerwald, Brian Stelfreeze, Cameron Stewart, Dave Stewart, Chic Stone, Karl Story, Lary Stucker, E. J. Su, Ardian Syaf, Pat Tan, Philip Tan, Romeo Tanghal, Babs Tarr, Roberta Tewes, Art Thibert, John Timms, Marcus To, Anthony Tollin, Dwayne Turner, Michael Turner, George Tuska, Ethan Van Sciver, Lynn Varley, José Villarrubia, Dexter Vines, Matt Wagner, Brad Walker, Lee Weeks, Chris Weston, Bob Wiacek, Wildstorm FX, Freddie E. Williams II, J. H. Williams III, Scott Williams, Ryan Winn, Stan Woch, Walden Wong, Wally Wood, Pete Woods, Gregory Wright, Jason Wright, Xermanico, Patrick Zircher, Tom Ziuko

Writers: Brian Azzarello, Mike W. Barr, Brian Michael Bendis, Marguerite Bennett, Don Cameron, Paul Dini, Chuck Dixon, Ray Fawkes, Bill Finger, Brenden Fletcher, Christos N. Gage, Alan Grant, Ed Herron, Kyle Higgins, Geoff Johns, Tom King, John Layman, Jeph Loeb, Royal McGraw, Brad Meltzer, Frank Miller, Alan Moore, Denny O'Neil, Stephanie Phillips, Ram V, Frank Robbins, Greg Rucka, Tim Seeley, Jerry Siegel, Gail Simone, Scott Snyder, Cameron Stewart, Mariko Tamaki, Tom Taylor, Peter J. Tomasi, James Tynion IV, Len Wein, Joshua Williamson, Judd Winnick